GOVERNING MODERN SOCI

Edited by Richard V. Ericson and N~~ico S~~

The essays collected in *Governing Modern Societies* arose from a lecture series of the same name held at Green College, University of British Columbia, in 1997 and 1998. Distinguished scholars in political science, philosophy, sociology, and economics from Canada, the United States, England, Germany, and Australia advance not only the most recent theories of how modern societies are governed, but also the ideological and political relevance of these theories.

The focus of this collection is on the extent to which the nature and practice of governance has dramatically changed. The realities of cutbacks in social security expenditures, changes in technology, shifts in labour markets, politics of identity and group rights, loss of political autonomy by nation-states, and management by surveillance and audit all underscore the evolution of governing. The fact that such shifts are also connected to new forms of governance beyond the state (at the community level, for example, within corporate institutions and through the influence of social movements and economic markets) makes the task of governing modern societies all the more challenging.

RICHARD V. ERICSON is Principal of Green College, University of British Columbia, a centre for interdisciplinary scholarship and graduate education.

NICO STEHR is Senior Research Associate in the Sustainable Development Research Institute of the University of British Columbia and DAAD Professor at the Universität Duisburg, Germany. He is a Fellow of the Royal Society of Canada and editor of the *Canadian Journal of Sociology*.

The Green College Thematic Lecture Series

GOVERNING
MODERN SOCIETIES

Edited by
Richard V. Ericson and Nico Stehr

UNIVERSITY OF TORONTO PRESS
Toronto   Buffalo   London

© University of Toronto Press Incorporated 2000
Toronto   Buffalo   London
Printed in Canada

ISBN 0-8020-4392-5 (cloth)
ISBN 0-8020-8198-3 (paper)

Printed on acid-free paper

Canadian Cataloguing in Publication Data

Main entry under title:

Governing modern societies

(The Green College thematic lecture series)
Includes bibliographical references.
ISBN 0-8020-4392-5 (bound)   ISBN 0-8020-8198-3 (pbk.)

1. Political science.   I. Ericson, Richard V., 1948–   .   II. Stehr, Nico.

JA66.G68 1999   320   C99-932185-4

University of Toronto Press acknowledges the financial assistance to its publishing program of the Canada Council for the Arts and the Ontario Arts Council.

University of Toronto Press acknowledges the financial support for its publishing activities of the Government of Canada through the Book Publishing Industry Development Program (BPIDP).

Canada

Contents

Acknowledgments   vii

1 The Ungovernability of Modern Societies: States,
   Democracies, Markets, Participation, and Citizens
   NICO STEHR AND RICHARD V. ERICSON   3

Part One: Globalization and Governance

Introduction   29

2 The Changing Contours of Political Community: Rethinking
   Democracy in the Context of Globalization
   DAVID HELD   42

3 Thinking Global Governance and Enacting Local Cultures
   DAVID J. ELKINS   60

4 Hyperspace: A Political Ontology of the Global City
   WARREN MAGNUSSON   80

Part Two: Modern Regimes of Governance

Introduction   107

5 Divide and Govern
   BARRY HINDESS   118

6 Governing Liberty
NIKOLAS ROSE   141

7 'Homogeneity' and Constitutional Democracy: Can We Cope
with Identity Conflicts through Group Rights?
CLAUS OFFE   177

Part Three: Prospects for Social Democracy

Introduction   215

8 Is Social Democracy Dead?
RONALD BEINER   225

9 Democracy and Social Inequality
DIETRICH RUESCHEMEYER   242

10 Can Welfare States Compete in a Global Economy?
ANTHONY B. ATKINSON   259

11 Social Justice and Citizenship: Dignity, Liberty, and Welfare
EDWARD BROADBENT   276

Notes on Contributors   297

Acknowledgments

This book grew out of a series of public lectures entitled 'Governing Modern Societies' that was presented at Green College, University of British Columbia, during the 1997–8 academic year. We are most grateful to Green College, the *Canadian Journal of Sociology*, and the Goethe-Institut of Vancouver for their generous financial support of these lectures and their publication. We would also like to thank Carolyn Andersson and Dene Matilda of Green College for being so helpful in organizing lectures and assisting with the preparation of this book.

RICHARD V. ERICSON and NICO STEHR

GOVERNING MODERN SOCIETIES

1

The Ungovernability of Modern Societies: States, Democracies, Markets, Participation, and Citizens

NICO STEHR AND RICHARD V. ERICSON

This book examines transformations as well as projected future trends in the governance of contemporary societies. It brings together scholars in the disciplines of political science, philosophy, sociology, and economics from Canada, the United States, England, Germany, and Australia. In the chapters they have written especially for this volume, they advance not only the most recent theories of how modern societies are governed, but also the ideological and policy relevance of these theories.

The chapters in this book are organized according to three broad themes: globalization and governance (Part One), modern regimes of governance (Part Two), and prospects for social democracy (Part Three). A summary of the contributions each chapter makes to the organizing theme, and of the relation among the contributions, is provided in the introduction to each part.

In this chapter we consider how the transformation of modern societies into knowledge societies has a fundamental impact on the political system. This impact has changed the ability of the state apparatus to govern – to the point that the state has become somewhat 'ungovernable.' This analysis is not a reiteration of assertions made several decades ago about the declining governability of modern society as a result of increasing demands on state institutions and the general expansion of the functions of the state – in other words, the well-known problem of corporatism. At the time, observers generally expressed regret about the loss of power of the state and set out to search for compensatory mechanisms to make up for the power deficit. The search for such mechanisms to reassert state authority is no longer typical. Instead, the loss of state efficiency and competence today is typically seen to be linked to the decline in the autonomy of the nation-state. In particular, this decline is said to result from an economization of society, that is, a displacement of politics by the market (see Habermas 1998). Hence some of the most recent debates about the governability of contemporary societies share with their predecessors a distinctive state-centered perspective. The disempowerment of the state, however, is now seen as a hopeful sign. For example, it offers a greatly needed response to the international linkage of political problems, and an impulse for the practice of transnational political functions.

Another line of argument about the decline in the autonomy of the nation-state is found in Niklas Luhmann's disparaging thesis ([1988] 1997) about the difficulties of steering a society that is composed of increasingly differentiated autopoietic institutions. Closed and self-referential institutions such as the economy, law, science, and religion have inherent difficulties intervening in each other's affairs (see Luhmann [1988] 1997). Luhmann's approach fails to concede that state intervention is now a routine matter.

More fundamentally, any inquiry into governability must address the efficacy of state intervention as judged against the political objectives of government itself. The government's efficacy will be assessed in terms of its ability to competently execute specific policies, such as in its attempts to reduce unemployment, increase social solidarity, police knowledge, and reduce violent crime. What we want to explore are the changing opportunities of the state and other large social institutions to effect and maintain social closure (Weber [1922] 1978, 314–43). This exploration entails an analysis of their ability to control (or even monopolize and deny access to) resources based on social attributes such as gender, class, generation, or ethnicity.

Some societal developments are systematically underrepresented in discussions of the governance of modern society. These developments are connected to the general extension of the capacities of individual citizens to act. This extension heightens the political consciousness of citizens and increases their ability to pass political judgment, which in turn extends the political community.

The mandate of democratic political systems is to enlarge *actual* political involvement and active citizenship in terms of a commitment to the *right* of citizens to take part in the governance of society. People's ability to make choices and resist choices made for them by major social institutions (i.e., their ability to 'govern' the course of their life and become more involved in political affairs), however, is not necessarily the intentional outcome of such democratic expressions. Although individual capacities for political involvement and citizenship rights are necessary for efficient or 'rationally' functioning economic markets, we do not claim that an efficient political market is on the horizon as well, even as the role of the state is being redefined in many countries. On the contrary, as a result of new resources now commanded by many individual and collective actors, politics are becoming more fragile.

The basis for social solidarity in modern society needs to be closely examined. In particular, one needs to ask whether knowledge offers the foundation for solidarity or contributes to its breakdown.

Until quite recently, social scientists were preoccupied with chronicling the immense and alleged inevitable growth of certain functions of the state, for example, in health care, education, science and technology policies, and redistributive programs. This chronicle included an attendant focus upon the centralization of power in society, the expanding economic role of governments, the enlarged role of governments as employers, and the immeasurably expanded function of public welfare. These developments were equally evident in societies with very different political regimes and leadership. They were regarded to be a result of specific sociostructural necessities of modern society, such as the enlarged complexity of economic systems and the more general increasing differentiation of societies.

The transformations observed and analysed by social scientists made reference to the fact that modern governments controlled half or even more of the national product. This control of economic resources profoundly affected the context within which modern politics occurred and societies were governed. The fascination with social, economic, and cultural forces that appeared to rationalize, concentrate, consolidate, and centralize led to notions such as the technical state as outlined by Herbert Marcuse (1964) and Helmut Schelsky (1961). The singular focus on the technical state deflected attention from structures and processes that sustain cleavages, conflicts, diversity, loss of power, traditional norms, and plurality. As Marcuse (1964, 48) feared, the 'decline of freedom and opposition is not a matter of moral and intellectual deterioration or corruption. It is rather an objective societal process insofar as the production and distribution of an increasing quantity of goods and services make compliance a rational technologic attitude.'

In contrast, any discussions of the political system, political participation, and political realities must be cognizant of the profound transformation of the modern economy. The widespread affluence it has

produced, the general decline in the fortune of purely economic matters, and the extent to which work has become a knowledge-based
activity, especially among politically active social strata, must all be
considered. Political participation, which includes a deliberate choice
to abstain from participation, is more effective if it is grounded in
knowledge. Many observers of present-day politics have recognized
the importance of such changes and focus their analyses on the proliferation of 'new' social movements, for example. The task new social
movements typically set as their agenda is to demand a more open
political process. The challenge of emerging social movements is not a
'revolutionary attack against the system, but a call for democracies to
change and adapt' (Dalton, Kuechler, and Bürklin 1990, 3).

In contrast, as public pessimism about the ability of the state to
govern became more marked in the early 1970s, conservative social
theorists investigated the crisis tendencies in industrial societies under
the general heading 'governability of society' or, even more broadly, in
terms of the 'stalled society' (cf. Crozier [1970] 1973; Crozier, Huntington,
and Watanuki 1975; Greven, Guggenberger, and Strasser 1975; King
1975, 1976). It was argued that the growing 'blockages' evident in
advanced societies are indicative of an increasing incapacity to effectively attend to 'problems' that must be solved collectively. Society is
likened to a stalled motor that is virtually incapable of moving a notch.
The authors of *Crisis of Democracy* (Crozier, Huntington, and Watanuki
1975) justify the title and urgent tone of their report by comparing the
climate of opinion in the West during the mid-1970s with the pessimistic mood of the early 1920s. Books such as Oswald Spengler's (1926)
immensely popular *The Decline of the West* served to reinforce a strong
and pervasive sense of social and political malaise.

The crisis tendencies in capitalism had long been a central topic in
Marxist analyses that located the sources of such conflicts in inherent
sociostructural tensions and contradictions. Ideological or cultural
sources of tensions that were neglected by Marxist perspectives achieved
prominence in analyses concerned with the governability of advanced
industrial societies (cf. Heidorn 1982). Interesting parallels between
neo-conservative and socialist critiques of Western industrial societies
became evident (cf. Offe [1979] 1984).[1] After reviewing a number of
political diagnoses of American society during the 1970s, Habermas
([1982] 1983, 76) concluded that the 'formerly liberal neoconservatives
are concerned with the alleged loss of authority of the central institutions, especially the political system. This phenomenon is presented

suggestively with key terms like governability, decline of credibility, the loss of legitimacy, etc.' Crozier ([1970] 1973, v) diagnoses severe 'blockages' that are not merely features of his primary interest, French society. He argues these to be essential features of modern advanced societies in general. The obstructions are not limited to large social institutions or 'collective management,' but are manifest even in day-to-day transactions. In everyday life, 'people are trapped in vicious circles; whatever their intentions, the logic of the system distorts their activities and forces them to collaborate in preserving the model' (Crozier [1970] 1973, vi). Analyses of the stalled society employ such terms as 'rigidity,' 'strait-jacket,' 'suffocation,' 'trap,' 'paralysis,' 'stagnation,' and 'involution.' These terms are designed to highlight the seriousness of the blockages and the urgency of ameliorative intervention.

We focus on three aspects of the politics of knowledge societies. First, we consider the broader social and economic conditions to which the political system must respond. Second, we examine the extent to which knowledge, as a differential capacity to act, becomes a component of politics and the ways in which political actors define and comprehend reality. As Haas (1990, 11) observes, 'science becomes a component of politics because the scientific way of grasping reality is used to define the interests that political actors articulate and defend.' Third, we analyse emergent changes in world-views and the meaning of citizenship in democratic societies.

The common understanding of citizenship in the past was not unlike the role expected of children in traditional family settings – namely, conformity to the legitimate demands of the parents. The role of the responsible citizen is to adhere to, facilitate, and conform to the state-prescribed responsibilities of such a role. Now political participation increasingly means to interpret, to review, or to resist government-initiated action, and/or to launch public action that wants to affect the decision-making process of state agencies. Any discovery, description, and analysis of the changing forms of political participation and of cognitive mobilization requires a growing familiarity with the 'micro-political' manifestations of the transformed reality as we are no longer subject to the primary influence of large-scale political movements.

Political actions are illustrated in the form of micropolitics, such as intervention that neither touches directly upon the state and its organs nor has immediate political results. Consequences for the political system and society at large become evident, at most, in the greater frequency and greater density of individual actions. Although often loosely organized, or even disorganized, such micro-political actions may, in the long run, help bring about far-reaching changes or effectively counteract the designs of larger institutions. As Feenberg (1995, 37) poignantly observes, micro-political activities constitute a new version of situation-specific politics that increasingly relies on local knowledge and local action: 'It implements no overall strategy and offers no global challenge to the society; instead, it involves a multitude of potentially converging activities with long-term subversive impacts' and therefore is a decisive component of the fragility of modern society.

The meaning of citizenship, as well as the explication of and efforts to enact the interests of a great variety of political actors, is increasingly oriented towards conceptions of society and nature articulated in the scientific community. Knowledge-based politics also becomes knowledge-based resistance to political action. Since modern scientific discourse lacks a monolithic quality, it becomes a resource of political action for individuals and groups who may pursue very diverse interests. Scientific discourse within practical contexts is often a source of uncertainty. What is therefore required is a highly differentiated conception of the interrelation between politics and science. This is a perspective that cannot be found in the typical portrait of the technical state. A perspective of science and politics that emphasizes contingencies cannot embrace such notions as a science of politics or the claim that science is a consensual form of knowledge that holds the key for lasting collective well-being or even social harmony. Nor is knowledge always disinterested, and politics always partisan. Knowledge *adds* to the capacity for action. It does so equally for opponents of a regime and for the administrative apparatus in power. Instead of being the source of reliable, trustworthy knowledge, science becomes a source of uncertainty. And contrary to what rational scientific theories suggest, this problem cannot be comprehended or remedied by differentiating between 'good' and 'bad' science or between pseudo-science and proper science. After all, who would be capable of doing this under conditions of uncertainty?

The thesis regarding the lack of governability of modern society is primarily concerned with the decreasing ability of politicians to carry out their mandate as the result of a heightened 'irrationality' of politics. As a result, there is a fundamental contradiction between concerns about the growing ungovernability of society and renewed warnings about the 'dangers of societal rationalization' in the postmodern age. Especially promoted are the notions of a 'deep and progressive disempowerment' of the clients of the modern welfare state and the subjects of corporate capitalism (White 1991, 7–8). And, as the choice of terms already signals, the 'loss of governability' thesis tends to be a state-centred approach.

The specific symptoms of the diagnosis usually involve reference to: (a) an *overload* of the political system with claims, expectations, and objectives, but also participants (e.g., Crozier 1975, 12),[2] and (b) the *disparity* between the 'inflation' in claims and ability of the state apparatus to deliver, and the state's steering and performance capacity.[3] As Huntington (1975, 104) argues, 'in the industrialized world, domestic problems thus become intractable. The public develops expectations that are impossible for government to meet. The activities – and expenditures – of government expand, but the success of government in achieving its goals seem dubious. In a democracy, however, political leaders in power need to score successes if they are going to stay in power.' As emphasized by at least some observers who diagnose a decline in the governability of modern societies, the 1960s witnessed an unprecedented surge in democratic spirit and participation. That surge, however, is not considered by these observers to be a satisfactory development, since it paradoxically results in an 'excess' of democracy responsible for the decline in the vitality and governability in the democratic system.

As Huntington (1975, 114) therefore underlines, the 'effective operation of a democratic political system usually requires some measure of apathy and noninvolvement on the part of some individuals and groups.' The redisciplining solution to the crisis brought about by the adversarial culture of the young, the mass media, and dissident intellectuals is, for neo-conservatives like Huntington, a greater reliance on 'expertise, seniority and experience' as a means of restoring the 'democratic balance' (Huntington 1975, 113).

The plausibility of such ungovernability appears to be widely shared, despite the absence of systematic and persuasive empirical analyses. Offe ([1979] 1984, 75), for example, refers to the 'highly descriptive value of the ungovernability thesis,' that is, the 'two components of the diagnosis fully and correctly circumscribe the functional problems that now confront the capitalist welfare and intervention state.' Moreover, there is persuasive empirical evidence of a wealth of symptoms concerning the growing disjuncture between demands made on governments and their actual capacity to satisfy such demands. These symptoms are manifest in new social movements, in the decline of the nation-state, in secular changes in the social structure and culture of modern society, and in the constant up-and-down public relevance and career of political topics (see Downs 1972).[4]

It needs to be emphasized that the aforementioned thesis often turns into a lament about the collapse of traditional institutions or social control and the need to increase state authority and power. The other side of the coin of the observation that social control processes have collapsed is, of course, as Crozier (1975, 250) recognizes, that 'everywhere in the West the freedom of choice of the individual has increased tremendously. With the crumbling of old barriers everything seems to be possible. Not only can people chose their jobs, their friends, and their mates without being constrained by earlier conventions, but they can drop these relationships more easily.' The conclusion – limiting our comments to but one of the neo-conservative laments Crozier advances – that the collapse of traditional social control patterns is replaced by a vacuum in which social control is entirely absent is, of course, a highly non-sociological observation.

Our own analysis, in contrast, is not in any way devoted to voicing regrets about the declining political authority of the modern state and the alleged moral and cultural crisis that presumably accompanies ungovernability. Nor do we have an affinity with efforts to locate those 'responsible' for the challenges faced by the state as the result of the 'decay' in the social basis of democracies.[5] Moreover, we are not concerned with the transformation of the foundations of the liberal state, especially the 'absolute' constitutional guarantees of freedom and equality that are often seen as undermining the 'discipline' citizens ought to demonstrate in order to ease the state's immense difficulties in coping with growing problems.

The following somewhat ambivalent warning by Wilhelm Hennis (1977, 16) is, in some ways, representative of views that may be interpreted as a justification for a dismantling of constitutional rights in an attempt to improve the capacity of the state to impose its will: 'Since all conduct, even existence itself, is based on our opinions, it is self-evident how difficult governing is or can be in communities based on absolute freedom and equality of all opinions … It is self-evident that the vast challenges now or soon faced by humanity and individual political systems can only be met with an unusual degree of *discipline, energy and moral stringency*' (emphasis added). In the end, *systemic* attributes of the liberal state such as the expansion of its social expenditures, are held responsible for its practical impotence. Thus, 'what Marxists erroneously ascribe to the capitalist economy is in reality [seen as] a result of the democratic political process' (Huntington 1975, 73). The conservative German historian Ernst Nolte (1993) shares such a diagnosis and calls it merely a realistic appraisal of modern liberal politics. Voicing his strong opposition to such views, Offe ([1979] 1984, 81) stresses that 'in the conservative world-view the crisis of governability is a disturbance in the face of which the false path of political modernization must be abandoned and nonpolitical principles of order, such as family, property, achievement, and science, must again be given their due.' A return to the past, especially to the early modern, or even premodern, world that derived its coherence from an adherence to centralized, hierarchical, and patriarchal religious sanctions is, of course, an absurd demand.

Initially, the thesis of the decreasing governability of modern society appears to imply that groups and individuals harbouring feelings of powerlessness and who still recall the former extensive power of the state or who have effectively resisted governmental decisions, now experience a greater sense of power. Those in power may well experience an inability to effectively cope with immediate problems of a loss of authority, such as those that result from the withdrawal of the public's normative consent. Since governability has mainly been examined from the state's perspective – namely, the agency of the state and its loss of political authority – most diagnoses primarily refer to a crisis brought about by the *disappearing* legitimacy of governments. Such diagnoses not only neglect to consider the gains and benefits of 'ungovernability,' but also often fail to examine the reasons behind the decline in the efficacy of the state, other than an alleged withdrawal of consent. It is also assumed that the *status quo ante* was characterized by extensive political authority by the state, and that ineffectiveness gives rise to a loss of consent rather than the reverse. In addition, much of the literature tends to be silent on the 'concrete objects of conflict that constitute the substance of the demands and expectations as they do about the character of those matters requiring regulation' (Offe [1979] 1984, 79).

Efficacy is about the ability to get things done. It is not only about decision making, but also about implementing decisions. To get things done means to be more or less in control of the general circumstances within which objectives need to be met.[6] Thus, a decline in governability primarily occurs as a result of a loss in control over conditions and circumstances of political action. Not only are government objectives extended in modern society, but the range of circumstances to which they apply are enlarged as well. In addition, the circumstances within which political objectives are realized are changing along with the subjects of these circumstances. Moreover, these varied circumstances are, to a lesser extent than in the past, subject to the control of state agencies. Generally, the recalcitrance of circumstances has risen. The relative loss of sovereignty or territoriality of the nation-state is but one element in the equation that produces a heightened recalcitrance of conditions conducive to political action.

The experience and perception of 'ungovernability' is, however, fundamentally linked to political conduct and administrative procedures that still aim to realize objectives based on the premise that changes in the recalcitrance of circumstances can be neglected as irrelevant or may be overcome in principle. In other words, the demystification of the state and the disenchantment with traditional modes of political representation, as well as the broad loss in confidence in governments, do not necessarily go hand in hand with a general cynicism about any kind of government. The conviction that the loss of efficacy of government can be recaptured, or that the contradiction between expectations and performance can be overcome, is still widely present among the public in developed societies (see Panitch 1993, 3). The accelerated, 'homemade' transformation of society generally has lowered sensitivity towards evolving limits and barriers against further (especially radical) transformations of society. The limits in question, that is, the growing recalcitrance of circumstances, are the product of these transformations and of their unanticipated consequences.

We will mention only one effort to quantify the massive erosion in confidence and trust in the American government in the last few decades: 'In 1964, three-quarters of the American public said that they trusted the federal government to do the right thing most of the time. Today [1997] only a quarter of Americans admit to such trust' (Nye 1997, 1; see also Inglehart, 1997b). The governments of developed societies may find some solace in the fact that the confidence of the public in all major social institutions is on the decline, and that the loss of trust in the political system can also be observed in all developed societies.

The economy's success in tackling relative material scarcity also leads to a change in the nature of political struggles and conflicts. The diminished relevance of traditional social constructs, such as property and labour, leads not merely to a shift in values (in the sense of particular objectives pursued by political actors), but, even more important, to an enlargement of resources at the disposal of actors. Politics, once viewed as a struggle between owners of the means of production and those who merely own their labour power, gives way to much broader political and social conflicts that increasingly involve such factors as lifestyle as well as a repositioning in the agendas of political parties.

Inglehart (1971, 1977, 1987, 1997a) has described such shifts in *values* that govern political preferences and class-based politics in advanced societies among younger cohorts as a movement away from primarily materialistic concerns towards a much more postmaterialistic outlook. Postmaterialist values are about personal and collective freedom, self-expression, and quality of life. Resonating with Karl Mannheim's ([1928] 1993) classical essay on the problem of generations, the overall speed of the transformation of values as a whole is tempered by the persistence of particular beliefs throughout an individual's lifetime. Inglehart combines a socialization hypothesis with a scarcity thesis. Echoing Mannheim, Inglehart argues that the fundamental world-view of an individual is linked to early socialization experiences. If the formative context in which value orientations are developed is characterized by economic security and prosperity, postmaterialistic values are likely to emerge. Periods of scarcity, on the other hand, are linked to a materialistic outlook. In the present age, the emergence of a postmaterialist world-view commenced with the postwar generations who experienced their formative years in conditions of relative economic and physical security. Younger, highly educated persons in developed societies tend to be the main proponents of a postmaterialist world-view (cf. De Graaf and Evans 1996). The trend towards postmaterialist values implies new political priorities, especially with regard to communal values and lifestyle issues, and leads to a gradual neutralization of political polarization based on traditional class-based loyalties (see also Inglehart and Abramson 1994). The result is that class-linked voting, for instance, 'in most democracies is less than half as strong as it was a generation ago' (Inglehart 1987, 1298).

Among the questions relevant in the context of the genesis and the correlates of postmaterialistic values are the relative importance of (formal) education and the mediating influence of the experience or the expectations of material well-being during the formative years. Indeed, some of the critics of Inglehart's assertion of a trend towards postmaterialistic values have argued that the origins of postmaterialistic value orientations are mainly located in an increase in the level of formal education among younger cohorts and, more generally, in improved economic conditions (for example, Duch and Taylor 1993). Inglehart rejects this interpretation. In his view, the extent of formal education has a weaker and a less immediate influence on the emergence of postmaterialistic values than has the experience of relative economic security.

On the whole, the persistent controversy about the exact role of education and/or the experience of existential security in the process of the emergence of postmaterial values among younger generations in modern societies has no immediate relevance for the generally accepted observation that postmaterialism is, in fact, on the rise. Whether educational, cultural, or economic backgrounds (or a figuration among these factors) is particularly significant does not detract from the now widely confirmed observation that a change in generational worldviews is under way. On the one hand, it seems to be argued that early and apparently largely unreflexive experiences with or without relative economic security have a decisive influence on the positioning of individual value orientations. On the other hand, the close association between education and postmaterial outlooks seems to indicate that a more conscious, reflexive process determines the value dispositions. The discussion refers to and is, for the most part, based on survey-type data that rarely allow for a precise factoring out of the processes stipulated to be at work. Abramson and Inglehart (1995, 85) admit as much, indicating that survey data relevant to 'formative security' are difficult to obtain in the first place. A decision about the nature of the social and cultural forces at work in the formation of generational word-views is, of course, also only possible once we have a clearer idea about the 'end points' of generational identities and how they may be subject to change over time.

Karl Mannheim ([1928] 1993, 374–5) has already issued a rather ambivalent opinion on this matter in his classical essay on generations. The controversy's opponents have largely ignored this essay. Mannheim questioned any precise determination of the formation of a generational outlook or the termination of primary socialization. He considered it to be entirely possible that individuals continue to encounter circumstances in their life-world that refashion and rewrite their value orientations. In addition, one cannot preclude from the beginning that there might not be altogether different paths that lead to the formation of a single world-view. In short, a definitive answer about the formative influence of education and familial existential security – and of collective, national expectations of the comparative state of economic well-being – is difficult to achieve.

Inglehart argues that the level of educational achievement is a valid indicator for the experience of existential security.[7] We know that the achieved educational level correlates with the material well-being of the parents. Inglehart points out that survey data show that 'Europeans with higher levels of education tend to be less likely to be Materialists and more likely to be Postmaterialists than those with lower educational levels' (Abramson and Inglehart 1995, 77). But the same correlation can be observed for older cohorts, even for groups that received their schooling during the Mussolini and Hitler eras. At the same time, a secular trend towards postmaterial values is noted. Such a trend is in evidence in survey data that show, for example, younger university-educated cohorts displaying a higher degree of affinity towards postmaterialism than older individuals with the same education. Abramson and Inglehart (1995, 81) stipulate that 'there is nothing inherent in education that automatically produces Postmaterialist values.' It is possible that present-day educational systems (that is, the teachers) are much more sympathetic towards postmaterial values when compared with schools and universities of a couple of generations ago. Inglehart is convinced, however, that fundamental economic changes and expectations that then work their way towards cultural responses and adaptations precede the formation of such preferences. In this sense, at least, Inglehart remains a materialist.

Inglehart, in other words, somewhat underplays the fact that the volume and quality of cognitive skills, knowledge, and the resources available to political actors have risen considerably. But this increase in the resources available to political actors is not the outcome of a redistribution of existing capacities of action. It is the result of an extension of capacities of action from which 'ordinary' citizens have primarily benefited. The extension of the state has paradoxically empowered its citizens by extending the private and personal spheres and by producing numerous structural indeterminacies. The very 'success' of the state – its original autonomy and differentiation, and the enlargement of the range, scope, and intensity of its functions has meant that individuals and non-state groups have gained resources that can potentially aid them in approaching, enticing, demanding, resisting, and deflecting efforts of state agencies. As a result of these developments, the state is losing its status as a monolithic entity.

The lament about the loss of authority of the state needs to be augmented by several realizations: the rapid expansion of education (especially tertiary education); the growing importance of cognitive skills; the enfranchisement or the extension and reconfiguration of citizenship

to previously marginal groups; the defusion of class conflict; the growth of wealth and entitlements; the expansion of and easier access to communication networks (including the enlargement of the mass media); the rapid growth of knowledge-based occupations (and therefore of knowledge and skills that can be utilized as a resource not only on the job, but in a variety of social and political contexts); and, finally, the exceptional growth of the role and the sheer number of professionals in many fields. The devolution and decentering of the state is, to a considerable extent, the result of its own success.[8] The changes now under way, however, are difficult to empirically document. To some extent, this is the result of the continued use of indicators developed under different social regimes and not necessarily appropriate for emerging structures and processes. With some justification one may speak of social indicators that are 'frozen in time.'

The controversial issue of the source of value change in modern society – what is sometimes called 'subjective modernization and the individual enlargement of capacities to act'– is significant in this context. However, the exact attribution of factors remains difficult to demonstrate, as is the determination of indictors that illustrate the heightened presence and relevance of cognitive skills. We are convinced that the growing volume of knowledge that is individually and collectively available not only is a constitutive factor of knowledge societies, but also plays a decisive role in the governance of present-day society.

Economists in search of an empirical clarification of these rapid changes of the labour market, in particular the stratification of wages, have in recent years turned to new explanatory dimensions that remain hidden in most conventional labour markets and unobserved in population surveys. Similarly, there has been considerable speculation about cognitive skills that may be increasingly important as industry and the service sector restructure or as capital accumulation moves from redundant Fordist structures to new flexible post-Fordist modes of production. Of interest in this context is research that regards the role of cognitive skills, in contrast to years of formal schooling, as the much more common and sometimes even exclusive indicator for ascertaining knowledge or skills. In this spirit, Murnane, Willett, and Levy (1995) inquire if basic cognitive skills are becoming more important in wage determination on an economy-wide basis in the United States. Their focus is on the question of how mathematics skills of graduating high school seniors affect their wages at age twenty-four. They ask this question for two cohorts, first for students who graduated from high school in 1972, and then for students who graduated in 1980.[9] By comparing the relationship between wages and mathematics score between the two cohorts, they claim to be able to address two questions: (1) 'Are basic cognitive skills becoming more important in determining wages on an economy-wide basis?' and (2) 'How much of the increase in the college-high school wage premium during the 1980s stems from a widening of the skill gap between college graduates and high school graduates who did not go to college?' (Murnane, Willett, and Levy 1995, 252).

Let us first turn to the results of the study which pertain to a number of more conventional attributes that have been associated with wage differentials in the past. The Murnane results replicate the well-known results of the effect of years of schooling on subsequent wages. For example, their estimate is that, for males in the 1972 cohort, each year of completed *college* is associated with a wage premium of 2.2 per cent above the wage earned by individuals without any college education. The corresponding figure for the 1980 male graduates is 4.5 per cent; for females it is even more substantial – namely, 5.5 and 6.7 per cent, respectively.The main finding of their study is that, on an economy-wide basis, 'basic cognitive skills were more important predictors of wage six years after high school in the mid-1980s than in the late 1970s' (Murnane, Willett, and Levy 1995, 263). The authors therefore conclude that the growing importance of cognitive skills as measured by the mathematics test scores for the younger cohort in the study is rooted in a *demands* shift towards basic cognitive capacities and primarily reflects changes within occupational groups.[10] The demand for cognitive skills is not limited to a few firms but is strong enough to show up in a nation-wide sample. The Murnane study can only be considered to be a beginning. Wages are a 'compositive compensation for a variety of skills' (Murphy and Welch 1993, 109) and the supply and demand for such skills varies.[11] An examination of the impact of basic mathematical skills acquired early on in high school can only be a first approximation of changes in the labour market.

Indeed, nothing else in the history of the industrialized countries of Western Europe and North America resembles the experience of the years between 1950 and 1995. By the end of this period, the perpetual possibility of serious economic hardship that in earlier periods had threatened the wellbeing of up to three-quarters of the population now affected only one-fifth. Although real poverty still existed in even the richest countries, the material standard of living for most people improved almost without interruption and quite rapidly for forty-five years (see Milward 1992). In addition, during the same period, access to higher education doubled or tripled in many countries. This unprecedented prosperity and the growing access to higher education mark this period as unique.

The focus on knowledge also implies a focus on the new bases for effective political participation (and conflicts).[12] What cognitive resources of action allow for the possibility of more practiced forms of participation? And how broadly do these resources need to be socially distributed in order to extend participation to the non-elite strata of a population? More concretely, how does knowledge function as a resource in struggles for status or dominance in cognitive representations?

Knowledge should be conceptualized in this context as a bundle of social competencies that drive the process of political participation and form as well as maintain social prestige and status. Knowledge as a broad and heterogeneous bundle of competencies has noticeable effects on the *process* of participation. In this sense, knowledge possesses qualities that are unlike earlier, more singular mechanisms of political participation.

Generally, the range of social competencies amount to stratified facilities for *mastering one's life*, for example, one's health (life expectancy), financial well-being, personal life, aspirations, career or long-term security, or the ability to locate and gain assistance towards mastering these tasks. They represent the generalized effects of a differential access to relevant knowledge bases.[13] The ability to mobilize defiance, exploit discretion, develop ways of coping, and organize protection are a significant part of such strategies, and therefore of the conviction that one is in charge and not merely the victim of fortuitous circumstances. Yet it is wise to conclude with Simmel ([1907] 1978, 440) that, while the widespread 'rise in the level of knowledge as a whole is indeed remarkable and its effect on the social inequality regime in modern societies is profound, it does not mean that inequality will be significantly lowered or is about to disappear.'

What is remarkable about the debate in the 1970s about the governability of modern democratic societies is an almost complete absence of reference to globalization processes as a possible major source of decline in the ability of the state to give direction, impose its will, or otherwise execute and realize policy decisions. For the most part, the decline of governability is seen as confined to the nation-state. The sovereignty of the nation-state itself is almost never questioned. Serious discussion about globalization and its varied consequences begins only after the period during which the thesis of a lack of governability had preoccupied political scientists and sociologists. Economists, on the other hand, were already pointing to globalization as the motor of societal changes. It took some time before the focus of the debate shifted in this direction among other social scientists as well. Today, the issue of governability is primarily framed in terms of the impact of globalization on the political system of the nation-state (e.g., Zürn 1996, 14). Globalization and (un)governability is the focus of Part One, and informs all of the essays in this volume.

Notes

1 John Keane (1988, 6–11) examines the apparent contradiction in neo-conservative discourse regarding the role of the state. On the one hand, such discourse favours a systematic reduction in the functions of the state and its policies. On the other hand, it is concerned about the loss of the state's moral and political authority (see also the excerpts of remarks made by Ralf Dahrendorf on the Governability Study, reprinted in Crozier, Huntington, and Watanuki 1975, 188–95).
2 One of the non-conforming accounts of the reasons for the apprehended difficulties of the state that reduce its ability to effectively execute its mandate and refers, as most observers do, to the magnitude of societal demands and the impatience of its clients, is Gianfranco Poggi's (1982) observations about the persistence of bureaucratic organizational patterns. The ineffective functioning of state rule is linked to the sprawling gigantism, fragmentation, and introversion of the bureaucracy that account for 'the costliness of the state apparatus, and the tardiness and inefficiency of its mode of operation' (Poggi 1982, 359).
3 We will leave aside the question whether it is possible and sensible to attribute the decline of governability primarily to *domestic* issues. Huntington (1975, 104), for example, stresses that governments, as a result of the recognition of growing difficulties in attaining domestic policy objectives, move their attention increasingly to the field of foreign policy matters, where success is presumably easier to attain, although 'a decline in the governability of democracy at home means a decline in the influence of democracy abroad' (Huntington 1975, 106). In this particular instance, as well as in many other details of the thesis of the decline in

governability, it is difficult to disentangle (even with the benefit of hind-sight) political, economic, and cultural features that are historically highly context-specific from those that may be of a more lasting importance.

4 Few social scientists implicate the social sciences in these developments, especially in the genesis of the exaggerated expectation that the state is, in principle, capable of solving many of the problems social scientists have identified as needing solutions. One observer who has highlighted the importance of the social sciences in this respect is Friedrich Tenbruck (1977, 144), who points to the central role of the social sciences in concep-tualizing problems as social problems and in offering solutions based on social science constructs. According to Tenbruck, the social sciences there-fore ought to be credited with a long list of practical failures. Tenbruck holds the social sciences at least indirectly responsible for a growing gap between performance and expectations.

5 Crozier, Huntington, and Watanuki (1975, 6–7) identify an adversary cul-ture, for example, that democratic societies have spawned. This culture consists of opportunistic 'value-oriented intellectuals who often devote themselves to the derogation of leadership, the challenging of authority, and the unmasking and delegitimation of established institutions.' The threat to the traditional state ('as serious as those posed in the past by the aristocratic cliques, fascist movements, and communist parties'), if any such strata existed, appears to have been rather short-lived, as we know. Crozier (1975, 25, 33–7), in addition, blames the mass media and the break-down of traditional social control mechanisms, including the moral au-thority of churches, schools, and cultural organizations, in reinforcing the disintegration and drift in Western societies.

6 The distinction between social integration and system integration, or be-tween rules that are followed by individuals and regularities at the collec-tive level that are self-implementing, is discussed by Offe ([1979] 1984, 83), whose description of the loss of efficacy of the state takes both of these dimensions into consideration: 'Social systems may be said to be ungov-ernable if the rules their members follow violate their own underlying functional laws, or if they do not *act* in such a way that these laws can *function* at the same time' (Offe 1979, 313).

7 Abramson and Inglehart (1995, 86) propose a more differentiated enu-meration of characteristics and experiences that are linked to the level of formal education: 'We suggest that "education" actually taps a number of distinct variables: (1) indoctrination, both formal and informal; (2) the respondents' current socioeconomic status; (3) parental socioeconomic status during the respondent's formative years; (4) the historical era when

the respondent was born and educated; (5) the degree to which the respondent has acquired various skills; and (6) the respondent's information level, since these skills make it easier to acquire information.' The relative importance of each of these factors and experiences varies, depending on the specific dependent variable. At the same time, the list actually underplays the role of the education system in helping to bring about a secular transformation in the general level of cognitive skills, growth of knowledge, and overall increase in the level of education.

8 At the level of culture and politics, a shift can be observed in some countries towards a more pronounced celebration of the local, and a reassertion of traditional values. This shift perhaps resonates with the more general societal developments we have described. It may also represent, at least in the self-consciousness of the active participants in such movements, a 'protest against homogenization of state-bureaucratic capitalism – against creeping mediocrity, mass-culture, unisex society' (Friedman 1989, 54). However, such a diagnosis simultaneously perpetuates the myth of the efficacy of the power of the state in the past and underestimates the importance of fundamental transformations in the structure of society as a precursor for important cultural shifts.

9 The two samples on which their information is based are longitudinal studies of high school seniors. The samples include both women and men and are based on individuals who had completed their formal education and who engaged in paid work for six years after graduation. In their last year of high school, the participants in the two samples took a mathematics test. The test assessed students' skill in following directions, working with fractions and decimals, and interpreting line graphs. In other words, the test measured elementary mathematical concepts and not advanced mathematical knowledge. The average math scores for the 1980 high graduates is lower than for the 1972 cohort.

10 As the authors of the study emphasize, the nature of the tested mathematics skills of high school seniors (age seventeen to eighteen) pertains to curriculum matters that are taught in American high schools no later than the eighth grade, or at about age fourteen.

11 For an analysis of the college-wage premium, see Katz and Murphy (1992) and Murphy and Welch (1992).

12 Daniel Bell (1973, 44) remarks that any new system generates hostility among those who feel left out or threatened by it. Among the primary cleavages and sources of tension in the 'emerging post-industrial society is the conflict generated by a meritocracy principle which is central to the allocation of position in the knowledge society.'

13 In the United States, the social location of many of these activities can be
    found in what Peter Drucker (1989, 187) calls the 'third' sector of non-
    profit, non-governmental, 'human change' institutions (or, the 'civil soci-
    ety sector' as Salomon and Anheier [1997] have called it). The third sector
    is actually the 'country's largest employer, though neither its workforce
    nor the output it produces show up in the statistics. One out of every two
    adult Americans – a total of 90 million people – are estimated to work as
    volunteers in the third sector' (Drucker 1989, 197).

References

Abramson, Paul R., and Ronald Inglehart. 1995. *Value Change in Global Perspec-
    tive*. Ann Arbor: University of Michigan Press.
Bell, Daniel. 1973. *The Coming of Post-Industrial Society: A Venture in Social
    Forecasting*. New York: Basic Books.
Crozier, Michel. [1970] 1973. *The Stalled Society*. New York: Viking Press.
Crozier, Michel. 1975. 'Western Europe.' Pp. 11–57 in Michel Crozier, Samuel
    P. Huntington, and Joji Watanuki, eds., *The Crisis of Democracy: Report on the
    Governability of Democracies to the Trilateral Commission*. New York: New York
    University Press.
Crozier, Michel, Samuel P. Huntington, and Joji Watanuki, eds. 1975. *The Crisis
    of Democracy: Report on the Governability of Democracies to the Trilateral Com-
    mission*. New York: New York University Press.
Dalton, Russell J., Manfred Kuechler, and Wilhelm Bürklin. 1990. 'The Chal-
    lenge of New Movements.' Pp. 3–20 in Russell J. Dalton, and Manfred
    Kuechler, eds., *Challenging the Political Order: New Social and Political Move-
    ments in Western Democracies*. New York: Oxford University Press.
De Graaf, N.D., and G. Evans. 1996. 'Why Are the Young More Postmaterial-
    ist? A Cross-national Analysis of Individual and Contextual Influences on
    Postmaterial Values.' *Comparative Political Studies* 28: 608–35.
Downs, Anthony. 1972. 'Up and Down with Ecology – The "Issue Attention
    Cycle".' *The Public Interest* 28: 38–50.
Drucker, Peter F. 1989. *The New Realities: In Government and Politics/In Econom-
    ics and Business/In Society and World View*. New York: Harper & Row.
Duch, Raymond M., and Michael A. Taylor. 1993. 'Postmaterialism and the
    economic condition.' *American Journal of Political Science* 37: 747–79.
Feenberg, Andrew. 1995. *Alternative Modernity: The Technical Turn in Philosophy
    and Social Theory*. Berkeley: University of California Press.
Friedman, Jonathan. 1989. 'Culture, Identity, and World Process.' *Review* 12:
    51–69.

Greven, Michael T., Guggenberger, Bernd, and Johano Strasser, eds. 1975. *Krise des Staates? Zur Funktionsbestimmung des Staates im Spätkapitalismus.* Darmstadt: Luchterhand.

Haas, Ernst B. 1990. *When Knowledge Is Power. Three Models of Change in International Organizations.* Berkeley: University of California Press.

Habermas, Jürgen. [1982] 1983. 'Neoconservative Culture Criticism in the United States and West Germany: An Intellectual Movement in Two Political Cultures.' *Telos* 56: 75–89.

– 1998. 'Die postnationale Konstellation und die Zukunft der Demokratie.' Public Lecture, Kulturforum of the Social Democratic Party, 5 June 1998, Willy-Brandt-Haus, Berlin.

Heidorn, Joachim. 1982. *Legitimität und Regierbarkeit. Studien zu den Legitimitätstheorien von Max Weber, Niklas Luhmann und Jürgen Habermas und der Ungleichheitsforschung.* Berlin: Duncker & Humblot.

Hennis, Wilhelm. 1977. 'Zur Begründung der Fragestellung.' Pp. 9–21 in Wilhelm Hennis, Peter Graf Kielmansegg, and Ulrich Matz, eds., *Regierbarkeit. Studien zu ihrer Problematisierung.* Band 1. Stuttgart: Klett-Cotta.

Huntington, Samuel P. 1975. 'The United States.' Pp. 59–118 in Michel Crozier, Samuel P. Huntington, and Joji Watanuki, eds., *The Crisis of Democracy. Report on the Governability of Democracies to the Trilateral Commission.* New York: New York University Press.

Inglehart, Ronald. 1971,'The Silent Revolution in Europe: Intergenerational Change in Post-Industrial Outlook.' *American Political Science Review* 65: 991–1017.

– 1977. *The Silent Revolution.* Princeton, NJ: Princeton University Press.

– 1987. 'Value Change in Industrial Society.' *American Political Science Review* 81: 1289–1303.

– 1997a. *Modernization and Postmodernization: Cultural, Economic and Political Change in 43 Societies.* Princeton, NJ: Princeton University Press.

– 1997b. 'Postmaterialist Values and the Erosion of Institutional Authority.' pp. 217–36 in Joseph S. Nye, Philip D. Zelikow, and David C. King, eds., *Why People Don't Trust Government.* Cambridge, MA: Harvard University Press.

Inglehart, Ronald, and Paul R. Abramson. 1994. 'Economic Security and Value Change.' *American Political Science Review* 88: 336–54.

Katz, Lawrence F., and Kevin M. Murphy. 1992. 'Changes in Relative Wages, 1963–1987: Supply and Demand Factors.' *Quarterly Journal of Economics* 107: 35–78.

Keane, John. 1988. *Democracy and Civil Society: On the Predicaments of European Socialism, the Prospects for Democracy, and the Problem of Controlling Social and Political Power.* London: Verso.

King, Anthony. 1975. 'Overload: Problems of Governing in the 1970s.' *Political Studies* 23: 284–96.

– ed. 1976.*Why Is Britain Harder to Govern?* London: BBC.

Luhmann, Niklas. [1988] 1997. 'Limits of Steering.' *Theory, Culture and Society* 14: 41–57.

Mannheim, Karl. [1928] 1993. 'The Problem of Generations.' pp. 351–95 in Kurt H. Wolff, ed., *From Karl Mannheim*, 2d expanded ed. New Brunswick, NJ: Transaction Books.

Marcuse, Herbert. 1964. *One-Dimensional Man: Studies in the Ideology of Advanced Industrial Society*. Boston: Beacon Press.

Milward, Alan S. 1992. *The European Rescue of the Nation-State*. Berkeley: University of California Press.

Murnane, Richard J., John B. Willett, and Frank Levy. 1995. 'The Growing Importance of Cognitive Skills in Wage Determination.' *Review of Economics and Statistics* 77: 251–66.

Murphy, Kevin M., and Finis Welch. 1992. 'Industrial Change and the Rising Importance of Skill.' Pp. 101–32 in Sheldon Danziger and Peter Gottschalk, eds., *Uneven Tides: Rising Inequality in the 1980s*. New York: Russell Sage Foundation.

– 1993. 'Inequality and Relative Wages.' *The American Economic Review: Papers and Proceedings* 83: 104–9.

Nolte, Ernst. 1993. 'Die Fragilität des Triumphs. Zur Lage des Liberalen Systems nach der neuen Weltordnung.' *Frankfurter Allgemeine Zeitung* 151, 3 July.

Nye, Joseph S. 1997. 'Introduction: The Decline of Confidence in Government.' Pp. 1–18 in Joseph S. Nye, Philip D. Zelikow, and David C. King, eds., *Why People Don't Trust Government*. Cambridge, MA: Harvard University Press.

Offe, Claus. 1979. '"Ünregierbarkeit": Zur Renaissance Konservativer Krisentheorien.' Pp. 294–318 in Jürgen Habermas, ed., *Stichworte zur 'Geistigen Situation der Zeit.'* Band 1: *Nation and Republik*. Frankfurt am Main: Suhrkamp.

– [1979] 1984. 'Ungovernability: On the Renaissance of Conservative Theories of Crisis.' Pp. 67–88 in Jürgen Habermas, ed., *Observations on 'The Spiritual Situation of the Age'*. Contemporary German Perspectives. Cambridge, MA: MIT Press.

Panitch, Leo. 1993. 'A Different Kind of State?' Pp. 2–16 in Gregory Albo, David Langille, and Leo Panitch, eds., *A Different Kind of State? Popular Power and Democratic Administration*. Toronto: Oxford University Press.

Poggi, Gianfranco. 1982. 'The Modern State and the Idea of Progress.'

Pp. 337–69 in Gabriel A. Almond, Marvin Chodorow, and Roy Harvey Pearce, eds., *Progress and Its Discontents*. Berkeley: University of California Press.

Salomon, Lester M., and Helmut K. Anheier. 1997. 'The Civil Society Sector.' *Society* 34: 60–5.

Schelsky, Helmut. 1961. *Der Mensch in der wissenschaftlichen Zivilisation*. Köln/ Opladen: Westdeutscher Verlag.

Simmel, Georg. [1907] 1978. *The Philosophy of Money*. London: Routledge and Kegan Paul.

Spengler, Oswald. 1926. *The Decline of the West*. New York: Knopf.

Tenbruck, Friedrich H. 1977. 'Grenzen der staatlichen Planung.' Pp. 134–49 in Wilhelm Hennis, Peter Graf Kielmansegg, and Ulrich Matz, eds., *Regierbarkeit. Studien zu ihrer Problematisierung*. Band 1. Stuttgart: Klett-Cotta.

Weber, Max. [1922] 1978. *Economy and Society*. Edited by Guenther Roth and Claus Wittich. Berkeley: University of California Press.

White, Stephen K. 1991. *Political Theory and Postmodernism*. Cambridge: Cambridge University Press.

Zürn, Michael. 1996. 'Globalisierung von Ökonomie und Gesellschaft.' pp. 9–24 in Werner Fricke, ed., *Jahrbuch für Arbeit und Technik 1966: Zukunft der Industriegesellschaft*. Bonn: Dietz.

Part One:

Globalization and Governance

Introduction

In Part One, David Held, David Elkins, and Warren Magnusson address core features of globalization and their implications for governance. David Held provides conceptual clarifications and analytical distinctions for more refined analyses of globalization and democratic government. David Elkins and Warren Magnusson offer sustained critiques of particular conceptions of globalization and their implications for governance. Prior to discussing each of these contributions, it is important that we clarify key issues in globalization and governance.

Modern societies are characterized by an awareness that government is not, and will not be, what it used to be, even in the recent past. This awareness is sharpened by the realities of cutbacks in social security expenditures, technological changes, shifting labour markets, greater emphasis on individual responsibility, intensified politics of identity and group rights, the loss of political autonomy by nation-states, and management by surveillance and audit. These realities are interconnected with new forms of governance beyond the state, for example, in the community, corporate institutions, social movements, and markets. Political interests from left to right are advocating reduction, or even removal, of many areas of governance from state control and supply. This advocacy is based not only on negative warnings about the perils of the intrusion of the state into the life of the individual. It is also a positive development of institutional forms and technologies that create an environment of economic, cultural, and political freedoms to enhance personal autonomy and enterprise. Of course, these developments are complex, ambiguous, shifting, uneven, and contradictory. There are counter-ideologies, for example, in support of stronger social rights and the welfare state; and counter-tendencies, for example, new forms of concentration, rationalization, and consolidation of power in both state and non-state institutions.

The transformations observed are widely attributed to globalization. Globalization is an abstraction that serves a wide variety of purposes simultaneously.

Globalization is a theoretical category of social science. It is a concept through which social scientists are trying to understand macro-level social, cultural, political, and, above all, economic forces that are bringing about the transformations noted above.

At the same time, globalization is a popular term that is useful in various contexts of everyday life. It is a political category of blame, justification, and excuse. For example, politicians use it freely in declaring that they must do something – reduce the deficit, promote free trade, allow incursions on their country's cultural industries – because of 'world order' forces beyond their control. In these political uses, globalization involves a denial of responsibility in order to shift responsibility onto something or someone else. One aggregate effect of this political use of globalization is the constitution of a new image of sovereignty at the level of world order.

Globalization is also a cultural category of fear. It is used to express grave concerns about those forces beyond the capacity of humans and their collectivities that are believed to be affecting long-term prospects for civility, economic security, health, well-being. and democracy. These fears are compounded by the current ideological strength of neo-liberalism, with its peculiar emphasis on individual responsibility. Every person is to be his or her own risk manager, own political economy, in a context of declining state social security provision and rapid social change.

Globalization is also an economic category of opportunity and enterprise. It is a discourse that moves people to economic action, to create mini-capitalist enterprises that allow self-sufficiency, economic advancement, and personal security. Ideally, *the* political economy is to wither away, or to be constituted solely out of the billions of individual political economies that meet in agreeable market transactions.

Globalization also serves as a social category of new forms of interaction, especially technologically mediated interaction. It expresses the fact that new electronic communication orders such as the Internet have fostered new forms of meaningful interaction at a distance, and collapsed space and time. People now routinely interact with no sense of place.

These changes in social interaction patterns in space and time, combined with the above-noted political, cultural, and economic elements, give globalization its geographic dimension. New conceptions of territory have arisen, which in turn create new questions about belonging: to communities, nation-states, institutions, and cultural identity configurations. Conceptions of past, present, and future alter. Traditions are variously erased, rewritten, and invented. Insecurities generate reflexivity about risk and a new future orientation in both individuals and social institutions. The physical environment becomes a particular focus of concern, both the dark sides of the urbanscape and the seeming inability to escape to a more natural environment.

These discourses and experiences of globalization are embedded in new regimes and practices of governance, which in turn amplify the experiences and elaborate the discourses. Private corporate institutions have acquired new roles and responsibilities in governance. For example, governance is increasingly accomplished through privately authorized and controlled electronic technologies of surveillance and accounting technologies of audit. State regulatory agencies pull back from direct intervention in the affairs of private corporations, and instead emphasize the nurturing of corporate cultures and the facilitation of self-governance. Multinational insurance companies – with their panoply of associated financial, legal, medical, and preventative security institutions – take over and commodify many aspects of security provision that are also recognized as responsibilities of the liberal state.

The discourses and practices of globalization are also articulated in various community-based contexts beyond the state. New social movements promote communitarian solutions to problems of collective civility, responsibility, and well-being. State-backed programs of health, welfare, and deviance management are decentred into local settings to foster more community-based responsibility and control, including especially cost control. New communication technologies facilitate new communities of interest at a distance, whether built around market identities of consumers or the political identities of group interests and rights.

These new private corporate and community-based articulations of governance also constitute and are constituted by individual self-governance. The individual is to become his or her own risk manager through reflexive awareness of risk in all spheres of governable life. He or she is to sustain awareness through professional expertise, popular media, the Internet, special courses, and any other means for making reasonable choices as a responsible agent of consumption. Health is to be consumed as a matter of constant exercise, diet, and drug management. Culture is to be consumed as a matter of constant vigilance regarding bad effects, for example, from the Internet and television regarding foreign content, pornography, violence, information overload, and new physical disabilities associated with excessive use. Financial markets are to be consumed through instant electronic access to mutual fund and securities transactions that ostensibly allows better choice about one's financial future. Consuming the future is to be a reasonable blend of risk management and risk taking. This sensibility also applies to individual participation in the political sphere, for example, environmental movements that inform individuals about how their market choices will incrementally influence the sustainable future.

The new forms of governance on state, private corporate, community, and individual levels make it clear that democracy is something that cannot be managed from above. Globalization holds no promise that a new world order backed by supranational sovereignty will provide more democracy, equality, and security in alliances with capitalism. There remains a strong need for the correct mix of state, private corporate, community, and individual responsibilities in blending capitalism with social democracy.

David Held considers how globalization as 'the progressive enmeshment of human communities with each other' results in an ongoing refiguring of liberal democracy and its economic, cultural, environmental, legal, and national security dimensions. He initially demarcates how the foundations of modern democratic theory are embedded in modern ideas about nation and territory. There is a long-standing belief that national political communities can be relatively autonomous because they have the capacity to control their own destinies, and the attendant ability to make their citizens believe in their common good. Moreover, this belief in collective self-determination is made geographic by relating systems of governance to a defined territory, and by constructing what is outside that territory as external, foreign, the other. At least in theory, democratic technologies (e.g., elections) and representations (e.g., the meaning of citizenship) can be connected to territorial boundaries to yield consent by citizens to the legitimacy of nationally bounded decision makers.

Held observes that the main problem with these national and territorial foundations of modern democratic theory is a geographical bias. It is more cogent to view political communities sociologically, as overlapping networks of interaction, rather than geographically, as bounded territorial totalities. These social networks are organized around multiple sites and forms of economic, political, and cultural power that have no obvious sense of place. They spiral through interregional and transcontinental patterns of activity across space and time.

Globalization has been with us for a long time; indeed, it is a characteristic feature of modernity. In Held's view, the contemporary conjuncture is different and worthy of the 'globalization' rubric because of the rapidly increasing *extensiveness* of social networks, the *intensity* of activity within these networks, and in turn their impact on previously more bounded communities. These features of globalization must be analysed within each of several domains, including the economic, cultural, environmental, legal, and national security domains. These domains overlap, but it is best to keep them analytically distinct if one is to understand the specific relation between the global and the local.

Global economic processes are characterized by an enormous growth in trade, financial flows, and dominance of multinational corporations. Held offers several examples of the consequences of these processes that have appeared on an unprecedented scale. There are major price fluctuations based on speculation above and beyond the fundamentals of asset value. Finance has become hyper-competitive, based on differential interest rates available across worldwide capital markets. Employment is increasingly transitory and mobile, shifting to regions that offer lower employment costs. Shifts in employment and in financial strength also occur through technological transformation, with concentration in the most efficient centres of advanced technology. Changes in the global markets of speculation, competition, and technology also provide many more exit options for capital than was the case even in the recent past.

Held makes the important point that these real changes are accompanied by changes in the mentalities and sensibilities of decision makers. It is the template of international economies and global financial markets that is paramount in everyday political and business decisions.

Held is quick to observe, however, that the pressure is not simply one-way. Nation-states individually and in blocs still have substantial control over how they risk-manage the present economy and variously conserve and consume the future. We are far from the neo-liberal dream of a 'world market order' of minimally regulated free trade as the guarantor of efficiency and liberty, regardless of how much politicians use such rhetoric to escape some of their own political responsibilities.

In the cultural arena, nationally based culture and identity is being decentred by changes in telecommunications infrastructures, the reach of multimedia conglomerates, and the spread of tourism. Multinational corporations provide new forms of identity via consumption, including especially consumption of their corporate signs and slogans. Political communities and identities are reconfigured in transactional and transnational processes involving myriad commercial and cultural institutions.

Transboundary interactions also characterize the environmental arena, whether the issue is pollution, biodiversity (demographic expansion and resource consumption), or ecosystem integrity (respect for the 'global commons'). Held emphasizes that the risk-management responses to environmental problems are also transboundary, involving complex transactions among networks of scientific expertise, social movements, legal conventions, and political institutions. These social-network transactions have profound implications for the idea of political community, especially regarding the locus of decision making and deciding the political good.

In the realm of law, Held points to developments in international law conventions that are encroaching upon the sovereignty of nation-states. For example, the European Convention on Human Rights not only allows cases to be brought against violators between member states, but also allows an individual to initiate proceedings against his or her own government. Held observes that individuals, groups, and organizations now have an inroad on state sovereignty, albeit within the institutional constraints of law. On the other hand, compared to the other spheres analysed by Held, in terms of its scale and influence legal globalization is in its infancy. Some areas, such as the regulation of new communication technologies, are proving especially difficult for legal regimes. Other efforts, such as the current attempt to establish an international criminal law regime, evidence the continuing strength of the sovereignty of individual nation-states. Law has a peculiar habit of remaining domestic.

The domain of national security is being reconfigured by the forces of globalization, although it has always been subject to strategic alliances for specific challenges (e.g., international wars) as well as longer-term defensive posturing (e.g., the Cold War). The present emphasis is on collective defence and cooperative security. This emphasis has resulted not only from the dramatic change in borders in Europe and elsewhere over the past decade, but also from new technological connections among nation-states and multinational corporations.

Held argues the combined effect of these changes from each domain is that governments are no longer the locus of power or of self-determination for a collectivity. The myriad changes identified criss-cross in ways that substantially reduce the autonomy, and hence the sovereignty, of nation-states. They create problems of boundary and accountability. The boundaries of accountability are no longer evident, with attendant consequences for democratic consent and legitimacy. The categories of the nation-state are no longer capable of containing fundamental processes of governance. This situation creates an almost desperate need for new institutions and mechanisms of accountability *among* nation-states that in effect pool their resources of sovereignty. There is also a need for new social movements to constitute a 'cosmopolitan democracy' of citizens who mediate among their own traditions and alternative forms of life.

David Elkins points to the many ways in which globalization as the progressive enmeshment of human communities does not inevitably lead to the convergence and homogenization of these communities. Globalization has brought new forms and relations of governance, each with varied consequences for transactions within and between the communities involved.

Elkins characterizes modernity as a quest for standards and norms that are ahistorical, context-free, and universal. There is an emphasis on universality rather than diversity. In the ideals of modernity, globalization will yield progressive technological advance and refinement. However, in reality, technological advances, especially in transportation and communication, have resulted in varied processes and consequences. Globalization has in fact problematized the territorial basis of governance and fostered diversity.

In the contemporary world, two fundamentally different bases of governance have emerged. On the one hand, there is governance in terms of non-territorial identities and interests. There is a global 'virtual neighbourhood' of those with common identities and mutual interests: highly focused, specialized communities, networks, organizations, and institutions that nevertheless have a global reach and interact with each other via electronic communications. Governance within and among these virtual communities is diffuse, fragmented, multidimensional, and targeted. It is also local in the virtual sense of conducting parochial affairs within the community concerned, albeit across widely dispersed places and spaces. On the other hand, there are territorially rooted identities, formed among contiguous communities that coexist in particular places and that manage to conduct their affairs in a more or less orderly and civilized manner. The territorially based transactions of these contiguous communities have very different implications for convergence and diversity compared to the non–territorially based transactions among virtual communities.

For Elkins, globalization involves 'increasing widespread awareness of other parts of the world, the logical end of which finds each culture or group available to each other culture or group on a global scale.' However, 'available to' in no way means 'convergence with.' Much of the debate about globalization centres on convergence or divergence, but there are no solid measures of these concepts, and conclusions are often based on presumptive evidence and perceptual biases.

Elkins observes that the meeting of cultures often leads to the reinforcement of differences. This fact is signified by the values of toleration and pluralism in Western cultures. Toleration does not mean acceptance. Rather, it nurtures, enables, and sustains diversity. Diversity is often masked by what superficially appears to be convergence in cultures. Convergence on a single cultural form is highly unlikely because cultures are hybrid, evolve and change, respond to diverse global influences, and are always creating new niches.

Elkins enumerates how the forces of globalization foster diversity. Modern transportation and communication technologies create awareness of diversity, oppression and the mixing of values and interests across the cultures of groups, organizations, institutions, regions, and nation-states. Electronic media, often taken to be the driving force of convergence and homogeneity, also work in the opposite direction. Television programs from other cultures are typically viewed within one's own cultural framework, which results in solidification of one's own cultural identity in relation to 'the other' represented in the 'foreign' content. This is true even between similar cultures, for example, British people watching American television programs. Television narrowcasting on cable networks features special ethnic channels, and there are ethnic, linguistic, and religious minority programs on broadcast channels. These special channels and programs are culturally reinforcing and create virtual ethnic and religious communities. Electronic media of all types foster non-territorial identities, which may in turn diverge across different territories (i.e., have different national manifestations). The effects of electronic media involve a complex interplay among both territorial and non-territorial dimensions.

Elkins counsels against simple determinism when it comes to the analysis of globalization of culture. Cultures are never very coherent.

Convergence on some cultural traits is sometimes compatible with divergence on others. Cultural traits are bundled with other cultural traits. For example, the liberal-democratic tradition defines religion as in the private sphere and politics as public, but the Islamic tradition has no public-political, private-religious boundary.

There is divergence as well as convergence in every field of culture. Science and technology are differently received and resisted. Resistance to technology is one of the great moral discourses of our time. The move from production to consumption in the contemporary period has not resulted in a simple assimilation of corporate advertising culture. Many products that are subject to globalized mass production and marketing processes have also yielded greater product diversity. The running-shoe industry is a case in point: while Nike urges that you 'just do it,' the hedonistic rush is at least temporarily interrupted by the incredible range of shoes to choose from. In political culture, the current existence of the United States as the only model superpower may actually give other political elites around the world a wider choice of governance models and alliances.

Social movements exemplify the fact that knowledge of other cultures may be used for counter-culture purposes within one's own milieu. The globalizing world is a lot less precise, logical, consistent, and systematic, and a lot more plural, fragmented, and diverse, than most globalization theorists suggest.

Warren Magnusson finds troublesome many of the concepts employed to understand contemporary governance in the global context, including the three concepts that form the title of this volume. In a globalized world, 'governance' is especially problematic because of the increasing difficulty in defining the relation between governance and freedom that has been central to the liberal-democratic tradition. There is growing uncertainty about whether we can call ourselves 'modern.' Perhaps we are postmodern, or maybe we have never been modern. For Magnusson, globalization and modernization are, respectively, spatial and temporal descriptions of the same civilizing process. But globalization means that differences are now expressed in terms of space rather than time, and as distance itself collapses into new communication orders so too do modern distinctions of space and time. The very notion of 'society' is also called into question, especially as it has been identified in social science as being coterminous with the nation-state.

Magnusson urges us to break out of our conventional, liberal, modern thinking in order to resist globalization and the undesirable political communities it is fostering. Globalization is in part an ideology that attempts to come to terms with the crisis in modernity, which is a crisis in modern thinking. It expresses fears that seemingly cataclysmic forces beyond control of a given political community are profoundly changing individual and collective lives and a sense of security. A particular focus in this regard is on the withering away of the security promises of the state. As Magnusson notes wryly, when statelessness was visualized by Marxists it was deemed a fantasy, but it is 'now presented as a logical consequence of the global triumph of capitalism' and deemed a realistic possibility. People are led to ask how, without the state, they are to communicate collective identity and security, and create values of human dignity.

The modern liberal state proffers security in the form of a political ontology of sovereignty. The belief is created that people are autonomous decision makers who can create order by surrendering their own sovereignty to an authority they trust, in particular the state and its domain of citizenship and liberal democracy. In this context civil society is the state's 'other' and helps to define the collective values that are consistent with good citizenship. The authority in turn provides for the needs, especially regarding moral freedom, of the autonomous Kantian self. The self is also treated as king-like, as sovereign, with the effect that 'the political ontology of sovereignty is prior to and constitutive of our understandings of individual and social differences.'

The ontology of sovereignty is common sense. It itself is in a sense sovereign, even though it is an artificial political construct. It not only provides the template for constitutional democracy, but also for radical or progressive politics of resistance, difference, and transformation. As Magnusson expresses it, gays, women, indigenous peoples, and others try to 'rewrite Mill's classic *On Liberty* in terms of a more adequate understanding of cultural differences and privileged identities.' The ontology of sovereignty is also embedded in politics associated with 'post' thinking: postmodernism, post-Existentialism, post-Wittgensteinianism, and post-structuralism, all of which are part of the nostalgia industry that has formed around the sovereign self.

The sovereign individual is the state-governed individual, and thus not free. He or she is entrapped in the political ontology of sovereignty. Individuality is but self-sovereignty, making the person king-like. Self-discipline is to blend with political discipline. Any alternative conception is of course a threat to the integrity, unity, and identity of both the self and its political community. Magnusson feels that there is too much focus on the self, which itself has political effects. For example, per-ceived failures in the liberal-democratic state are projected onto the self. Self-discipline, evidenced in the contemporary emphasis on individual responsibility under neo-liberalism, is seen as the solution to the prob-lems of liberal democracy because of the persistence of the Kantian liberal-democratic dream that constraints from above are the ones that we give to ourselves. 'The presumption is that consent legitimates external discipline, not that it makes it unnecessary.'

With Western thinking so framed, globalization is treated as the new sovereign within the same logic of sovereignty that has trapped us up until now. The new sovereigns of globalization are, for example, 'world cities' such as New York, London, and Tokyo, or 'the global economy' or 'the market.' These, like the state before them, are surro-gates for God, reflecting how 'God-like control is at the heart of our dream of sovereignty and hence of our conceptions of personal and social identity.'

The focus on these new global sovereigns is augmented by the col-lapsing of time and space distinctions noted previously. Sovereignty for both individuals and communities is now present-tense, created out of the unity in the present environment and its peculiar sense of imme-diacy. Therefore, the focus on the market as sovereign seems obvious and natural. It offers an immediate means of constituting a tangible sovereignty, one that is consistent with absolute security of property. It offers the newly constituted sovereign individual the opportunity to market his or her self and identities, although as market commodities these may be destroyed as quickly as they are invented.

Magnusson argues that neither the state nor the market can provide popular sovereignty. The state is perpetually 'out of control' because its juridical order is always limited by other states, and by its subjects who have their own economic, social, and cultural orders and forms of institutionalized resistance. As Magnusson remarks pithily, the state is forced to 'legitimize what it cannot control for fear of forfeiting what control it has.' In the case of the market, the forcefulness of a 'Hobbe-sian sovereignty' backs up the 'Lockean idyll' of market sovereignty. That is, the contracts of global markets require the deployment of state authority, sometimes with deadly consequences. Consumer sovereignty also falls short of its liberating potential because it produces obviously unattractive identity-effects on 'consumers who must then be workers, entrepreneurs, rentiers, thieves or beggars if they are to survive.' Roll-ing back the state lays bare the downward disciplinary force of the market as sovereign, and at some point the state as sovereign must return to discipline the market and those individuals displaced by it. Magnusson concludes that sovereignty of any kind will not liberate, and that indeed the very problematic of liberation is just an effect of the ontology of sovereignty.

Magnusson advances the view that we can only overcome our puzzles and fears if we recognize that we are entrapped in the ontology of sovereignty, and try to break out of this ontological trap with something radically different. The 'something different' he offers is the idea of hyperspace from physics, combined with the idea of the global city from political science. These imaginative possibilities offered by Magnusson have some parallels with Elkins's previously noted distinction between a global 'virtual neighbourhood' of non-territorial identities and interests, and a more local, territorially rooted set of contiguous communities that interact directly.

Magnusson develops the idea of hyperspace based on physicists' theories of relativity, uncertainty, and chaos. He is drawn to these theories because they have enhanced understanding and control in the physical realm by highlighting the dynamics of what appears to be out of control. He reasons that since the twentieth century has been governed by science, science may be more helpful in explaining the globalized present than seventeenth-century categories of modern liberal-democratic theory and the ontology of sovereignty. The idea of hyperspace from physics can lead to a new understanding of a self-organizing system in which there is an implicit, equivocal order without sovereignty. In this order the self-governance of anyone or anything – individuals, organizations, institutions, regions, states, the globe – is embedded in the logic of the system itself, over which each self-governing unit has no effective control. In any effort to establish sovereignty through self-governance within this order, there is a loss of sovereignty which Magnusson says is a loss of 'an ideological effect of our assumptions about space, time and destiny.'

The global city is conceived as myriad interacting social movements, including modern movements of capitalism, scientific rationalism, liberal individualism, statism, and Western imperialism. Each social movement has its own logic, including peculiar spatial–temporal domains. These logics intersect, and are encompassed by urbanism. Magnusson accords urbanism a special place in the civilization process. The global city has become the hyperspace of human life, both an effect of criss-crossing social movements and in turn having an effect upon them.

Global cities have the above-noted features of an implicit and equivocal order without sovereignty: never fully contained by any movement or entity, or by states, economies, and cultures. The global city is more than the sum of the movements that make it tick, yet it does not rule over them either. Indeed, it disrupts sovereignty projects, generates openness, and thereby creates a hyperspace with potential for escaping the downward disciplinary effects of neo-liberalism and for enhancing human freedoms. In the global city a politically productive form of identity politics emerges, one in which the sovereign self is moved aside and a plurality of identities is celebrated and used to enrich humanity.

2

The Changing Contours of Political Community: Rethinking Democracy in the Context of Globalization

DAVID HELD

Political communities are in the process of being transformed. Of course, transformation can take many forms. But one type of transformation is of particular concern in this discussion: the progressive enmeshment of human communities with each other. Over the last few centuries, human communities have come into increasing contact with each other; their collective fortunes have become intertwined. I want to dwell on this and its implications.

My focus in this analysis is on the changing nature of political community in the context of the growing interconnectedness of states and societies – in short, globalization. This chapter is divided into a number of parts.[1] In the first part, I explore some of the key assumptions and presuppositions of liberal democracy; above all, its conception of political community. In the second part, I examine changing forms of globalization. In my view, globalization has been with us for some time, but its extensity, intensity, and impact have changed fundamentally. In the third and final part, I consider the implications of changing forms of globalization in relation to the prospects of democratic political community.

The Presuppositions of Liberal Democracy

Until the eighteenth century, democracy was generally associated with the gathering of citizens in assemblies and public meeting places. From the late eighteenth century, it began to be thought of as the right of citizens to participate in the determination of the collective will, but now through the medium of elected representatives (Bobbio 1989). The theory of liberal or representative democracy fundamentally shifted the terms of reference of democratic thought: the practical limits that a size-able citizenry imposes on democracy – which had been the focus of so much critical (anti-democratic) attention – were thought to be erradicable. Representative democracy could now be celebrated as both account-able and feasible government, potentially stable over great territories and time spans (see Dahl 1989, 28–30). As one of the best-known advo-cates of the representative system put it, 'by ingrafting representation upon democracy' a system of government is created that is capable of embracing 'all the various interests and every extent of territory and population' (Paine 1987, 281). Representative democracy could even be heralded, as James Mill wrote, 'as the grand discovery of modern times' in which 'the solution of all difficulties, both speculative and practical, would be found' (quoted in Sabine 1963, 695). Accordingly, the theory and practice of democratic government broke away from its traditional association with small states and cities, opening itself to become the legitimating creed of the emerging world of modern nation-states.

Built, as it was, against the background of the formation of the modern nation-state, the development of liberal democracy took place within a particular conceptual space (cf. Walker 1988; Connolly 1991; McGrew 1997). Modern democratic theory and practice was constructed upon national, territorial foundations. National communities, and theo-ries of national communities, were based on the presupposition that political communities could, in principle, control their destinies and citizens could come to identify sufficiently with each other such that they might think and act together with a view of what was best for all of them, that is, with a view of the common good (Sandel 1996, 202). It was taken for granted that, bar internal difficulties, the *demos*, the extent of the franchise, the form and scope of representation, and the nature and meaning of consent – in fact, all the key elements of self-determination – could be specified with respect to geography: systems of representation and democratic accountability could be neatly meshed with the spatial reach of sites of power in a circumscribed territory. Moreover, as a consequence of this, clear-cut distinctions could be elabo-rated – and national institutions built upon – the difference between 'internal' and 'external' policy, between domestic and foreign affairs.

Of course, the construction of a national democratic community was often deeply contested as different social, economic, and cultural groups fought with each other about the nature of this community and about their own status within it. Nonetheless, the theory of democracy, par-ticularly as it developed in the nineteenth and twentieth centuries, could take for granted the link between the *demos*, citizenship, electoral mechanisms, the nature of consent, and the boundaries of the nation-state. The fates of different political communities may be intertwined, but the appropriate place for determining the foundation of 'national fate' is the national community itself. Accordingly, modern democratic theory and democratic politics assumes a symmetry and congruence between citizen-voters and national decision makers. Through the ballot box, citizen-voters are, in principle, able to hold decision makers to account; and, as a result of electoral consent, decision makers are able to make and pursue law and policy legitimately for their constituents, ultimately, the people in a fixed, territorially based community.

Changing Forms of Regional and Global Order

At the centre of the dominant theoretical approaches to democratic politics is an uncritically appropriated concept of the territorial political community. And the difficulty with this is that political communities have rarely – if ever – existed in isolation as bounded geographical totalities; they are better thought of as overlapping networks of interaction. These networks crystallize around different sites and forms of power – economic, political, military, cultural, among others – producing diverse patterns of activity which do not correspond in any simple and straightforward way to territorial boundaries (see Mann 1986, ch. 1). Modern political communities are, and have always been, locked into a diversity of processes and structures that range in and through them. The theory and practice of the democratic sovereign state has always been in some tension with the actuality of state sovereignty and autonomy. How, then, should one understand these patterns of interconnections, and their changing form over time? And how should one understand their political implications, in particular, for sovereignty, autonomy, and the democratic political community?

The term 'globalization' captures some of the changes that shape the nature of the political and the prospects of political community; unpacking this term helps create a framework for addressing some of the issues to be explored. Globalization can be understood in relation to a set of processes that shift the spatial form of human organization and activity to transcontinental or interregional patterns of activity, interaction, and the exercise of power (see Held et al. 1999).[2] It involves a stretching and deepening of social relations and institutions across space and time such that, on the one hand, day-to-day activities are increasingly influenced by events happening on the other side of the globe and, on the other, the practices and decisions of local groups or communities can have significant global reverberations (see Giddens 1990). It is possible to distinguish different *historical forms of globalization* in terms of: (1) the extensiveness of networks of relations and connections; (2) the intensity of flows and levels of activity within these networks; and (3) the impact of these phenomena on particular bounded communities. It is not a case of saying, as many do, that there was no globalization, there is now; rather, it is a case of recognizing that forms of globalization have changed over time and that these can be systematically understood by reference to points 1–3 above. Such a historical approach to globalization contrasts with the current fashion to suggest either that globalization is fundamentally new – the 'hyper-globalization school,' with its insistence that global markets are now fully established (see Ohmae 1990) – or that there is nothing unprecedented about contemporary levels of international economic and social interaction since they resemble those of the gold standard era, the 'sceptical school' (see Hirst and Thompson 1996).

Globalization is neither a singular condition nor a linear process. Rather, it is best thought of as a multidimensional phenomenon involving domains of activity and interaction that include the economic, political, technological, military, legal, cultural, and environmental. Each of these spheres involves different patterns of relations and activities. A general account of globalization cannot simply predict from one domain what will occur in another. It is necessary to keep these distinctive domains separate and to build a theory of globalization and its impact on particular political communities from an understanding of what is happening in each and every one of them.

At least two tasks are necessary in order to pursue this objective, although, of course, not to complete it. First, it is important to illustrate some of the fundamental alterations in the patterns of interconnectedness among political communities. Second, it is important to set out some of the political implications of these changes. In what follows, I start by illustrating some of the transformations which have brought a change in the organization and meaning of political community.

1. Among the significant developments which are changing the nature of political community are global economic processes, especially growth in trade, production, and financial transactions, organized in part by rapidly expanding multinational companies. Trade has grown substan-

tially, reaching unprecedented levels, particularly in the post–Second World War period. Not only has there been an increase in intraregional trade around the world, but there has also been sustained growth among regions as well (see Perraton et al. 1997). More countries are involved in global trading arrangements, for instance, India and China, and more people and nations are affected by such arrangements. If there is a further lowering of tariff barriers across the world, along with a further reduction of transportation and communication costs, these trends are likely to continue and to further the extension, intensity, and impact of trade relations on other domains of life. The expansion of global financial flows has, moreover, been particularly rapid in the last ten to fifteen years. Foreign-exchange turnover has mushroomed and is now around $1.2 trillion a day. Much of this financial activity is speculative and generates fluctuations in prices (of stocks, shares, futures, etc.) in excess of those which can be accounted for by changes in the fundamentals of asset values. The enormous growth of global financial flows across borders, linked to the liberalization of capital markets from the late 1970s, has created a more integrated financial system than has ever been known.

Underpinning this economic shift has been the growth of multinational corporations, both productive and financial. Approximately 20,000 multinational corporations now account for a quarter to a third of world output, 70 per cent of world trade, and 80 per cent of foreign direct investment. They are essential to the diffusion of skills and technology, and they are key players in the international money markets. In addition, multinational corporations can have profound effects on macroeconomic policy. They can respond to variations in interest rates by raising finance in whichever capital market is most favourable. They can shift their demand for employment to countries with much lower employment costs. And in the area of industrial policy, especially technology policy, they can move activities to where the maximum benefits accrue.

It is easy to misrepresent the political significance of the globalization of economic activity. There are those, earlier referred to as the 'hyperglobalizers,' who argue that we now live in a world in which social and economic processes operate predominantly at a global level (see Ohmae 1990; Reich 1991). According to these thinkers, national political communities are now immersed in a sea of global economic flows and are inevitably 'decision takers' in this context. For many neo-liberal thinkers, this is a welcome development; a world-market order based on the principles of free trade and minimum regulation is the guarantee of liberty, efficiency and effective government (see Hayek 1960, 405–6). By contrast, however, there are those who are more reserved about the extent and benefits of the globalization of economic activity. They point out, for instance, that for all the expansion in global flows of trade and investment, the majority of economic activity still occurs on a more restricted spatial scale – in national economies and in the OECD countries. They also point out that the historical evidence suggests that contemporary forms of international economic interaction are not without precedent – and they refer to the gold-standard era for some substantial and interesting comparisons (see Hirst and Thompson 1996; cf. Perraton et al. 1997).

But the claims of the hyper-globalizers and their critics misstate much of what is significant about contemporary economic globalization for politics. Nation-states continue to be immensely powerful, and enjoy access to a formidable range of resources, bureaucratic infrastructural capacity, and technologies of coordination and control. The continuing lobbying of states by multinational corporations confirms the enduring importance of states to the mediation and regulation of economic activity. Yet it is wrong to argue that globalization is a mere illusion, an ideological veil, that allows politicians simply to disguise the causes of poor performance and policy failure. Although the rhetoric of hyper-globalization has provided many an elected politician with a conceptual resource for refusing political responsibility, globalization has significant and discernible characteristics that alter the balance of resources, economic and political, within and across borders.

Among the most important of these characteristics is the tangible growth in the enmeshment of national economies in global economic transactions (i.e., a growing proportion of nearly all national economies involves international economic exchanges with an increasing number of countries). This increase in the extent and intensity of economic interconnectedness has altered the relation between economic and political power. One shift has been particularly significant: 'the historic expansion of exit options for capital in financial markets relative to national capital controls, national banking regulations and national investment strategies, and the sheer volume of privately held capital relative to national reserves. Exit options for corporations making direct investments have also expanded … the balance of power has shifted in favour of capital *vis-à-vis* both national governments and national labour movements' (Goldblatt et al. 1997, 74). As a result, the autonomy of democratically elected governments has been, and is increasingly, constrained by sources of unelected and unrepresentative economic power. These have the effect of making adjustment to the international economy (and, above all, to global financial markets) a fixed point of orientation in economic policy and of encouraging an acceptance of the 'decision signals' of its leading agents and forces as a, if not the, standard of rational decision making. The options for political communities, and the costs and benefits of them, ineluctably alter.

2. Within the realms of the media and culture there are also grounds for thinking that there is a growing disjuncture between the idea of the democratic state as an independent, accountable centre of power bounded by fixed borders – in this case, a centre of national culture, able to foster and sustain a national identity – and interlinked changes in the spheres of media and cultural exchange. A number of developments in recent times can be highlighted. English has spread as the dominant language of elite cultures throughout the world: it is now the dominant language in business, computing, law, science, and politics. The internationalisation and globalization of telecommunications have been extraordinarily rapid: international telephone traffic has increased more than fourfold between 1983 and 1995; there has been a massive increase in transnational cable links; there has been an explosion in satellite links; and the Internet has provided a remarkable increase in the infrastructure of horizontal and lateral communication capacity within and across borders. Moreover, substantial multimedia conglomerates have developed, such as the Murdoch Empire and Time Warner. In addition, there has been a huge increase in tourism. For example, in 1960 there were 70 million international tourists, while in 1994 there were nearly 500 million. And in television and film there are similar trends.

None of the above examples, or the accumulative impact of parallel cases, should be taken to imply the development of a single global, media-led culture (consider the impact of Star television in India). But certainly, taken together, these developments do imply that many new forms of communication media range in and across borders, linking nations and peoples in new ways. The creation and re-creation of new forms of identity – often linked to patterns of consumption and the entertainment industries – are not to be underestimated. In this context, the capacity of national political leaders to sustain a national culture has become more complex and difficult. Even in China, for example, where the authorities sought to restrict access to and use of Western media, films, and the Internet, it has found this extremely difficult to do, especially with regard to young people. All independent states may retain a legal claim to 'effective supremacy over what occurs within their territories,' but this is significantly compromised by the growing enmeshment of 'the national' with transnational influences (see Keohane 1995). The determination of political community and the nature of political identity within it become less a territorial matter and more a matter of transaction, exchange, and bargaining across a complex set of transnational networks. At the very least, national political communities by no means simply determine the structure, education, and cultural flows in and through which citizens are cultivated. Citizens' values and judgments are now formed in a complex web of national, international, and global cultural exchange.

3. Environmental problems and challenges are perhaps the clearest and starkest examples of the global shift in human organization and activity, creating some of the most fundamental pressures on the efficacy of the nation-state and state-centric democratic politics. There are three types of problems at issue: (a) the first is shared problems involving the global commons, that is, fundamental elements of the ecosystem, and among the most significant challenges here are global warming and ozone depletion; (b) a second category of global environmental problems involves the interlinked challenges of demographic expansion and resource consumption. Pressing examples under this heading include desertification, questions of biodiversity, and threats to the existence of certain species; (c) a third category of problems is transboundary pollution such as acid rain, or river pollutants, or the contaminated rain that fell in connection with the Chernobyl nuclear disaster.

In response to the progressive development of, and publicity surrounding, environmental problems in the last two decades, there has been an interlinked process of cultural and political globalization as illustrated by the emergence of new cultural, scientific, and intellectual networks; new environmental movements with transnational organizations and transnational concerns; and new institutions and conventions like those agreed in 1992 at the Earth Summit in Brazil. Not all environmental problems are, of course, global; such an implication would be entirely false. But there has been a striking shift in the physical and environmental conditions – that is, in the extent and intensity of environmental problems – affecting human affairs in general. These processes have moved politics dramatically away from an activity which crystallizes first and foremost around state and interstate concerns. It is clearer than ever that the fortunes of political communities and peoples can no longer be simply understood in exclusively national or territorial terms. As one commentator aptly noted, 'in the context of intense global and regional interconnectedness, the very idea of political community as an exclusive territorially delimited unit is at best unconvincing and at worst anachronistic. In a world in which global warming connects the long-term fate of many Pacific islands to the actions of tens of millions of private motorists across the globe, the conventional territorial conception of political community appears profoundly inadequate. Globalization weaves together, in highly complex and abstract systems, the fate of households, communities and peoples in distant regions of the globe' (McGrew 1997, 237). Political communities are locked into a diversity of processes and structures that range across them. It can be no surprise then that national communities do not make decisions and policies exclusively for themselves, and that governments today do not simply determine what is right or appropriate for their own citizens alone. While it would be a mistake to conclude that political communities are without distinctive degrees of division or cleavage at their borders, they are clearly shaped by multiple cross-border interaction networks and power systems. Thus, questions are raised both about the fate of the idea of political community and about the appropriate locus for the articulation of the democratic political good. The proper 'home' of politics and democracy becomes a quite puzzling matter.

4. Changes in the development of international law have placed individuals, governments, and non-governmental organizations under new systems of legal regulation. International law recognizes powers and constraints, and rights and duties, which have qualified the principle of state sovereignty in a number of important respects; sovereignty per se is no longer a straightforward guarantee of international legitimacy. Entrenched in certain legal instruments is the view that a legitimate state must be a democratic state that upholds certain common values (see Crawford 1994). One significant area in this regard is human rights law and human rights regimes.

Of all the international declarations of rights, the European Convention for the Protection of Human Rights and Fundamental Freedoms (1950) is particularly noteworthy. In marked contrast to the Universal Declaration of Human Rights and the subsequent U.N. covenants of rights, the European Convention was concerned, as its preamble indicates, 'to take the first steps for the collective enforcement of certain of the rights stated in the Universal Declaration.' The European initiative was and remains a most radical legal innovation: an innovation which, against the stream of state history, allows individual citizens to initiate proceedings against their own governments. Within this framework, states are no longer free to treat their own citizens as they think fit (see Capotorti 1983, 977). Human rights regimes have also been promoted in other regions of the world, partly in response to U.N. encouragement that such rights should be entrenched at regional levels (see Evans 1997).

Each of the main U.N. human rights covenants has now been ratified by over 140 out of 190 states, and more are expected to ratify them. Increasing numbers of states appear willing to accept, in principle, general duties of protection and provision, as well as of restraint, in their own procedures and practices (see Beetham 1998). Clearly these commitments are rarely backed by coercive powers of enforcement. However, the demands of the new international human rights regimes – formal and informal – have created a plethora of transnational groups, movements, agencies, and lawyers all engaged in reworking the nature of national politics, national sovereignty, and state accountability.

In international law, accordingly, there has been a gradual shift away from the principle that state sovereignty must be safeguarded irrespective of its consequences for individuals, groups, and organizations. Respect for the autonomy of the subject, and for an extensive range of human rights, creates a new set of ordering principles in political affairs which can delimit and curtail the principle of effective state power. Along with other international legal changes (see Cassese 1986; Held 1995, ch. 5), these developments are indicative of an alteration in the weight granted, on the one hand, to claims made on behalf of the state system and, on the other hand, to those made on behalf of an alternative organizing principle of world order, in which an unqualified state sovereignty no longer reigns supreme.

5. While all the developments described so far have helped engender a shift away from a purely state-centred international system of 'high politics' to new and novel forms of geo-governance, a further interesting example of this process can be drawn from the very heart of the idea of a sovereign state – national security and defence policy. There has

been a notable increase in emphasis upon collective defence and cooperative security. The enormous costs, technological requirements, and
domestic burdens of defence are contributing to the strengthening of
multilateral and collective defence arrangements as well as international military cooperation and coordination (see Held et al. 1999,
chs 2 and 3, for an extensive discussion). The rising density of technological connections between states now challenges the very idea of
national security and national arms procurement. Some of the most
advanced weapons systems in the world today, for example, fighter
aircraft, depend on components which come from many countries.[3]
There has been a globalization of military technology linked to a
transnationalization of defence production. And the proliferation of
weapons of mass destruction makes all states insecure and problematizes
the very notions of 'friends' and 'enemies.'

Even in the sphere of defence and arms production and manufacture,
the notion of a singular, discrete, and delimited political community
appears problematic. Indeed, even in this realm, any conception of
sovereignty and autonomy which assumes that they denote an indivisible, illimitable, exclusive, and perpetual form of public power – embodied within an individual state – is increasingly challenged and
eroded.

Democracy and Globalization: In Sum

At the end of the second millennium, as indicated previously, political
communities and civilizations can no longer be characterized simply as
'discrete worlds'; they are enmeshed and entrenched in complex structures of overlapping forces, relations, and movements (cf. Fernández-
Armesto 1995). Four points can be noted to help characterize the
changing relationship between globalization and democratic nation-
states.

First, the locus of effective political power can no longer be assumed
to be national governments – effective power is shared, bartered, and
struggled over by diverse forces and agencies at national, regional, and
international levels. Second, the idea of a political community of fate –
of a self-determining collectivity – can no longer meaningfully be located within the boundaries of a single nation-state alone. Some of the
most fundamental forces and processes that determine the nature of
life-chances within and across political communities are now beyond
the reach of nation-states. The system of national political communities

persists of course; but it is articulated and rearticulated today with complex economic, organizational, administrative, legal, and cultural processes and structures which limit and check its efficacy. If these processes and structures are not acknowledged and brought into the political process themselves, they will tend to bypass or circumvent the democratic state system.

Third, it is not part of my argument that national sovereignty today, even in regions with intensive overlapping and divided political and authority structures, has been wholly subverted – not at all. But it is part of my argument that there are significant areas and regions marked by criss-crossing loyalties, conflicting interpretations of rights and duties, interconnected legal and authority structures, and so on, which displace notions of sovereignty as an illimitable, indivisible, and exclusive form of public power. The operations of states in increasingly complex regional and global systems both affects their autonomy (by changing the balance between the costs and benefits of policies) and their sovereignty (by altering the balance between national, regional, and international legal frameworks and administrative practices). While massive concentrations of power remain features of many states, these are frequently embedded in, and articulated with, fractured domains of political authority. Against this background, it is not fanciful to imagine, as Bull once observed, the development of an international system which is a modern and secular counterpart to the kind of political organization found in Christian Europe in the Middle Ages, the essential characteristic of which was a system of overlapping authority and multiple loyalties (1977, 254–5).

Fourth, the late twentieth century is marked by a significant series of new types of 'boundary problem.' If it is accepted that we live in a world of overlapping communities of fate, where the trajectories of each and every country are more tightly entwined than ever before, then new types of boundary problem follow. In the past, of course, nation-states principally resolved their differences over boundary matters by pursuing reasons of state backed by coercive means. But this power logic is singularly inadequate and inappropriate to resolve the many complex issues, from economic regulation to resource depletion and environmental degradation, which engender an intermeshing of 'national fortunes.' In Zimbabwe, it is said, many villagers used to believe that weather patterns were due to 'acts of God' and, accordingly, climate shifts had to be accepted; today, the same people believe that their weather is affected by Western energy policy, patterns of pollution, as well as some local practices and, of course, some bad luck. In a world where powerful states make decisions not just for their peoples, but for others as well, and where transnational actors and forces cut across the boundaries of national communities in diverse ways, the questions of who should be accountable to whom, and on what grounds, do not easily resolve themselves. Overlapping spheres of influence, interference, and interest create fundamental problems at the centre of democratic thought, problems which ultimately concern the very basis of democratic authority.

Rethinking Democracy in the Context of Globalization

In the liberal democracies, consent to government and legitimacy for governmental action are dependent upon electoral politics and the ballot box. Yet, the notion that consent legitimates government, and that the ballot box is the appropriate mechanism whereby the citizen body as a whole periodically confers authority on government to enact the law and regulate economic and social life, become problematic as soon as the nature of a 'relevant community' is contested. What is the proper constituency, and proper realm of jurisdiction, for developing and implementing policy with respect to health issues such as AIDS or BSE (bovine spongiform encephalopathy), the use of nuclear energy, the management of nuclear waste, the harvesting of rain forests, the use of non-renewable resources, the instability of global financial markets, the reduction of the risks of chemical and nuclear warfare? National boundaries have demarcated traditionally the basis on which individuals are included and excluded from participation in decisions affecting their lives; but if many socio-economic processes, and the outcomes of decisions about them, stretch beyond national frontiers, then the implications of this are serious, not only for the categories of consent and legitimacy, but for all the key ideas of democracy. At issue is the nature of a constituency (how should the proper boundaries of a constituency be drawn?), the meaning of representation (who should represent whom and on what basis?), and the proper form and scope of political participation (who should participate and in what way?). As fundamental processes of governance escape the categories of the nation-state, the traditional national resolutions of the key questions of democratic theory and practice are open to doubt.

Against this background, the nature and prospects of the democratic polity need re-examination. The idea of a democratic order can no longer be simply defended as an idea suitable to a particular closed political community or nation-state. We are compelled to recognize that we live in a complex interconnected world where the extensity, intensity, and impact of issues (economic, political, or environmental) raises questions about where those issues are most appropriately addressed. Deliberative and decision-making centres beyond national territories are appropriately situated when those significantly affected by a public matter constitute a cross-border or transnational grouping, when 'lower' levels of decision making cannot manage and discharge satisfactorily transnational or international policy questions, and when the principle of democratic legitimacy can only be properly redeemed in a transnational context (see Held 1995, ch. 10). If the most powerful geopolitical interests are not to settle many pressing matters simply in terms of their objectives and by virtue of their power, then new institutions and mechanisms of accountability need to be established.

It would be easy to be pessimistic about the future of democracy. There are plenty of reasons for pessimism; they include the fact that the essential political units of the world are still based on nation-states while some of the most powerful sociopolitical forces of the world escape the boundaries of these units. In reaction to this, in part, new forms of fundamentalism have arisen, along with new forms of tribalism – all asserting the *a priori* superiority of a particular religious, or cultural, or political identity over all others, and all asserting their sectional aims and interests. In addition, the reform of the United Nations that is currently contemplated by the most powerful countries is focused on efforts to include other powerful countries, above all, Germany and Japan. This would consolidate the power of certain geopolitical interests, but at the expense of many other countries which have some of the fastest rates of economic growth and some of the largest populations. I believe this position to be unsustainable in the long run.

But there are other forces at work which create the basis for a more optimistic reading of democratic prospects. A historical comparison might help to provide a context for this.

In the sixteenth and seventeenth centuries, Europe was marked by civil conflict, religious strife, and fragmented authority; the idea of a secular state, separate from ruler and ruled, and separate from the church, seemed an unlikely prospect. Parts of Europe were tearing themselves to pieces and, yet, within 150–200 years, a new concept of politics became entrenched based around a new concept of the state.

Today, we live at another fundamental point of transition, but now to a more transnational, global world. There are forces and pressures which are engendering a reshaping of political cultures, institutions, and structures. First, one must obviously note the emergence, however hesitatingly, of regional and global institutions in the twentieth century. The United Nations is, of course, weak in many respects, but it is a relatively recent creation and it is an innovative structure which can be built upon. It is a normative resource which provides – for all its difficulties – an enduring example of how nations might (and sometimes do) cooperate better to resolve, and resolve fairly, common problems. In addition, the development of a powerful regional body such as the European Union is a remarkable state of affairs. Just over fifty years ago, Europe was at the point of self-destruction. Since that moment, Europe has created new mechanisms of collaboration, human rights enforcement, and new political institutions in order not only to hold member states to account across a broad range of issues, but to pool aspects of their sovereignty. Furthermore, there are, of course, new regional and global transnational actors contesting the terms of globalization – not just corporations, but new social movements such as the environmental movement and the women's movement. These are the 'new' voices of an emergent 'transnational civil society,' heard, for instance, at the Rio Conference on the Environment, the Cairo Conference on Population Control, and the Beijing Conference on Women. In short, there are tendencies at work seeking to create new forms of public life and new ways of debating regional and global issues. These are, of course, all in early stages of development, and there are *no* guarantees that the balance of political contest will allow them to develop. But they point in the direction of establishing new modes of holding transnational power systems to account – that is, they help open up the possibility of what I call 'cosmopolitan democracy.'

If this possibility is to be consolidated, each citizen of a state must learn to become a cosmopolitan citizen – a person capable of mediating between national traditions, communities, and alternative forms of life. Citizenship in a democratic polity of the future must increasingly involve a mediating role: a role which encompasses dialogue with the traditions and discourses of others with the aim of expanding the horizons of one's own framework of meaning and prejudice, and increasing the scope of mutual understanding. Political agents who can reason from the point of view of others are likely to be better equipped to resolve, and resolve fairly, the new and challenging transboundary issues that create overlapping communities of fate. Moreover, if many contemporary forms of power are to become accountable and if many of the complex issues that affect us all – locally, nationally, regionally and globally – are to be democratically regulated, people must have access to, and membership in, diverse political communities. Put differently, democracy for the new millennium should describe a world where citizens enjoy multiple citizenships. They should be citizens of their own communities, of the wider regions in which they live, and of a cosmopolitan, transnational community.

Against this background, democracy must be thought of as a 'double-sided process' (Held 1996). By 'a double-sided process' I mean not just the deepening of democracy within a national community, but also the extension of democratic processes across territorial borders. Democracy for the new millennium must involve cosmopolitan citizens able to gain access to, and mediate between, and render accountable, the social, economic, and political processes and flows which cut across and transform their traditional community boundaries. The notion of cosmopolitan democracy recognizes our complex, interconnected world. It recognizes, of course, certain problems and policies as appropriate for local governments and national states; but it also recognizes others as appropriate for specific regions, and still others – such as the environment, global security concerns, world health questions, and economic regulation – that need new institutions to address them. Such political arrangements are not only a necessity but also a possibility in the light of the changing organization of regional and global processes, evolving political decision-making centres such as the European Union, and growing political demands for new forms of political deliberation, conflict resolution and decision making.

Notes

1 This is a revised and abridged version of 'The Transformation of Political Community,'prepared for publication in Ian Shapiro and Casiano Hacker-Cordon, eds., *Democracy's Edges* (Cambridge: Cambridge University Press, 1999).

2 The conception of globalization along with many of the examples in this section are drawn from this volume. I should like to acknowledge my debt

58   David Held

to my co-authors, with whom I have collaborated over the last four years on
these issues.
3 I'm indebted to Anthony McGrew for this point.

References

Beetham, D. 1998. 'Human Rights as a Model for Cosmopolitan Democracy.'
    Pp. 58–71 in D. Archibugi, D. Held, and M. Köhler, eds., *Re-Imagining Politi-
    cal Community*. Cambridge: Polity Press.
Bobbio, N. 1989. *Democracy and Dictatorship*. Cambridge: Polity Press.
Bull, H. 1977. *The Anarchical Society*. London: Macmillan.
Capotorti, F. 1983. 'Human Rights: The Hard Road towards Universality.' In
    R. St J. Macdonald and D.M. Johnson, eds., *The Structure and Process of
    International Law*. The Hague: Martinus Nijhoff.
Cassese, A. 1986. *International Law in a Divided World*. Oxford: Clarendon
    Press.
Connolly, W. 1991. 'Democracy and Territoriality.' *Millennium* 20/3: 463–84.
Crawford, J. 1994. *Democracy in International Law*. Inaugural Lecture. Cam-
    bridge: Cambridge University Press.
Dahl, R.A. 1989. *Democracy and Its Critics*. New Haven, CT: Yale University
    Press.
Evans, T. 1997. 'Democratization and Human Rights.' Pp. 122–48 in A.
    McGrew, ed., *The Transformation of Democracy?* Cambridge: Polity Press.
Fernández-Armesto, F. 1995 . *Millennium*. London: Bantam.
Giddens, A. 1990. *The Consequences of Modernity*. Cambridge: Polity Press.
Goldblatt, D., D. Held, A.G. McGrew, and J. Perraton. 1997. 'Economic Glo-
    balization and the Nation-State: Shifting Balances of Power.' *Soundings* 7
    (autumn): 61–77.
Hayek, F.A. 1960. *The Constitution of Liberty*. London: Routledge and Kegan
    Paul.
Held, D. 1995. *Democracy and the Global Order: From the Modern State to Cosmo-
    politan Governance*. Cambridge: Polity Press.
Held, D., A. McGrew, D. Goldblatt, and J. Perraton. 1999. *Global Transforma-
    tions: Politics, Economics and Culture*. Cambridge: Polity Press.
– 1996. *Models of Democracy*, 2d ed. Cambridge: Polity Press.
Hirst, P., and G. Thompson. 1996. *Globalization in Question*. Cambridge: Polity
    Press.
Keohane, R. 1995. 'Hobbes's Dilemma and Institutional Change in World

Politics: Sovereignty in International Society.' Pp. 165–86 in H.H. Holm and G. Sorensen, eds., *Whose World Order?* Boulder CO: Westview.

Mann, M. 1986. *The Sources of Social Power*, vol. 1. Cambridge: Cambridge University Press.

McGrew, A.G., ed. 1997. *The Transformation of Democracy?* Cambridge: Polity Press.

Ohmae, K. 1990. *The Borderless World*. London: Collins.

Paine, T. 1987. *The Thomas Paine Reader*. Harmondsworth: Penguin.

Perraton, J., D. Goldblatt, D. Held, and A. McGrew. 1997: 'The Globalization of Economic Activity.' *New Political Economy* 2/2: 257–77.

Reich, R. 1991. *The Work of Nations*. New York: Simon and Schuster.

Sabine, G.H. 1963. *A History of Political Theory*. London: Harrap.

Sandel, M. 1996. *Democracy's Discontent*. Cambridge, MA: Harvard University Press.

Walker, R.B.J. 1988. *One World, Many Worlds*. Boulder, CO: Lynne Reinner.

3

Thinking Global Governance and Enacting Local Cultures

DAVID J. ELKINS

Many commentators on the 'new global order' imply or explicitly state that local cultures will evolve into one global culture sometimes referred to dismissively as 'McCulture.' Others argue to the contrary that 'the clash of civilizations' will ensure that one hybrid culture is an extremely remote possibility. A variant of each position might lead to the prediction that, while small or weak or isolated cultures may disappear, a few major cultures may consolidate and survive indefinitely. 'Culture' in these scenarios has several possible meanings, including customs and way of life, religion, language, society, country, and nation.

This chapter argues that, regardless of the definition of 'culture,' a proper understanding of the process of globalization will lead to an outcome at variance with all of the predictions or possibilities noted above. Globalization should, I argue, assist the preservation of some aspects of many cultures, many aspects of some cultures, and a few aspects of all cultures. This result derives from technological innovations, evolution of governance, new concepts of identity, and adaptation to physical and conceptual niches.

Before developing my own position, it is necessary to clear away some conceptual and methodological underbrush. Some of these points may seem pathetically trite or obvious, but unfortunately some other observers have failed to take them into account, and so I must belabour them, at least briefly. All of these caveats concern hidden assumptions that underlie my own analysis or those of other scholars. It is crucial that these assumptions be brought to the level of consciousness so that they may be accepted or rejected openly and explicitly rather than surreptitiously.

For several hundred years in Europe, and for shorter periods in the rest of the world, territoriality has been assumed as the basis of governance, especially at the level of the national state. I have argued elsewhere that this orientation grew out of a series of technological changes and the intellectual concepts built on them.[1] Although military in important ways, the technologies and concepts also integrated trends in economics, finance, religion, and nationalism.

The concept of the territorial state won a Darwinian struggle with other forms of governance long established in Europe. These included the Roman Catholic Church, feudalism, and the commercial trading cities. Kings and their regional barons successfully invoked the concept of sovereignty to justify their claims to exclusive political control of all people and activities within a discrete, contiguous, and continuous territory. Through conquest, settlement, and imperialism, the European understanding of the territorial state became the hegemonic model for political organization throughout the world, although not all cultures accepted the alien concept willingly.

In recent decades, technological changes have rendered this territorial model problematic. Jet aircraft and rockets have changed strategic military considerations. Radio, television, and satellites have allowed global information dissemination. Personal computers, e-mail, the Internet, the World Wide Web, and related technologies constituting the Information Superhighway have facilitated non-territorial forms of organization, commerce, and governance which require that we reconsider assumptions about the role of territorial political institutions. This rethinking takes many forms, and I explore one of them in this chapter.

The very idea of unique cultures is an assumption that had its origin in early modern times in Europe, roughly parallel to the Reformation and the establishment of the territorial state as the model of governance and of the concept of the individual as the basic unit of analysis in each state. During the Enlightenment, the earlier idea of natural law was transformed into the notion of universal laws and social norms. Such universalizing tendencies would – as Reason spread – ensure that all societies converged on the same rules. 'The white man's burden' was also a product of this mindset. The historian and philosopher Stephen Toulmin (1990) has characterized 'modernity' precisely in terms of these beliefs in laws, rules, or norms that are ahistorical, context-free, and universal.

If this line of argument has merit, it should be especially difficult for those of us who participate in 'modernity' to 'see diversity' because our world-view presupposes a universalizing effort to uncover the rational way of doing things, including political and social organization. One way around this blind spot might involve the intellectual currents called 'post-modern' or 'post-structural' analysis. Another avenue involves a deeper historical understanding of how we got to where we are.

Another methodological point concerns how one might compare the degree of similarity or difference among cultures at widely separate times. Specifically, how much divergence or convergence was there before the construction of cities, and thereby of agricultural productivity? How might we compare that degree of convergence with the gulf between hunter-gatherer cultures and settled urban and agricultural cultures?

Every society for which we have any historical evidence has evolved in ways that might appear to entail convergence. In oversimplified terms, each society has become more 'modern' and 'developed': settled rather than nomadic; technically more adept; with monetized economic exchanges rather than barter; with longer life expectancies; and with more interdependence. Must one conclude, without any further analysis, that these trends prove that societies are more similar today than 1,000 or 10,000 years ago?

Looking at the broad historical sweep of most societies, why would one wish to say that the major industrial countries are more similar to Somalia, Saudi Arabia, or Papua New Guinea today than these areas were to each other a few centuries ago? The divergence over time in life expectancy, affluence, style of dwellings, consumer goods, and types of religious expression seems so obvious to me that I hesitate to conclude that homogeneity is just around the corner because of the spread of McDonald's and television.

The points that I believe are most crucial in this preliminary excursion are these: no one has any systematic data on convergence or divergence in the long run; no one has any 'metric measure' or yardstick by which to assess whether there is more or less diversity today than at other periods of recorded history; and everyone reaches a conclusion about convergence or divergence on the basis of *presumptive* evidence or perceptual biases. I mentioned above the 'optical illusion' built into 'modernity' as a result of its assumption that history moves in the direction of manifesting universal laws and norms. Hence, we must be wary of our assumptions and search for evidence of our own biases.

Whatever unconscious assumptions I may harbour, I shall try to be explicit about alternative possibilities. Thus, a large part of this chapter will focus on rates of change in different cultures, and conceptual distinctions among the units that 'carry' those cultures. Let me preview some of the argument so that readers may assess what is explicit and thereby be attentive to assumptions they may not yet have brought to consciousness. The title of the chapter contains the keys to certain conceptual clarifications.

'Thinking global governance' involves recognizing that countries or territorial states no longer do all the governing, if they ever did. Thinking global governance thus requires making conceptual space for non-territorial communities, networks, organizations, and institutions, each of which plays some role in global governance.

These new forms of governance (if they are really new) share a common characteristic. They are relatively narrow in focus, or 'targeted,' even though they are often global in scope or reach. Thus, they force us to redefine what we mean by 'local.' 'Local' will continue to mean close physical proximity, but it will also mean narrow or focused or targeted in a global 'virtual neighbourhood.'

On the basis of these distinctions, I argue that more and more governance will involve two parallel sets of communities: global networks with targeted interests, and physically contiguous communities which endeavour to encompass a broad range of interests. Both forms of governance, I will argue, could underpin different types of diversity; and even if that is not sufficient, the fact that both forms of governance coexist should sustain some degree of diversity. Globalization is not a uniform process, because it may affect differently these two types of 'local' communities.

The primary emphasis of this chapter, at least in terms of number of words, consists of an explication of a particular meaning of 'globalization.' That leads to a set of hypotheses about how diversity might be masked – especially in modern eyes – by features that appear superficially to favour convergence of cultures. These hypotheses in turn lead me to consider briefly a series of answers to the question of what threatens local cultures, and obversely what might sustain them.

Globalization and Globalism

For many people, globalization means larger or more inclusive political units. Thus, the European Community, the North American Free Trade Agreement, and the United Nations would be examples of globalization. I will stipulate instead that these more inclusive units of governance will be called 'globalism,' the suffix '-ism' establishing a parallel with 'nationalism,' which involved the consolidation of countries out of smaller or overlapping or less inclusive communities and populations. Globalization will be used here in the sense of increasingly widespread awareness of other parts of the world, the logical end of which finds each culture or group available to each other culture or group on a global scale. Globalization in my sense has always occurred. Migration has always resulted in contact and awareness. The voyages of exploration in the fifteenth and later centuries greatly expanded global awareness and contributed profoundly to modern notions of scientific knowledge. Recently, the scale has increased by orders of magnitude, as mass travel, mass media, formal education, the spread of literacy, and interdependent economic activities have forced people everywhere to come to grips with how they might relate to people in other places or from different backgrounds. If Magellan's circumnavigation of the globe in the sixteenth century led to the designation of the Age of Magellan, then I suggest that today's global electronic linkages should be thought of as a Second Magellanic Age.

Several developments have created opportunities for almost limitless explorations, and hence greater global awareness. Think especially of the expanded and expanding number of channels on televisions in many countries, and eventually global coverage as a result of the proliferation of satellite transmissions from the so-called Death Stars with 500-channel capacity or more. Think also of the personal computer – and its convergence with other digital media – which will allow personal interactions with targeted individuals and groups on a global scale through e-mail, the Internet, World Wide Web, and other innovations. Of course, it will be quite some time before every human being has a computer and modem, but by the beginning of the next century approximately 800 million businesses and households will be able to go online. That is worlds different from Columbus or Magellan and their small boats and scores of crew members, and yet all of these events constitute part of the long and continuous process of globalization.

One might be tempted to say that globalization cannot lead to homogeneity of culture on a global basis because it has obviously not happened after thousands of years, or at least centuries since Magellan. There is much force in that argument, and I wish to underline a couple of its strengths before moving on to consider the arguments for convergence.

The first point simply involves noting that diversity often grows out of awareness of special situations. One has only to think of many 'settler societies' around the world: although all are predominantly English-speaking outposts of Great Britain, there are many significant differences among the United States, Canada, Australia, New Zealand, Bermuda, and South Africa. Some have asserted their independence – as the United States did in the American Revolution – but those which did not do so through revolution still evolved into remarkably different countries while retaining the 'family resemblance' to the mother country.

A second and perhaps related point reminds us that almost every country in the world – with a few exceptions like Japan, Korea, and Finland – contains very substantial internal diversity. Usually we focus on regional economic or cultural units – as with England, Scotland, and Wales in Great Britain; Quebec in Canada; northern and southern Italy; Brittany, Burgundy, Provence, and other areas of France – but one can equally well comment on ethnic, religious, linguistic, and other kinds of diversity that are not tied to territory and that often are subsumed under the label 'multiculturalism.'

If virtually all countries retain extensive diversity and if countries 'descended' from a common origin exhibit major differences in culture, why would one even speculate about whether globalization (or globalism) could result in a uniform or homogeneous global culture? Perhaps the answer lies in our desire to 'see' universality rather than diversity, as I suggested above. But rather than dismiss these concerns, I propose to look at various hypotheses about what threatens (or sustains) local cultures, and I will mention how differential rates of change play key roles in sustaining diversity. In order to do so systematically, I propose to specify more clearly what *diversity* among cultures might look like so that we know what to look for in evaluating arguments about convergence. As will become clear, one must also inquire what are the 'culture-bearing units,' that is, the relatively homogeneous groups or communities across which we find diversity.

Varieties of Diversity

Diversity is diversity, but it can manifest itself in several different formal patterns, some of which mask its extent. This will be especially likely if we assume that diversity should occur primarily between territorial units. On the contrary, cultural diversity increasingly occurs within and not just between territorial units – whether cities, regions, or countries – and will do so even more in the future.

The lack of diversity is complete homogeneity between and within all countries. I will not discuss this possibility since the other patterns I discuss make complete homogeneity virtually impossible as an outcome of globalization. Of course, one must allow for the possibility that any simple cultural trait (such as wearing blue jeans or having an elected legislature) might become universal, but that still allows for diversity on an unlimited number of other traits.

A second pattern could involve the break-up of existing states into more homogeneous, smaller states ('successor states'). This second pattern of diversity looks more like what people imagine to be the pattern which they say is being undermined by globalization. Even if it does succumb to globalization to some degree, its description in formal terms helps us see why diversity might be more resistant than some believe. As diverse countries have broken up into smaller and somewhat more homogeneous countries, at least two processes sustain diversity among them. First, the resulting units have a cultural majority more clearly dominant – as in the Czech Republic and the Slovak Republic; or if Quebec separates from Canada, the two (or more) resulting units would be less internally diverse. Note, however, that in most such cases, the succeeding state and the rump state will still be internally diverse, and previous 'fault-lines' may simply diminish in salience and allow attention to be diverted to new dimensions less obvious in the previous country. For example, if Quebec secedes from Canada, the visibility of the cleavage between French and English may decline while that between the francophone majority and aboriginal minorities will increase, as the latter demand to remain within Canada.

Since majorities in one country are usually minorities elsewhere, the second product of redrawing boundaries to make countries internally less diverse will increase the apparent diversity between countries. If this logic holds, globalization aids the awareness of internal diversity, oppression, or mixing, which in turn results in new borders that reduce internal diversity, which in turn increases variation between successor states. This holds whether one compares single cultural traits or compares 'packages' such as ethnic groups or cultures.

The third major way diversity may be manifested involves increasing internal diversity in most or all countries. Internal diversity will increase for several reasons, some of long-standing and others just now under way. Immigration (legal or illegal) has occurred in all countries, although some countries have experienced very little of it. Even if immigration does not increase, multiculturalism is already a fact of life almost everywhere. Note that in relatively homogeneous countries with little immigration – such as Japan – dominance of one culture leads to variance from one country to another as noted above, and thus diversity is sustained in another form.

Besides immigration (i.e., movement of people), one can increase cultural diversity within a country by 'importing' ideas or products from places with different cultures. In the past, border controls served to limit this means of sustaining or increasing internal diversity. As information technology changes, however, borders become more and more permeable. To offer only one example, satellite broadcasting of television cannot be easily 'jammed,' and the receiving 'dishes' have become smaller and cheaper. Thus, the advent of Death Star satellites will allow dedicated channels of targeted transmissions to be readily available throughout most of the globe. Since it is in the interests of major countries representing large numbers of speakers of particular languages to launch their own satellites or to rent channels on commercial ones, in a few years most major ethnic, linguistic, and religious minorities will be able to receive culturally reinforcing transmissions. This should result in what I have described elsewhere as 'virtual ethnic communities' even when local populations of a particular group are very small and previously vulnerable to assimilation.

Whether such broadcasting actually increases diversity within a given country or simply sustains existing diversity, the result runs contrary to predictions of convergence in the normal sense. Note the dilemma this poses for the hypothesis that globalization leads to homogeneity: if it results in more internally homogeneous countries, globalization enhances intercountry variation; but if it results in greater or sustained internal diversity, that is a significant form of diversity. Note also that I have used television as only one example; many other forms of digital transmission will operate in these ways with similar effects on internal diversity. Some of them – such as the Internet – are even more difficult to disrupt or interdict than is television broadcasting. Travel and other forms of direct and indirect experience will presumably have effects that parallel or amplify those of the media.

Carry this logic one step further. If cultural transmissions in English, French, Spanish, Russian, Chinese, Arabic, Hindi, and other languages are available to most residents of almost every country, then the *profile* or distribution of cultural influences will be increasingly similar in all countries (Elkins 1997). That is, the type and degree of internal diversity may be similar in several countries. For many observers, I suspect that such similar profiles of cultural influences constitute globalization; that is, they assume that similar or identical profiles indicate or cause similarity of cultural practices within a country. But in a perverse sense, the greater the similarity of cultural influences on each country, the more internal diversity we may expect. If every Spanish-speaking resident of every country in the world has access to virtually identical profiles of transmission, ideas, entertainment, and advertising, the diversity among Spanish speakers should decrease because they will be watching more of the same programs than they do currently. Since they will presumably watch different programs than speakers of other languages, internal diversity within each country should increase. One way or another, cultural diversity appears to be very difficult to stamp out.

Diversity between some countries may increase while internal diversity may also increase in other cases. Indeed, the picture will very likely be much more complex than this analysis portrays: internal homogeneity of language and ethnicity (as in Japan) may be coupled with greater diversity of lifestyles or popular cultures; or obversely, very large differences in language, religion, and popular culture may coexist with greater homogeneity in style of daily life (in North America, for example), as the economies of Canada, the United States, and Mexico integrate more fully.

Non-territorial Diversity

So far, I have discussed patterns and effects of globalization on the assumption that *countries* or other territorial units were relevant 'containers' of culture or culture-bearing units. For some purposes that is a defensible usage. In many other respects, however, one must make explicit 'room' for non-territorial social, economic, and political formations. Let us consider briefly some implications of non-territorial governance for long-term diversity.

Many dimensions of diversity within a given country represent linkages across borders between countries. The diasporas of ethnic groups, for example, may be viewed as sources of diversity within any one country, but each ethnic group can also be considered as a simple, non-territorial, culture-bearing unit. Likewise, several of the major world religions – including Christianity, Islam, Hinduism, Confucianism, and Buddhism – can serve as integrating forces of a non-territorial sort while simultaneously constituting elements of diversity in any given territorial unit. Languages, too, have both territorial and non-territorial bases and effects on diversity.

When Marx and Engels exhorted the workers of the world to unite, they were implicitly playing down the diversity of social class at the local or territorial level and emphasizing the non-territorial integration of one of those classes. By the same token, feminist pleas to support oppressed 'sisters' in other countries build on and help to sustain an important non-territorial identity and may even sharpen gender-based tensions or conflict in any one country. Increasingly common have been cross-border alliances and information-sharing by aboriginal groups, environmental movements, consumer groups, and even municipal politicians.

As digital information technology becomes cheaper and more accessible, and as it penetrates more deeply into areas little touched so far, the opportunities for non-territorial networks, groups, and organizations will be virtually unlimited. Not all of these developments will be beneficial – think of how drug cartels and terrorists might make use of them – but for good or ill, non-territorial dimensions of diversity should compete with territorial forms or at least share the stage with them on more even terms.

I wish to emphasize only a few of the many consequences these trends have for governance and for cultural diversity. The most obvious consequence concerns the increase in the number of culture-bearing units when one examines non-territorial organizations as well as countries. Equally crucial, as individuals look to a wider range of reference groups and not just to territorial states, governance becomes more fragmented, more specialized, and more targeted, while sovereignty becomes more widely shared.

Indeed, for many people in many countries, non-territorial identities and the digital networks and social relationships underlying them may eclipse the territorial identities and institutions traditionally at the centre of attention. Whether that shift of loyalties turns out to be rare or dominant, most people will find that they participate in more and more non-territorial groups. One should not prejudge which types of groups will become the major culture-bearing units or whether they will be internally cohesive rather than differing according to their geographic contexts. There have been and continue to be historic differences among the national manifestations of the Catholic Church in different parts of the world, and also among Muslims in the Middle East and Asia. Thus, it may turn out that such non-territorial cultural units may diverge along geographic lines. Territorial states will experience sustained or increased internal diversity because of greater salience of these and other non-territorial groups within their borders. An accurate and complete assessment of sustainable diversity (or its obverse, convergence) will therefore require that territorial and non-territorial dimensions of diversity (or convergence) be examined simultaneously.

There are, of course, many other aspects of governance that siphon away bits of sovereignty from territorial states. Some are themselves territorial in nature, such as the European Community. Others, however, are non-territorial and specialized, such as the World Trade Organization (formerly GATT), the International Air Transport Association, the Organization for Economic Cooperation and Development (OECD), the Organization of Petroleum-Exporting Countries (OPEC), and Amnesty International. My focus on sociological, religious, or other such groups should not be seen as slighting these more formal organizations. Instead, they reinforce my broader points by showing that many non-state and non-territorial organizations exist and more are being created or enhanced every day.

Let me sum up the argument so far by referring to the title of this chapter. 'Thinking global governance' involves thinking differently about governance and the organizations, institutions, and networks that it encompasses. In particular, each non-territorial organization is potentially global in scope in ways that countries can never be, and yet they are not comprehensive in the sense that one needs only one of them in the way a country needs only one state. Governance is more diffuse, fragmented, multidimensional, and targeted. Likewise, 'enacting local cultures' entails multiple perspectives: enabling rather than coercing or sponsoring; local in not only a geographic but also a 'virtual' sense, in which neighbours in a given country (or building, even) may operate or conduct many of their affairs in different cultures; and culture in the sense of including everything integral to the many facets of human existence.

What Threatens Local Cultures May Sustain Them

Unless one accepts that globalization (or globalism, for that matter) can operate in an abstract way to change cultures and lead to their convergence, one must inquire about specific mechanisms and processes that might threaten or sustain local cultures. Without trying to be comprehensive, let me assess a number of 'threats' others have identified and how there may be countervailing forces or processes, or even how the threats themselves may have effects that help to sustain local cultures.

One cultural assumption almost universal among social observers is that the economy has a major influence on lifestyle and thus culture. Hence, one mechanism that could explain why globalization or globalism should lead to cultural convergence is that a global economy causes a global culture. Without specifying the linkages more fully, let me just observe that even in a country with a fully integrated economy, there may still remain several cultures. By extension, one may assume that a global economy might occur at different rates in different places, or among different social groups in one place, and thus that globalization in the economic realm need not result in a homogeneous global culture. One might hypothesize that lags and differential rates of change should help to sustain diversity as much as to undermine it.

Scientific thinking or 'rationalism' would lead to convergence as more and more parts of the world give up 'folk' understandings and embrace scientific methods. Of course, many areas of the world resist science as alien or Western, and there are quite different theories and approaches within the scientific world-view. A stronger argument, however, focuses on technological products of science. Historical examples suggest this is a very unlikely source of convergence, since different cultures have reacted differently to the same technology. Ancient China invented gunpowder but used it for firecrackers – a form of entertainment – but when imported into Europe, gunpowder became the basis of military dominance. Even today, one may observe one culture embracing and another rejecting or fearing particular technological devices, ranging from condoms to robotics. Furthermore, many of the world's religions have endeavoured to foment backlashes against some technological innovations, and science more broadly. Finally, diffusion of innovation occurs at different speeds in different countries or groups; and with the rate of technological innovation observed today, that should sustain diversity for some time to come.

Greed, consumerism, materialism, capitalism, and manipulative advertising are sometimes seen as a 'culture' of their own. Whether these forces are a culture, or whether they are distinct mechanisms, people who predict a more homogeneous world usually attribute causal importance to some or all of them. I do not wish to dismiss all of these possibilities, especially to the degree they implicitly boil down to motives or incentives to improve one's physical well-being and enhance one's affluence. There are, however, quite varied ways of improving one's situation, and there are quite divergent starting points. Hence, convergence must be at least a distant possibility. More cogent counter-arguments, such as selective adoption of culture traits or adaptation of alien influences to existing cultures, suggest that great caution should be exercised in the use of outward manifestations (such as riding snowmobiles) and 'inward' cultural meanings (to Inuit hunters, for example, compared with recreational skiers or search-and-rescue teams). The current diversity of culture among countries and groups who are avowedly capitalist and consumerist should serve to caution us against simple processes of assimilation in these terms.

Although not always clearly distinct from the previous point, Western culture ('McCulture'), values, and religion have been granted a prominent place in predictions about global cultural convergence. Besides the counter-arguments made above, let me note that there have been backlashes in many places against these cultural traits, not the least of which have been 'counter-culture' movements within Western societies themselves. Such movements remind us that cultural change may be endogenous or internally generated, and most of them have been motivated by knowledge of different values in other cultures. All existing cultures are hybrids of earlier versions. Furthermore, one may question the validity of the label 'Western.' Although it conveys some cultural content – for example, in origin the European or Western culture is roughly coextensive with Christianity – one finds at any given historical period great variation (even in type of Christianity) among the areas called Western. Think about the varieties of lifestyles, economies, and religiosity of the United States, Australia, Spain, and Sweden. Indeed, one of the deepest values in Western culture – although not perfectly implemented in all situations – is pluralism or toleration of diversity. Western culture (to the extent there is such a thing) may therefore nurture, enable, and sustain diversity.

A more specific prediction focuses on U.S. military and political dominance. As the only Superpower, the influence exerted by the United States must lead to convergence. No doubt the United States 'gets its way' more often than any other country in one-on-one disputes; but one must also recall that the United States was extremely more dominant in the immediate post–Second World War period than today, and this did not 'homogenize' the world.

If the United States as Superpower is an unsatisfactory explanation, the end of the Cold War is equally so. Some observers (mainly American) allege that the end of the Cold War resulting from the collapse of the Soviet Union means that the world now has only one 'role model,' so convergence is assured. That may be the view from Washington, DC, but local elites around the world realize instead that they can now choose from a wider menu rather than from only one (or formerly two) models. Globalization, in this sense, enables local cultures more than it restricts them.

The spread and greater use of English has been offered as a sign that homogeneity or convergence was more likely. Indeed, most of the six mechanisms just reviewed implicitly rely on the importance of English as a cause or indicator of other trends. Leaving aside the question of numbers – for example, there are many more speakers of Chinese or Hindi or Arabic and their relative growth rates are high compared to those of speakers of English – one must query the equation of language with culture. Of course, sharing a language may aid communication, and having no common language can be a barrier to communication. However, I would not want to equate the cultures of the United States, Canada, Australia, New Zealand, and Great Britain. One reason concerns linguistic diversity within each country (more in some than others); another can be called the 'intent' of these countries to remain 'distinct societies'; and the most crucial is that the major culture-bearing units may be smaller in scale but more global than either countries or languages – namely, the focused, non-territorial networks and groups discussed above.

To amplify the last point about non-territorial cultural units, consider the allegations that television, the Internet, World Wide Web, and other digital technologies more generally are really 'Western' and will exacerbate any other forces leading to convergence. The first and most crucial point is the one I have already made about 'varieties of diversity.' These technologies will, I predict, create global non-territorial communities of great salience to their members because of their specific nature as targeted media meeting personal needs. For example, a feminist lawyer working on issues of family law or immigration will be able to deal directly with most counterparts in every part of the world through e-mail, web sites, Internet files, specialized television channels, and digital databases. This will be feasible because most communication is in English. The lawyer in the next office may deal with a similar network and support system but with no or almost no overlap in content or personnel because the concerns are focused on intellectual property.

If imitation and related processes are vitally important, why assume that there is only one model to imitate? What little research I have found on the effects of usage of the Internet, World Wide Web, and the like favours the view that they liberate people from existing habits, allow them to consider a wider menu of options, and enable them to adopt (or adapt) a wider rather than a narrower set of lifestyles. Of course, these are empirical questions, so future research may reveal a different outcome. But if existing cultures – whether territorial or non-territorial – are hybrids formed on the basis of past emulation or adaptation, why would one expect those same processes of hybridization to lead to the extinction of all but one culture?

Evolution and Sustainability

To drive home my analysis, let me recast it in two other forms or metaphors. The two are market analysis in economics and neo-Darwinism evolution. Both lead to the conclusion that globalization should lead to greater diversity rather than to less diversity because both identify ways in which economic actors or other organisms exploit niches, both show that use of niches need not involve universal knowledge or cultures, and both confirm that initial conditions affect later conditions.

Producers and consumers have, at first glance or in a general sense, the same motives – looking for a good deal. Producers want profits, and consumers want value for money. In reality, preferences diverge much more than a general analysis suggests. Some producers have long-term and others short-term perspectives on profits. Consumers differ profoundly in tastes and revealed preferences, and such variation is evident within particular cultures as well as between them.

The means by which producers try to meet consumer demands have varied over time in ways that help explain arguments about convergence versus diversity. In earlier eras – and today in some places – most consumer products have been one-of-a-kind: homemade by the poor or specially tailored for the rich. As a result of the Industrial Revolution, where it has occurred, the balance shifted towards mass-produced goods (and hence standardized products) although the rich still have had access to tailor-made goods. More recently – and especially in the most affluent areas – the balance is shifting back to 'targeted' goods that are not one-of-a-kind but are not standard, mass-produced products either. With a local market, there would be too few customers for certain items, but in a global or near-global market, any particular product can have sufficient demand to induce an entrepreneur to produce and sell it. For example, when I was growing up, there were at most a handful of athletic shoes available, even in large cities. Now, even in many small towns, there are scores, if not hundreds, of types designed for different activities and tastes.

Because we have not left the age of mass-production behind, and may never fully do so, it is easy to imagine that global economies of scale lead to, or indeed are equivalent to, homogeneous products. But over time we have moved away from such standardization in many product areas and moved towards 'value-added' and 'targeted' products. These are still produced in large numbers compared with, say, the fifteenth century, but the numbers are small proportionately compared with the 1950s, which saw many copies of few products. Today in many countries, and eventually in even more, we will find many more products and a smaller market share for each specific product.

Some products are still standardized and still mass-produced. McDonald's hamburgers are an obvious example; but one is hard-pressed to think of many others. And even at McDonald's, one can sometimes find some different products in different markets, adjusted to local tastes; and, indeed, find a wider selection (chicken, pizza, etc.) than previously.

Economic theory explains all of these patterns in terms of competition along several dimensions. One dimension involves price, but consumers who are even moderately well-off financially no longer buy purely on price. Another dimension derives from product quality, and a third from product–purpose fit. A cheap running shoe which does not have the cushioning for distance jogging will be replaced by a more expensive one with appropriate cushioning – and perhaps also a choice of colours. Market 'niches' create zones of less competition, and thus the profit to produce greater varieties and styles.

Notice what lies behind words like preferences, targeted, styles, tailored, made-to-order, quality, and niche. The broader concept that encompasses all of these words is culture. This is so whether culture means religion (kosher hamburgers) or lifestyle (fast food for two-career families). Outward appearance and inner meaning may diverge, and perhaps too much attention has been focused on people buying or using similar objects when it would help to consider what those objects or actions mean in a local context. When the meanings are considered more explicitly, I suggest, cultural diversity will be more obvious and cultural convergence less so. What is true or best or desired in one culture may be a matter of indifference or even be actively disliked in another. Or the same product may be preferred for quite different reasons in different cultures.

Neo-Darwinian theories of evolution provide another domain in which a global environment does not lead to homogeneity but instead to a proliferation of forms and species. After all, adaptation to local environments created the diversity so apparent at any particular time or in any place. To introduce species to new habitats, to create new strains through breeding or genetic engineering, or to disrupt or even devastate a local region may at first reduce the diversity locally, but it often has a longer-term effect of enhancing diversity. The classic example involves Darwin's discovery of how many different types of finches populated the Galapagos Islands: each island fostered distinct species of finches because of their adaptation to an environment different in very subtle ways.

A global environment, of course, has always existed. In this context, it means more, however, than 'the total environment of Earth.' I will use it to refer to the greater interaction among and interdependence of what heretofore have been relatively distant, distinct, and isolated local niches. The spread of diseases, crops, plants, animals, and urbanization – among other examples – has rendered 'local niches' less local and subject to more influences. Yet the response of any one species to this interference has often been and presumably will be different from another species. Likewise, the spread of influences from area to area may create new niches – and hence new opportunities – for existing species to proliferate.

Very few, if any, ecological niches remain untouched by human activity. Indeed, it is easy to forget that much of what we label as 'wild' or 'natural' has been fashioned at least in part in response to human activity. Agriculture and urbanization are the most obvious examples and probably the ones with most impact on other species as well as our own. To take an example from what most observers would find most 'wild,' recall that the Australian bush or outback has been dramatically shaped by the conscious and intentional use of brush fires by the Aborigines. Because this apparently commenced at least 40,000 years ago, and continues today, European explorers did not understand how much of the Australian environment was created by human agency and was not 'natural.'

Most animate life forms, whether apes or viruses, adapt to existing (and evolving) niches. Humans do too, of course, but they create niches to a far greater degree than all other species combined. Hence, it seems preposterous to imagine that all human societies or groups will converge on a single culture or even on fundamentally similar cultures. Instead, they will create and adapt to niches, imitate or emulate other cultures' helpful ideas, and resist traits their culture defines as unworthy.

Considering that the original human gene pool must have consisted of a relatively small number of relatively similar mammals in a single, highly localized niche, the existing variety of human life is quite re-markable. Of course, logically one cannot rule out 'reverse evolution,' or alien invaders who choose to exterminate all but one culture, or some genetic experiment gone haywire; but there is no realistic way to get from current cultural diversity to McCulture. Ecological, social, and cultural constraints will continue to discipline cultural evolution; dif-ferential rates of evolution will help to sustain diversity; and all con-straints constitute opportunities for adaptation.

Traits and Bundles

Although many anthropologists have alleged that any given culture has coherence, that every element of a culture is somewhat related to every other, anyone not blinded by dogma knows that is not true. Instead, we can analyse cultural 'memes' (analogous to 'genes' in biol-ogy, as evolutionary theorists like Richard Dawkins [1978, 1983] have postulated). For some purposes, 'memes' might be analysed as single traits, but for other purposes they might be usefully seen as bundles of traits. Both are legitimate levels of analysis, but they will almost cer-tainly lead to contrary conclusions about sustainable diversity, as I will now show.

Suppose every city and most towns in the world boasted a McDon-ald's. Would one conclude that globalization leads to a homogeneous global culture? Of course not; and even if everyone wore blue jeans and spoke often about 'Seinfeld,' the conclusion about convergence would not hold. Instead one would point to the resilience of many religions, the millions of speakers of each of scores of languages, the great varia-tions in types of economic activities, and the consumer preferences which reveal diversity rather than mass conformity.

Indeed, how traits become bundled may be a cultural trait itself. For example, the European or Western or liberal-democratic culture defines religion as a private sphere and politics as public, with certain rights and protections inherent in the distinction. In some other world-views, such as the Islamic, there is no boundary at all between public–political and private–religious. Hence, my analysis may have less than universal validity, since I argue that cultures are never really coherent and that convergence on some traits may be compatible with divergence on others.

Short of a crystal ball, one can only speculate and theorize about future conditions. So what follows should be taken with the appropriate grain of salt. Breaking the very broad concept of culture into subcategories of governance, spirituality, and daily lifestyle, my argument amounts to an explanation of why aspects of lifestyle might see the most convergence, spirituality the least convergence, with governance converging in some ways but not in others and thus falling between these extremes.

Think about lifestyle first. Clothing is only partly a matter of taste or fashion, and so is food. They are determined in part by climate, occasion, affluence, and the like. Thus, one may expect some diversity regardless of cultural norms. Furthermore, except for decency norms, which vary widely, there are relatively few restrictions on clothing, food, leisure activities, and so, as compared with criminality or religion. Thus, emulation and affluence may lead to some convergence in this domain, while local cultural preferences sustain some diversity.

Spiritual activities and beliefs, on the other hand, severely constrain most individuals. Even educated, widely travelled, and open-minded individuals rarely convert from one religion to another. Although a reduction of religious fervour may occur among such persons, it is more than compensated for by zeal among other types of individuals.

Governance, then, seems likely to be an area where some convergence could occur. Already we find that almost every state has a legislature, although the details differ widely. Likewise, every state has a military or defense force of some kind. And so on. Hence, one might be led to think that, over time, convergence based on emulation and competition and bureaucracy should increase.

Note that this conclusion holds – if it does – only for territorial states. It seems less plausible for certain types of non-territorial regulatory bodies, such as the WTO, OPEC, the IATA (International Air Transport Association), and so on. And other networks and communities of a non-territorial sort look like very poor candidates for convergence, even though they perform functions of governance. Virtual ethnic communities, Amnesty International, Greenpeace, alliances of aboriginal groups, consortia of professional groups, and political parties have no incentive to emulate each other's values, norms, or customs, except in learning how to operate efficiently and gain political clout at minimum cost.

Conclusion

If we define globalization in terms of wider and wider awareness of global diversity, it is plausible to expect some emulation. But there are many models and no reason to assume only one will be emulated.

If we define globalism in terms of ever-more-encompassing units of governance, then diversity seems equally assured for at least two reasons. Nationalism failed to tame diversity, so why expect globalism to succeed in taming the even greater range of cultural diversities revealed by globalization? And non-territorial but global networks and organizations will exhibit extreme diversity because they target audiences with (by definition) distinct interests and purposes.

All cultures are hybrid. All cultures evolve and change. All cultures respond to global influences. All cultures fit a niche and create a niche. None of these observations offers any reason to expect convergence on a single cultural form or content.

Note

1 Several themes in this chapter are developed at greater length in Elkins 1995.

References

Dawkins, Richard. 1978. *The Selfish Gene.* New York and Oxford: Oxford University Press.

– 1983. *The Extended Phenotype.* New York and Oxford: Oxford University Press.

Elkins, David, J. 1995. *Beyond Sovereignty: Territory and Political Economy in the Twenty-first Century.* Toronto: University of Toronto Press.

– 1997. 'Globalization, Telecommunications, and Virtual Ethnic Communities.' *International Political Science Review* 18/2: 139–52.

Toulmin, Stephen. 1990. *Cosmopolis: The Hidden Agenda of Modernity.* New York: The Free Press.

4

Hyperspace: A Political Ontology of the Global City

WARREN MAGNUSSON

The puzzles that inspire this book are ontological. We no longer know what might be involved in governing modern societies, because we can no longer tell what a society is, we are no longer sure whether we are still (or ever were) modern, and we can no longer say where govern-ance ends and freedom begins.

If 'the state' were secure, we would not be so puzzled. The state is supposed to make society orderly and to set bounds between one society and the next. It is also supposed to organize governance. The state is a mark of modernity. It rationalizes human relations by forming people into citizens of separate, sovereign countries. However, the order produced by the state system seems secure only if sovereign identities fill the whole world and give it a unique history. There must be no surplus, no messiness that disrupts the system. Sovereignty-thinking suggests that people must be distinct and self-governing, both individually and collectively. If instead social and individual identities bleed into one another, and difference is expressed as an endless repeti-tion of the same, then we always have only a simulacrum of autonomy or sovereignty. If, moreover, there are no centres from which to govern ourselves individually or socially, then we lack any order that makes sense in sovereignty terms. This is both puzzling and frightening. It is significant that many of our contemporary fears are expressed in the ideology of globalization, which suggests that the state (and with it distinct societies, cultures, and economies) is about to wither away. The idea of statelessness, which two decades ago was dismissed as a Marx-ist fantasy, is now presented as a logical consequence of the global triumph of capitalism. Only the most sanguine look forward to such statelessness, because all of us have absorbed the lessons of Hobbes's

Leviathan. Without the state, we fear, the life of man will indeed be 'solitary, poor, nasty, brutish, and short' (Hobbes [1651] 1962, 100).

Sensitive thinkers realize that the crisis of the state is really a crisis of modernity. The whole edifice of modern identities is in question, from 'the individual' on up and from 'the state' on down. This edifice makes the world intelligible and enables us to communicate despite differences in language and culture. We can create values in such a world and learn to act accordingly. However, that activity is always premised on an 'ontology of sovereignty.' The latter is an understanding of what *must* exist for the world to be intelligible. According to the ontology of sovereignty, there must be autonomous decision makers (us) who can create order by surrendering their sovereignty to an overarching authority. In other words, if there are people, there must be autonomous individuals; if there is society, there must be sovereign authority; if there is a transcendent order, there must be a law of nature. Since the seventeenth century, our political ontology – the ontology of modernity itself – has been an ontology of sovereignty. This ontology depends on early modern assumptions about space, time, and identity, assumptions that have been challenged (if not refuted) by subsequent philosophical and scientific investigations, but that nonetheless have been fixed as common sense (Walker 1993). It is not just the most conventional forms of thinking that have been fixed in this way. Most of what passes now for radical or progressive politics – the politics of resistance, the politics of difference, the politics of social transformation – is premised upon an ontology of sovereignty. This is testimony to the political power of the latter. To coin a phrase, the ontology of sovereignty is sovereign. This is not a natural fact. As Hobbes certainly recognized, sovereignty is always an artificial *political* construct.

What follows is an effort to raise consciousness about the ontology of sovereignty and to suggest the importance of engaging with this ontology politically. I am a child of my time, and I cannot simply abandon the sovereignty-thinking that enables me to make sense of the world and to communicate with other people. However, I am going to try to lead the reader towards another way of thinking about space, time, and identity, a way that has helped me to unsettle my prior ontological assumptions. I invoke two contemporary images: one from physics (hyperspace) and one from social science (the global city). I try to combine these images and relate them to a conception of social movement that detaches the latter from its state-centric assumptions. I conceive of the global city as an ensemble of social movements in hyperspace, and attempt to locate the politics of the global city within and between those movements (Magnusson 1996). In so doing, I am trying to offer a political ontology that breaks free from sovereignty-thinking, or at least that problematizes the assumptions on which such thinking depends. Whether I am successful in this regard is less important than the fact that I am putting ontological questions at the centre of what I take to be the crucial political debate. As I argue in the first section, these questions have been raised again and again in twentieth-century art and literature, but have nonetheless been marginalized in political discussion. This is testimony to the ongoing power of the ontology of sovereignty. In the second section, I attempt to deal with the contemporary ideology of globalization, which appears to open up the questions I raise here, but then rephrases them just as quickly in terms of a problematic of sovereignty. Putting 'world cities' or 'the global economy' in place of the state in our thinking allows us to mark a difference that repeats the logic of sovereignty step by step. In the final section, I suggest a different political ontology, and so point towards a different politics. Whether or not my suggestions are persuasive, I will succeed in my purpose if I convince the reader that our puzzles and fears are indeed ontological.

Sovereignty and Identity

The modern citizen is an effect of the relation between the sovereign state and the sovereign individual, and it is this citizen who enters into other social relations, like the ones that produce 'markets' and 'cultures.' The domain of citizenship proper is the domain of the state, and hence of liberal democracy. This is a domain in which the transcendent ideal is always already defined by the conditions of citizenship. However, there are other ideals – of salvation or personal enrichment, for instance – that are enabled by civil society, which is the state's other. These ideals are supposed to be consistent with good citizenship. The disciplines of state and society are apparently the ones that flow logically from the needs of the autonomous Kantian self, the self that supposedly establishes its own morality freely and comes to knowledge of things independently. The latter is the self that sets our liberal hearts aflutter, and provides the rationale for the disciplines that run from top to bottom and from side to side within the order of sovereignty. But, what is this self that we seek to free, if it is not a miniaturized version of the Hobbesian sovereign?

It is not surprising that the ideal of sovereignty appeals to those who have heretofore been denied sovereign identities. Thus, we have powerful claims to sovereignty from women and gays, Africans and Asians, indigenous peoples and others who have been oppressed or marginalized. The temptation for people of enlarged sympathies is to defer uncritically to these claims, and thus to rewrite Mill's classic, *On Liberty* ([1859] 1972), in terms of a more adequate understanding of cultural differences and privileged identities. Unfortunately, even the revised versions of *On Liberty* are likely to repeat the ontology of sovereignty. As Foucault put it, 'We need to cut off the king's head: in political theory it has still to be done' (Rabinow 1984, 63). He might have added that our constant resort to a king-like conception of the self is a sign that the *political* ontology of sovereignty is prior to and constitutive of our understandings of individual and social difference. If we do not put those understandings to the test by questioning their ontological foundations, we repeat the logic of kingship or sovereignty in a particularly unhelpful way. Radical rhetoric comes to conceal conventional politics.

For a long time, philosophical attention has been directed towards the ontological assumptions of selfhood. Indeed, the assertion of the autonomous self (most usually associated with Descartes, but long foreshadowed in the Western tradition) is implicated in a discourse that poses selfhood as a problem (Taylor 1989). Twentieth-century speculations, following on from Nietzsche and Freud, have generated many ideas about the split self, the fractured self, the repressed self, the free self, the transcendental self, and so on. One of the positions enabled by this discourse is a radical denial of selfhood, a denial that takes the form of assertions about the impossibility of integrating human experiences into a single narrative. The narrative in question is both personal and political. Many recent analysts have said that we cannot tell a single story about an individual person, or about humanity in general (Lyotard 1984). In fact, a denial of the possibility of narrative or 'representation' is implicit in much of the great art, music, and literature of the twentieth century. The philosophical counterpart of this is to be found in post-Existentialist and post-Wittgensteinian thought. Post-structuralism expresses similar themes from within the historical and social sciences. One would think that such work would generate a different politics, a politics that broke free from the strictures of sovereignty-thinking. However, the politics that we have seen under these signs is usually one of childish self-assertion, motivated by nostalgia for the sovereign self.

However often the subject is decentred, it returns as a spectre: the ghost of freedom lost, or selfhood denied, to be revenged by an act of radical self-assertion. Thus, we have a politics of Nietzchean agonism that covers for ontological loss without ever addressing the problem of sovereignty.

The Foucauldian king can be regarded as the self projected into a position of rulership over others. However, this formulation can as well be reversed: the self is but the king projected into a position of rulership over the individual. Individuality is normally understood as the achievement of self-sovereignty: kingship at the level of the person. The microcosm of the self and the macrocosm of the state have a similar structure. Just as the individual is supposed to order his or her desires appropriately and thus to establish a rational plan of life, so the state is supposed to order the activities of desiring individuals and coordinate them in accordance with a rational plan. The economy/rationality of bodily desire and the economy/rationality of the market are modelled upon one another. So, too, are personal morality and the law. As Plato told us more than 2,000 years ago, rationality is a matter of *self*-discipline combined with *political* discipline. Christian and later liberal thought repeats this analysis with minor variations. To conceive of things differently is to suggest that the integrity, internal unity, and unique identity of the self or the *polis* (or God) is unnecessary. This is the frightful possibility that haunts us, and that makes the disintegration of the self our obsessive concern.

I know no way of avoiding this concern: It will come back to haunt me whether I like or not. However, I think we would do well to give less attention to the self as such, and more to the king on which the self is modelled. Our sense that things are falling apart and that there is no longer a central purpose to our lives (well expressed at mid-century by writers like Sartre, Beckett, and Pinter and now repeated even in popular entertainment) is to a large extent an effect of our *political* understanding. Most of us cope well enough with the fragmentation of the self and the absence of self-sovereignty in everyday life. More troubling for us is the sense that the world in which we live has no rational form and no rational purpose. It is not just that the world appears ungovernable. It often seems to lack identity, and hence to be utterly chaotic. If I am correct, this sense of the world is provoked by recognition that our god on earth – the king, the sovereign nation, the liberal-democratic state – has failed. This secular god is supposed to reassure us that rational form and rational purpose can be secured by human effort.

Unfortunately, although we have tried hard to make the king an expression of our desires, by reconstituting him as a liberal-democratic nation-state, we have been left with the same old order of sovereignty, which fails of its purpose in the late twentieth century as dramatically as it did in the early seventeenth century. The order of the state, the hierarchy of sovereign identities, the very ontology of sovereignty is a recipe for frustration.

It should be remembered that the Hobbesian Leviathan was intended to fill the existential void left by the death of God. It has succeeded, ideologically if not practically. The Great Chain of Being has been preserved, but at the top is the state, the market, or some other surrogate for God. God-like control is at the heart of our dream of sovereignty, and hence of our conceptions of personal and social identity. Clearly, our concern is partly with establishing the appropriate hierarchy of ends. However, it is also with discovering the means to those ends. The orderliness we seek is to be expressed in disciplines that would enable us to pursue the appropriate ends in right measure. The disciplines may be internalized, but we generally believe that the global order will not hold if self-discipline is not reinforced by constraints imposed from above. That these constraints might be ones that we give to ourselves is the Kantian or liberal-democratic ideal. Nonetheless, the presumption is that consent legitimates external discipline, not that it makes it unnecessary. Without either God or the state, it seems impossible to realize the dream of liberty, equality, and fraternity (or indeed any other universal ideal). It is frightening to think that individuals have to create order in a world that lacks a sovereign authority on earth or in heaven.

But, perhaps there is something wrong with identifying sovereignty with the order of the state? Perhaps we do live in a rational order of our own making, one that reflects our needs and desires. Is this not what Smith, Bentham, and Marx suggested, in their own very different ways? Isn't capitalism the order in which we live? Isn't the market the mechanism for rationalization? Isn't it also the mechanism for translating our desires into social outcomes? That certainly has been the claim of free-market liberals, up to the present day. Although Marx, for one, thought that this claim was ideological, he also thought that it expressed a truth. To the extent that there is order and rationality in a capitalist world, that order and rationality flow from the market. States do not create the capitalist order; they emerge within it, and help to secure the order of which they are part. Vital as states are, they are not perfect embodiments of capitalist rationality, any more than are joint-stock companies, banks, or brokerage houses. The organization of the state or state-system, like the organization of capitalist business, is constantly evolving, in accordance with the requirements of the mode of production. Thus, the Keynesian welfare state was only temporary. New forms of state have emerged since the 1970s, and they too will be temporary. We may be pleased or disappointed as these forms wither away, but we can be assured that other forms will emerge, more suited to the current phase of capitalist development – unless, of course, the long-promised socialist revolution occurs. The idea that the state is essentially capitalist can be articulated in either critical or celebratory terms. The implication still is that the state is to be understood as an effect of social order, rather than as its main source.

Both Marxist and pro-capitalist analysts have striven to show that states cannot be masters of the global order. In a way, we all accept this, but in another way we bow to statist thinking. The state remains at the centre of our political universe. To the extent that we have means of changing the order that is given in the market, these means appear to be connected to the power of the state. Like the absolute monarchs of the past, modern states appear to be the only authorities that can make things different by forcing people to obey laws that reflect a non-market rationality. To the extent that we can be other than what we appear to be when we allow our lives to be rationalized by the market, this difference can only be enforced by the state. Or, so it seems. Analysts who spend most of their time showing that the state cannot alter human nature or act against the laws of the market or serve the interests of the subordinate class, nonetheless tend to make the same assumption as the rest of us. High politics has to have the state at its centre, because the state is the ultimate *governmental* authority. So, despite the fact that Marx put capitalism and thus class relations at the centre of politics, he operationalized this view by substituting the state for capitalism and parties for classes. It was a short step from there to the parliamentary politics of the social democrats and the revolutionary statism of the Leninists.

Marx and Lenin were not unique. We are all caught between a form of political thinking that leads us inexorably towards the state and a mode of socio-economic analysis that tells us that states cannot be the source of fundamental change. Considered juridically or in terms of the means of violence, the state is obviously at the centre of government and politics. However, considered in any other way, it is evidently a particular aspect of social organization that can be changed only as part of a broader effort. The politics of action within the larger whole may be entirely different from what we are used to within the domain of the state. Only if we are thinking of overthrowing or changing the law does the state appear as the inevitable centre of our politics. Otherwise, we may imagine political action in quite different terms, as innovation, persuasion, popular mobilization, and so on. Such modes of action may occur at several removes from the state as normally conceived. More important, they may sweep across the boundaries between state and society, and government and politics, in ways that make nonsense of notions of sovereignty.

This oscillation in our thinking reflects the gap between the order of the state and the order of society. The order of the state is supposed to be juridical, and that juridical order is supposed to put every other entity in its place. The state's monopoly of legitimate violence is supposed to express and secure its supremacy. On the other hand, the state's capacity to create a juridical order is limited, in the first place by the presence of other states, and, in the second, by the presence of its own subjects. Those subjects generate other orders – economic, social, cultural – that are resistant both to the force of law and to the force of arms. These other orders have their own geographies or territories that are not amenable to direct control by the state. Thus, the state is always in an impossible position, in which it must legitimize what it cannot control for fear of forfeiting what control it has. Although no politician imagines that the state is actually sovereign, every politician – and indeed every citizen – has an interest in pretending that it is. How else can one make sense of the idea that one lives in a democracy, that the order of things is an expression of the will of the people, and that politics as it is now constituted really matters?

The trouble is that none but a few fanatics really believe that the state or the market provides for popular sovereignty. It is hard to imagine that a man as bright as Bill Gates actually believes that a Microsoft monopoly will facilitate consumer control. In any case, it is obvious that even under competitive conditions the main effect of market relations is to turn people into consumers – consumers who must then be workers, entrepreneurs, rentiers, thieves, or beggars if they are to survive. Consumer 'sovereignty' thus produces a particular and not very attractive array of identity-effects. The same is true for electoral sovereignty, which is the equivalent of consumer sovereignty in the domain of the state. The downward, disciplinary force of sovereignty is much more

evident than the autonomy it promises. Although we habitually respond to our frustrations by demanding to make 'our' sovereignty real,
we find that the consolidation of sovereignty in 'our' state or in the
'free' market actually intensifies the disciplinary force that we are seeking to control. So, we have rolled back the state in recent years only to
expose ourselves more completely to the disciplines of the market. This
should suggest to us surely that sovereignty is not the means to liberation: that the problematic of 'liberation' is just an effect of the ontology
of sovereignty.

We need to think again about the politics that gives us this insoluble
problem. Would it help to leave 'state' and 'society' behind us, and to
begin thinking of ourselves as inhabitants of the globe? Or, would we
just repeat the dream of sovereignty on another scale?

The Ideology of Globalization

Many of our hopes and confusions are expressed in the ideology of
globalization. As usually understood, globalization is supposed to be a
recent phenomenon, something bound up with the development of
global financial markets, the reorganization of production and distribution on a global scale, and the emergence of new systems of global
communication (Waters 1995). McLuhan (1964) and others may have
talked of the global village in the 1960s, but it was not until the 1980s
that it became a palpable reality. Or, so the story goes. Thus, the anxieties associated with the end of the Cold War security system; the disruption of the Bretton Woods arrangements; the closure of old mines,
mills, and factories; the collapse of public authority in various countries; retrenchments in public services elsewhere; and the general deterioration in the quality of life have all been associated in one way or
another with globalization. It matters remarkably little to most analysts
that the current phase of globalization, initiated by the original European voyages of discovery, began 500 years ago, before anyone quite
knew what the state, or capitalism, or the individual was. That there
were earlier phases of globalization, marked especially by the spread of
the world religions (Robertson 1992), is scarcely noticed. So, we have an
ideology of globalization that obscures as much as it reveals.

If it is true that people have been living in a globalizing world for
hundreds, if not thousands, of years, how are we to make sense of this
phenomenon? One way is to start is with the old idea of civilization, but
to keep the focus on the idea of city-building (rather than to be dis-

tracted by spurious notions of cultural superiority). If civilization in this sense is about building towns and cities, and if (as Jane Jacobs [1969] suggests) agriculture is better understood as an effect of cities rather than as a cause, then we have in the notion of urbanization a key to understanding both modernization and globalization. If (as Louis Wirth [1938] suggested) urbanism is a 'way of life,' then we can understand what we have been doing in terms of a shift from one way of life to another. As far as we can tell, that earlier way of life was nomadic, and it was dependent on hunting and gathering. Pastoral nomadism developed later, in constant tension with civilization, a way of life that involved both settled agriculture and settled towns and cities. We are the heirs of Cain, a cultivator whose hubris was inevitably displeasing to God, and who expressed his anger in an unfortunate way. We are also the heirs of Prometheus, an inventor who was also punished by the gods. What marks the project of civilization is the development of a man-made world, in which the natural order is made to serve human purposes, and in which an artificial environment for human life is constructed. Our capacity to create such an artificial environment is now much greater than it was. So, our cities are no longer like isolated enclaves, and we no longer need to condemn the majority of people to what Marx called 'the idiocy of rural life.' On the contrary, we have largely erased the distinction between the urban and the rural, and reorganized agriculture as a business like any other. We have spread our cities out more comfortably, organized agricultural regions as country retreats, developed the wilderness as a recreational area, and linked our cities into a seamless web, tied together by wires, pipes, roads, airplanes, and most recently by various forms of radio communication. What were distinct cities are in the process of integration into a single, global city, which will be the ultimate product of this process of civilization.

Civilization in this sense is beyond good and evil. It is so much an effect of what we are as humans that to call it back is impossible, and to condemn it is both pointless and hypocritical. We are engaged in a process of civilization because we are the sort of beings who can and do create civilizations. We cannot negate our own powers or prevent ourselves from wanting to create a better world. However, we can think about what we are doing, and criticize ourselves in a more serious way. This does not mean invoking a banal universalism that simply reaffirms some variant of what we are already doing. Nor does it mean translating Marxism into environmentalist or feminist terms. It certainly does not mean resorting to religious or genetic or cultural identities as fundamental. None of these forms of critique are adequate to the manifold project in which we are actually engaged.

The politically productive form of identity politics is the type that decentres the sovereign self, that enables us to see that we are all many in our sexual orientations, our ethnic origins, our relations to nature, our needs for individuality and community, our capacities for violence and peaceful cooperation, our destructiveness and creativity, and so on. It is that manyness that enables us to establish connections with others – collective identities – that offset the differences we feel. In giving up or at least moderating the quest to become a sovereign self, a person opens him- or herself to the possibility of connections that are not subject to the rule of sovereignty. Thus, one is free to be more than one person, if that manyness is necessary to the expression of our humanity. That, I take it, is what many writers of fiction have been trying to say to us for a long time. It is a lesson we have learned to expect in fictional representations: we cannot take seriously a character with no internal contradictions, or embrace a character who lives by a single rule, or accept a story that tells us that some one rule will enable us to live as we should. Unfortunately, we have more difficulty accepting such an ambiguous message in social and political theory.

One of the advantages of focusing on the project of civilization, rather than on capitalism or patriarchy or Western domination, is that we are drawn to recognize that this project has involved many cultures, with widely varying social relations, over a long period of time. We are talking about the ancient Egyptians and Sumerians, the Han and the Mexica, the Greeks and the Persians, the Moghals and the Incas, the Haida and the builders of great Zimbabwe. We are not talking about practices that are simply European or Christian. We are not talking only about the modern era. We are not talking about something in which only men have been implicated. We are talking about an ensemble of human practices in which we can discern a varied and variable effort to make the world over into a home for humans. Women's domestic practices are as much a part of this effort as men's labours in the fields. Over long years, in many different places, with different cultural assumptions and different social relations, people have transformed their environment, developed new technologies, learned to live in new ways. They have in the process become different from what their ancestors were. This civilizing effort began long before people began settling permanently, but the development of permanent settlements marked a significant change. From this permanence came the form of the urban, a form, significantly, that appears static, but that is in constant motion. By bringing large numbers of people in close proximity, cities intensified human activity. Cities became centres of innovation and differentiation. They enabled specialization. They facilitated learning and the preservation of learning. They created the conditions under which people could learn to make lives for themselves that were not governed by the immediate requirements of food-gathering. The urban is the mode of life that enables the development of agriculture and manufacturing. It is the mode of life within which modernity emerges.

It is pointless to enter into the endless debates about the origins of modernity. However, the historical record seems to make a few things clear. First, the practices and ideological orientations of modernity – capitalism, statism, scientific rationalism, and liberalism in particular – seem to have developed in concert with one another. They form an ensemble. Second, modernization was bound up with European expansionism. The Europeans changed as they moved outward, and they themselves became mediators of change within and between different parts of the world. Third, modernizing practices everywhere modified civilizations that were long in the making. Whatever the Europeans might have thought, modernization did not begin *ex nihilo*. Finally, the effect of modernization was to bring distant peoples into relation to one another, in ways that could not previously have been imagined. Globalization was implicit in modernization and vice versa. To use the term 'modernization' is to draw attention to the temporal character of civilizing activities. 'Globalization' shifts the focus to spatial relations. Ironically, the recent popularity of the latter term reflects the belief that time has finally triumphed over space, that we have at last come to the moment at which distance becomes meaningless, and that as a result we are now starting to live in the same space, and hence in the same time. However, the collapse of space is also the collapse of time. We are living, supposedly, in an eternal present, in which differences can be expressed only spatially. Thus, the Hobbesian problem appears to be reversed. Sovereign individuals and sovereign communities have to be created out of the unity that is always already present.

Let me expand on this idea. On the traditional analysis, the distance between people is always already given, and it is this distance that creates the Hobbesian problem. We do not feel pain and pleasure as one; we do not live or die as one; thus, our interests are always different. Given that the individual is an autonomous source of motion, the possibility of collision and even mutual destruction is always present.

Moreover, given the physical impossibility of global sovereignty – an impossibility that arises from the distances between people on earth – there will always be a plurality of political sovereignties. The Hobbesian solution reduces individuals to order, but only within a confined space. If global sovereignty becomes technically possible, thanks to instantaneous global communications and the dispersal of centrally controlled armed forces, then the claims to sovereignty by particular groups, nations, or states come to appear as problems subject to Hobbesian resolution. However, it is beyond belief that formerly sovereign authorities would surrender their power without a struggle. The struggle is evidently going on now. The key to it is the creation of two states of nature that exist in uneasy relation to one another. The first of these states is in the form of the Hobbesian dystopia, which seems to exist in the 'no-go' zones that journalists have identified in various parts of the world. (Whether conditions conform to the Hobbesian dystopia or not is less important than the fact that outsiders believe that such conditions prevail there.) The twin to this Hobbesian world is a Lockean state of nature, in which people's lives, liberties, and estates are secured by mutual enforcement of a natural law. Market relations are the supreme embodiment of the natural law, for they preserve such sovereignty as is consistent with absolute security of property. What is hidden in the Lockean idyll is the fact of Hobbesian sovereignty. That is, it is the power of the sovereign that ensures that the rules of the market are everywhere observed within the Lockean world. We are all Lockeans now, because the only other choice is the Hobbesian dystopia.

What social contract theory has always obscured is that the contract that is supposed to solve the problem only becomes possible when the problem is already solved. Thus, the formalization of global sovereignty will become possible only when sovereign authority has been deployed again and again with such deadly force that it becomes apparent to all that obedience is the only rational option. The punishment of Iraq, the humiliation of Indonesia and Korea, and the adoption of the Multilateral Agreement on Investment are all aspects of the same process, by which a new global regime is being created. The aim, clearly, is sovereignty, but sovereignty will not the take the form of statehood (if only because the form of the state is necessary to secure the dignity of formerly sovereign countries: in this respect, ongoing statehood is akin to ongoing medieval institutions like the British monarchy). To be effective, global sovereignty must take its own shape, and this will inevitably be rather different from the familiar form of the nation-state.

Various commentators, like David Held (1995), have attempted to respond to this reality by offering more benign models of global sovereignty. Intriguing as some of these models are, they all seem premature, since the messy work of crushing the opposition is still going on. There is a consensus among the most powerful authorities in the world today that everyone must be obliged to obey the Lockean rules. Only when the great majority of people in the world have accepted that 'there is no alternative' will it be possible to formalize arrangements and allow for a more meaningful show of democracy. Un-Lockean behaviour has to be rendered unthinkable, and this is not a task that can be entrusted to people who have too many democratic scruples. Liberal democracy may come at the end of the process, but at the beginning people must be terrorized into submission by threats of starvation, imprisonment, displacement, destruction, dismemberment, and death. People must learn proper market behaviour or face exclusion from the civilized world. The price of exclusion is much as Hobbes indicated.

The globalization literature tells us that sovereignty has already been secured: that we are already inhabitants of one world, in which there is one law, and ultimately only one way of being human. The sovereign consumer – the king-like individual in his or her most potent (but most fragile) form – is the identity-effect of the law of the market. However, in the market, identities can be purchased and sold, and as such they are established only to be destroyed. There is no logical limit to the proliferation of identities, and this means that each person can be (and indeed is encouraged to be) unique. On the other hand, there is no need for identities to be permanent or total. People can assume new guises in different contexts, and can make firm transitions from one totalizing identity to another. The production of identities (like the production of everything else) is subject to the laws of the market, and so entrepreneurs are encouraged to fabricate and sell identities that seem to have popular appeal. The market for most goods becomes saturated quickly, unless those goods are configured as symbols of identity. Once everything is so configured, then the problem of market saturation is resolved. New markets can be created by generating new identity-needs, and the latter appears to be a fairly simple process. Although some identities (especially of a religious or ethnic character) seem to be generated by non-market processes, this is becoming the exception rather than the rule. The hope (or fear) implicit in the globalization literature is that market-mediated identities will become of such overwhelming importance that people can no longer imagine life outside the market, except as a life of extreme deprivation. In this context, monasteries and wilderness retreats are symbols of a good life suitable only for saints, whereas the street people and the unfortunate inhabitants of anarchic zones elsewhere (observed on television and re-created imaginatively in the movies) are symbols of the extra-market life that emerges when unsaintlike people make a claim to it. These alternative spaces thus come to reinforce the one space that civilized people can inhabit.

Let us put it this way. It is becoming clear now that 'globalization' and 'modernization' have to be understood as 'spatial' and 'temporal' descriptors of the same process. These descriptors draw attention to certain features of the project of civilization. 'Sovereignty' is evidently one of the ideological effects of this project. It appears first in the sixteenth and seventeenth centuries, as a way of understanding the relationship between human identity, political authority, and divine law. The individual, the ruler, and the divinity were all understood in the same terms, as autonomous persons with a capacity to rule in accordance with a rational plan. Given the remoteness of God and the natural difference of interest between individual human beings, it was assumed that, for practical purposes, 'sovereignty' would have to be conferred on a ruler whose authority would be accepted by his subjects. This idea has been elaborated with great subtlety in the last 300 years. It has been shown, for instance, that sovereignty can be organized in a way that is consistent with individual self-government, provided that everyone conforms to certain rules (rules that allow both citizens and rulers to exercise considerable discretion within their own spheres of activity). It has also been shown that sovereignty can be divided in a way that enables rulers to live in harmony with one another. The key to this is the creation of a modern/global order that includes most people in the world. To be viable, this order must not only offer a better life than what is possible 'outside' (so that people naturally choose to be within it), but it must also engender, naturally, the disciplines required to sustain it. What is required to be successful in this world must be fairly plain, and the basic habits and skills must be ones that people in most if not all cultures tend to acquire. Moreover, it must be clear that children of the new entrants will be able to develop more advanced skills that will enable them to do better than their parents. Such conditions have by no means been universally achieved, but it seems clear that globalization/modernization will not be complete until this does happen. People who are not now 'sovereign selves' of the right kind have to transformed into such beings, if sovereign authority is to work as expected within and between states. Sovereignty is, in a sense, the ultimate objective of globalization and modernization.

Or, so it seems.

The City as Hyperspace

In the previous section, I presented sovereignty as the logical outcome of civilization. But, earlier, I implied that sovereignty was an illusion. Can these two lines of thought be resolved?

Sovereignty-thinking involves a particular ontology, and thus a particular conception of space and time. The theory that influenced Hobbes and Locke was the one that they got from Galileo and (later) Newton. It posited an empty space in three dimensions, within which the position of objects could be plotted geometrically. Objects were thought to fill space, and to move through space. Time was the measure of movement through space. A person could be construed as an object in space, with an inherent capacity for motion. The fact that only one object could occupy a particular space at any given moment meant that persons were necessarily separate from one another. The fact that persons (like other objects) were in motion meant that they could collide with one another. Only in so far as people surrendered to a ruler their right to regulate their own motions could an order free from collision be established. The need for sovereignty was implicit in spatial relations thus conceived. So too, was the possibility of sovereignty. On this model, one could well imagine that particular domains were susceptible to enclosure and hence to autonomous government.

On any of the models of space and time that we might take from twentieth century physics, the possibility of autonomous government seems much less likely. Significantly, the physicists have invoked concepts of 'relativity,' 'uncertainty,' and 'chaos' to make sense of their discoveries. Those of us who lack the necessary mathematical understanding are invited to conceive of the basic principles of physics in terms of Einstein's theory of 'relativity,' Hiesenberg's 'uncertainty' principle, and the more recent theory of 'chaos.' Few of us really understand what the physicists mean by these terms, and it is clear that the physicists themselves are taking ideas from cultural and social theory and applying them in accounts of physical processes. Be that as it may, it is significant that the twentieth-century physicists found that they could only make sense of what they could observe experimentally if they abandoned the idea that space and time were qualitatively different (in favour of the notion that time was a dimension of space: or, what it is to say the same thing, that we experience the second, third, and fourth dimensions of time as 'space'), if they dropped the assumption that objects had to be in a unique space at any time, and if they recognized that the key relationships they had to understand were nonlinear (and hence alternated between chaos and order in an unpredictable but not indeterminant way). The resultant theories displace the fixities of space, time, matter, energy, order, and chaos in favour of concepts that explain patterns, relations, contingencies, and transformations. Although the public has been frightened by concepts like relativity, uncertainty, and chaos, the physicists keep assuring us that the theories that invoke such concepts make the world more intelligible, not less. What is more, these theories enable human beings to do things that were unimaginable a century ago. That some of these unimaginable things proved to be horrific is no reason for losing sight of the fact that our environment is now more susceptible to human control thanks to our understanding of relativity, uncertainty, and chaos.

The work of the physicists is in various ways complementary to the work of the biologists, biochemists, and theoreticians of artificial life and artificial intelligence. As Donna Haraway (1991) has argued, the individual is no longer the entity to be explained in modern science. The body, the group, and the species are contingent effects of more complex systems that can be understood only when we drop the distinctions between 'whole' and 'part,' 'internal' and 'external,' 'living' and 'dead,' 'individual' and 'group,' 'human' and 'animal,' 'animal' and 'plant,' 'organic' and 'inorganic.' Modern biology, like modern physics, requires categories that make nonsense of the distinctions that were shared between the human and natural sciences from the seventeenth to the early twentieth century. The categories concerned – like system and network – were not developed by natural scientists working in isolation from the social sciences. As Haraway notes, some of the most crucial innovations were made by the people planning the bombing campaign against Germany during the Second World War. It was impossible for these planners to understand the effects of the bombing without modelling flows in a way that made little or no reference to Germany as such, let alone to Hitler or other individual Germans. Although the analysts were only dimly conscious of what they were doing, the effect of such an approach was to make nonsense of the hierarchy of sovereign identities. No sense could be made of the effects of the bombing on the assumption that Hitler was in control of Germany. What had to be understood were flows of energy and materials, patterns of communication and transportation, and so on. In this context, one could identify ways in which the flows could be disrupted, and also see how these disruptions could and would be overcome by systemic adaptation. The more sophisticated the analysis became, the clearer it was that the model of sovereign identities was absolutely useless for analytical purposes. So, modern war planning, like modern biological theory, demands an ontology that breaks free from seventeenth-century categories. Haraway's famous 'Manifesto for Cyborgs' grows out of a recognition that the seventeenth-century categories that inform most political theory will not work in a world that is governed with the assistance of twentieth-century science.

Eighteenth-century political economy and nineteenth-century sociology anticipate some of the insights of twentieth-century science. The focus is on flows, systems, structures, equilibria, and so on. However, these social sciences pre-suppose a seventeenth-century theory of government that flows from seventeenth-century ideas of space, time, and individual identity. One effect of this is that we have innumerable accounts of Canadian society or the Canadian economy – accounts written in face of the recognition that 'Canada' is an inappropriate unit of analysis for sociological or economic purposes. Although we know that the boundaries around Canada are about as useful for contemporary analytical purposes as were the boundaries of Germany for the military analysts half a century ago, we keep insisting on their importance. Only if we do can we make 'Canada' work as a sovereign identity, and only then will our 'citizenship' make sense to us in terms of the seventeenth-century dream of self-government. That dream – the dream of sovereignty – still has a powerful grip on our political imagination. It informs not only the idea of sovereign nationhood, but the ideal of individual freedom. It is not a dream that we know how to abandon, no matter how unrealistic it may seem.

Some of the most interesting writing on globalization focuses on the world city as a node of global domination (Sassen 1991; Knox and Taylor 1995). Urban geographers long ago noted that individual towns and cities functioned within systems of cities. Analysts showed that there were local, regional, national, and global hierarchies of urban settlements. In the last twenty-five years, the boundaries that separated local, regional, and national systems from one another (and that contained subordinate systems within larger ones) have become much more porous, and the relevant hierarchies have been differentiated and de- or re-spatialized. In terms of finance, Toronto may be higher in the urban hierarchy than Calgary, but in terms of the oil business, the relation is reversed. And, in terms of the operation of a big bank or oil company, it is not clear that Calgary or Toronto or indeed Houston or New York has much meaning. However, the globalization of the urban system – by which people mean the disruption of the established spatial hierarchies – has led to an almost obsessive interest in identifying the global command centres. It is somehow reassuring to think that we now have a tricephalous urban system, with New York, Tokyo, and London each governing the world for eight hours a day. A comforting 'sovereignty' is thus reinstalled in a world that is at once exploding and imploding (and in the process destroying the sovereignties that we once knew).

I have learned much from the literature on world cities, but I am disappointed by the way in which analysts revert to the seventeenth-century categories when they are confronted with political issues. Although the analysis always suggests that the urban system can no longer be analysed in terms of a neat hierarchy of cities, there are persistent attempts to impose such a hierarchy on the data. Some cities have to be on top; some cities have to be world cities; some cities have to be 'major league'; otherwise, there is no order to which people can relate. That the world is not like that – or, rather, that 'major league' or 'world city' status is something that can be commodified and sold, as it is by Major League Baseball or the International Olympic Committee – is at once acknowledged and denied in an effort to impose an intelligible hierarchy of sovereign identities. The assumption seems to be that we need to identify the hierarchy in order to determine where and how we should act politically. If the capital of the world is the tricephalous megalopolis centred in New York, London, and Tokyo, then we have to focus our politics at this sovereign centre, and not elsewhere. If, instead, the capital is in Washington (or, perhaps, in Washington–Brussels–Tokyo–New York), then our politics has to be organized differently. The global-city literature, like the literature on global civil society, the globalized economy, and global culture, draws our attention to the possibility that the governance of the world is no longer mediated by states, so much as by other institutions. Out of these literatures have come claims about the decline of sovereignty and the withering away of the nation-state. These claims are rarely posed in hopeful terms. Rather, there is great nostalgia for the world we have lost and great anxiety about the world to come. It is in this context that the search for a sovereign centre becomes particularly anxious. If no such centre now existed, that would be a matter for concern. But, if no such centre could ever be created – at the level of the individual, the state, or the world as a whole – that would be a much fearful prospect. For good or ill, that is precisely the prospect that is before us.

Sovereignty is an illusion in the sense that the king is never in control of his own domain. Whenever we ask, 'Why is this happening?' or 'How could this be changed?' we are forced to abandon the idea that the sovereign is in control. At best, the sovereign (self or state) is a site at which various forces interact, but more likely it is not a site at all, for analytic purposes. We have to construct different categories and identify the space–time of action in some other way to make sense of what is going on. And, as a result, the sovereign disappears in the analysis. On the other hand, sovereignty-*thinking* is of crucial importance, because people still tend to model themselves and the political entities that concern them with reference to the sovereignty-model. So, we have a paradox. Sovereignty is an illusion, but it is an illusion that people are constantly trying to put into effect. It seems clear that the most powerful people in the world would like to reconfigure sovereignty in the form of what Steven Gill (1991) calls 'disciplinary neo-liberalism.' There has been much progress in this direction, and no doubt it will continue. If there is a hopeful aspect to this, it comes not from the prospect of 'world governance'– since the only form of world governance imaginable is the kind Newt Gingrich and Jesse Helms would like to establish – but from the fact that any sovereignty-project is unachievable.

The sovereignty-project with which we have become familiar has a number of anticipated effects, including the state system, representative government, and the modern individual. All of these effects are now in question. The new sovereignty-project seems to involve creation of institutions of governance that are at once 'global' (in the sense that they are all-pervasive and all-encompassing) and 'local' (in the sense that they are articulated in the form of local practices). The capacity to create, shape, or transform these emergent institutions is by no means equally distributed, but it is not evident that there is any centre from which the process could be managed. If sovereign authority emerges, it will be from the interaction of agencies that lack sovereignty. The contemporary sovereignty-project appears to be an effect of processes that cannot be modelled in sovereignty-terms. The immediate consequence of the project is to disrupt traditional sovereignties, and its ultimate effect (if successful) will be to establish conditions in which there is an implicit order, but no recognizable sovereignty. The world will be self-governing only in the sense that it can be modelled as a self-organizing system. The self-governance to which any entity (individual, state, region, globe) could aspire will be conditioned by the logic of a system over which it has no effective control. So, the most evident effect of the contemporary sovereignty-project would appear to be the 'loss' of sovereignty. Or, at least, that is way that we could construe the effect, if we were to suppose that we had sovereignty to lose.

If my argument to this point has been clear, it should be apparent that the sovereignty we are about to lose was always only an ideological effect of our assumptions about space, time, and identity. This is not to say that ideological effects are unimportant: on the contrary. However, it is to suggest that we need to get some critical distance from the political ontology of sovereignty, if we are to understand our political possibilities. If sovereignty is always only a project, if its forms are always changing, if what it establishes is only ever a simulacrum of sovereignty, then our approach to contemporary political struggles has to be very different from what is indicated by sovereignty-thinking. There is no sovereign centre to be captured, and there is no point in trying to create such a centre. There is rather a multiplicity of different centres, nodes, zones of activity in which we can engage creatively. Our problem is not so much that there is no place to act politically, but rather that the sites at which we can engage are so diverse, so particular, so contingent, so local, so momentary that we can never draft any satisfying rules of engagement. The appropriate course of action has to be worked out *ab initio*, over and over again. This is certainly frustrating for anyone with aspirations to sovereignty. On the other hand, it involves the sort of freedom that we associate with creativity.

I have suggested elsewhere (1996) that it might be useful to begin thinking of the global city (or 'urbanism as a way of life') as a political hyperspace. 'Hyperspace' is a term taken from contemporary physics (Kaku 1994). It refers to n-dimensional space, of which our universe is supposed to be a particular domain. Contemporary string theory suggests that space actually has ten, rather than four, dimensions. According to this theory, the four-dimensional world in which we live is in a sort of giant, expanding bubble on the surface of a six-dimensional space curled up in a tiny ball. Whether or not this theory is correct is of less interest to me than the fact that it can be shown mathematically that the four fundamental forces of the universe would operate in the way that we observe if space were configured in the way indicated. In other words, the theory of hyperspace offers a possible account of the world in which we live. As I understand it, there is no such possible account of the fundamental forces in a strictly four-dimensional space. The theory of hyperspace offers an explanation of the way that relativity, uncertainty, and chaos can be produced by the interaction of the four fundamental forces in a space that transcends any particular domain, but that is internally differentiated so that the particular space–time of a domain like our own universe appears distinct, self-subsistent, and self-governing, even though it is overdetermined (to borrow a term from Althusser) by its relations with other domains that can be posited theoretically but not detected empirically.

I find the theory of hyperspace helpful in so far as it loosens the hold of sovereignty-thinking (and seventeenth-century physics) on my brain. Other people will find more assistance in different tropes and figures. When I try to imagine the global city, I see a variety of social movements that have constituted and are constituting various institutions, practices, and forms of identity. I begin from Marx's idea that the most powerful of the contemporary social movements is capitalism. Clearly, he thought that most of what we associate with modernization and globalization could be understood as an effect of capitalism. His argument along these lines was extremely insightful, but he was too much in the grip of sovereignty-thinking to accept the possibility that there were other, powerful social movements that developed in conjunction with capitalism and were neither its cause nor its effect. When we think of scientific rationalism, statism, liberal individualism, and Western imperialism developing in conjunction with capitalism and each influencing or 'determining' the others in infinitely complicated ways, we get a better sense of the origins of modernity or globalism. However, this means learning to think of each of these movements on its own terms. Rather than imagining a space–time that encompasses them all (which is what we do when talk about modernity), it is more helpful to think of each of these movements *producing* a space–time of its own. Capitalism has its own history and its own geography, but so too do scientific rationalism and the rest. The various spatio-temporal domains of these movements are not independent of one another, but the relations within each domain have a logic peculiar to it. This logic is, in a sense, constituted by relations that traverse the particular domain, but those relations are not usually apparent within the domain itself. To comprehend the most powerful movements (like capitalism) we have to relate them back to the architectonic movement, of which moderni-zation and globalization appear to be particular effects. This is how we come to an idea of civilization or urbanism as the movement that somehow encompasses all the other movements. Hence, the idea of the global city as the hyperspace of human life.

Already I seem to have been led into a trap. The effort to comprehend the whole leads me to posit a sovereign space ('the hyperspace of the global city') within which the particular movements like capitalism, statism, and the like appear as domains governed by the overdetermining logic of urbanism. However, if I am saved (to use a Christian metaphor) it is by the illogic of the city. One can certainly interpret the city teleologically, as I have done above: that is, to say of the city that it is an effect of human efforts to humanize the human environment. But, this is not to say anything very specific. In any case, it is to attribute to human actions a purpose that can only be assigned *post factum*. What seems clear is that the hyperspace of the global city is an effect of the various movements that constitute it. On the other hand, the form that it takes itself has an effect on those movements. Among those movements are not only the ones that I think of as *governing* move-ments – movements like statism, capitalism, Western imperialism, and so on – but also the various movements of *resistance*. The latter are what we usually think of as social movements, for they are not so obviously constitutive of the world in which we live and they seem to be moving against what is already there. Each of these movements of resistance constitutes its own space–time: It defines an object of attack, gives that object a history and a geography, defines itself in relation to the object, and tells a story of its own struggles, struggles that hopefully lead towards ultimate victory. The governing movements take shape in face of these movements of resistance, and so the hyperspace of the global city is by no means an effect of governance in isolation. Instead, new spaces are always in formation, as people struggle to give effect to what has been excluded or devalued. Although we can read the politics of the last half-century in terms of the progress of sovereignty, we should also be able to see that there has been a proliferation of new political spaces. The hyperspace of the global city is not fixed in a way that it suppresses every possibility. On the contrary, it is surprisingly open to political innovation.

This is where the hope lies in the politics of the global city: not in the prospect of global sovereignty, but in the ongoing possibilities for something different. In the wake of totalitarianism, Hannah Arendt (1961) wrote eloquently about the practice of politics as freedom. Her work is a reminder that the sovereignty-project is never complete, and the resources of hope are always present. What attracts me to the concept of hyperspace is that it is a reminder of openness. The city, to me, offers the same reminder. Cities are never fully contained by states, cultures, economies, or religions. To be cities they must reach beyond themselves, draw new things in, rework what they have been given, produce themselves anew over and over again. The city cannot be conceived as a determinate, tightly bounded, three-dimensional space. It is an ensemble of movements, movements that produce an order that transcends, but does not govern them all. The whole does not determine the parts, nor do the parts determine the whole. The order that emerges is dynamic, fluid, mutative, chaotic: not amenable to understanding in terms of hierarchies and enclosures. And yet, the effort to establish hierarchies and form enclosures is always present. If we understand that effort with reference to ongoing sovereignty-projects, we can see that the city is the form of order that disrupts such projects. The city generates the excesses, the proliferation of new domains of activity, that open up the enclosed spaces of *oikos* and *polis*, church and state, self and other, and thus constitute a proliferative hyperspace that is, at least potentially, a domain of human freedom.

The current sovereignty project – the project of disciplinary neo-liberalism – is not something permanent. It is not a project that can ever be completed. It will fail, because it is based on assumptions about the world and about humans that simply make no sense. In the end, sovereignty-thinking is profoundly disabling, both for those who pursue sovereignty-projects and for those who resist them. We have been captivated by the dream of sovereignty for far too long, and we need to exercise our imaginations to conceive of the world in a way that enables us to identify political problems and political possibilities realistically. The king is dead. Long live the free city.

References

Arendt, Hannah. 1961. *Between Past and Future*. New York: Viking Press.
Gill, Steven. 1991. 'Reflections on Global Order and Sociohistorical Time.'
   Alternatives 16: 275–314.

Haraway, Donna. 1991. *Simians, Cyborgs, and Women: The Reinvention of Nature*. New York: Routledge.

Held, David. 1995. *Democracy and the Global Order: From the Modern State to Cosmopolitan Governance*. Stanford, CA: Stanford University Press.

Hobbes, Thomas. 1962. *Leviathan: Or the Matter, Forme and Power of a Commonwealth Ecclesiastical and Civil*. Edited by Michael Oakeshott. New York: Collier Books.

Jacobs, Jane. 1969. *The Economy of Cities*. New York: Random House.

Kaku, Michio. 1994. *Hyperspace: A Scientific Odyssey through Parallel Universes, Time Warps, and the Tenth Dimension*. New York: Oxford University Press.

Knox, Paul L., and Peter J. Taylor, eds. 1995. *World Cities in a World-System*. Cambridge: Cambridge University Press.

Lyotard, Jean-François. 1984. *The Postmodern Condition*. Minneapolis: University of Minnesota Press.

Magnusson, Warren. 1996. *The Search for Political Space: Globalization, Social Movements, and the Urban Political Experience*. Toronto: University of Toronto Press.

McLuhan, Marshall. 1964. *Understanding Media: The Extensions of Man*. New York: New American Library.

Mill, John Stuart. 1972. *Utilitarianism, On Liberty and Considerations on Representative Government*. Edited by H.B. Acton. London: Dent.

Rabinow, Paul, ed. 1984. *The Foucault Reader*. New York: Pantheon.

Robertson, Roland. 1992. *Globalization: Social Theory and Global Culture*. London: Sage..

Sassen, Saskia. 1991. *The Global City*. Princeton, NJ: Princeton University Press.

Taylor, Charles. 1989. *Sources of the Self: The Making of Modern Identity*. Cambridge: Cambridge University Press.

Walker, R.B.J. 1993. *Inside/Outside: International Relations as Political Theory*. Cambridge: Cambridge University Press.

Waters, Malcolm. 1995. *Globalization*. London: Routledge.

Wirth, Louis. 1938. 'Urbanism as a Way of Life.' *American Journal of Sociology* 44: 1–24.

Part Two:

Modern Regimes of Governance

Introduction

In Part Two, Barry Hindess, Nikolas Rose, and Claus Offe ground the broader theoretical concerns of this book in specific aspects of modern regimes of governance. They each focus on governance as population management, albeit with markedly different emphases.

Barry Hindess joins Warren Magnusson in observing that each of the concepts in the title of this book is troublesome. Hindess's approach is to problematize these concepts through a critique of Foucault's theories of governance. Foucault's focus was on the government of populations as it occurred within states as distinct territories. This focus exemplifies the sovereignty-thinking addressed by Magnusson. In Foucault's work, the government of others and the government of self are conceived as coterminous. The analytical focus is on the everyday 'conduct of conduct' that facilitates self-governance.

Hindess argues that, in Foucault's theory, the closer one gets to a system of self-governance, the more one approaches the model of a perfectly ordered market. The more one has a perfectly ordered market, the more one has efficient government at-a-distance: population members regulating their own and others' behaviour through fine-grained calculation and knowledge. Government is the practices of myriad centres and activities that attain the ends of prosperity by means that are immanent to the bounded population itself.

Hindess objects that this narrow focus on intrastate population management ignores the lessons of globalization theory and practice. There are now many dispersed regimes of governance by multistate, multicorporate, and multicommunity institutions that constitute and regulate human populations beyond the individual state.

Hindess problematizes society as a concept that connotes political and governmental unity, and an independent reality subject to its own laws and mechanisms. He notes that this concept is a relatively recent invention, and that social scientists studying societies as nation-states involved in population management have been important contributors to this invention.

Foucault examined how this conception of society as nation-state arose from modern liberal critiques of 'police,' that is, from critiques of surveillance and disciplinary control. Liberalism offered individual liberty as a crucial concept not only for the mobilization of the well-being of individuals, but also for the mobilization of the well-being of the state itself. In a sense, individual liberty was to be the most sophisticated application of *raison d'état*. As such, well-being was formulated in terms of the ideal of self-regulation. Well-being results from the refined practices of self-regulating domains, each with its own laws of interaction and organization that give participants freedom. The task of state government is to secure the conditions of self-regulation necessary to achieve well-being and freedom.

Hindess criticizes Foucault for overemphasizing the importance of the nation-state in marshalling self-regulation, well-being, and freedom. Foucault's work suggests a self-contained unity that simply is not present in any society/state. Private corporations, community groups, social movements, and other social institutions are underanalysed by Foucault as important contributors to self-regulation, well-being, and freedom.

Hindess points out that Foucault identifies the project of society, state, and liberalism with the project of modernity itself. Modern science, technology, legal norms, and bureaucratic norms were studied by Foucault in terms of their contributions to detailed immanent knowledge of the population (police), and to the more abstract knowledge of social science (society as nation-state) as these constitute the governable order of things. Again, the state, its territory, and its population are conceived as self-contained.

Hindess juxtaposes Foucault's view of the modern, liberally governed society with his own analysis of the modern global arena. The modern global arena is usually depicted as a liberally governed society. It is politically presented as international, that is, as merely a social contract of independent states that enter into agreements with each other, just like individuals and groups acting within each state form contractual agreements. However, Hindess says this political presentation ignores the governmental character of the system of states, which

is based on varying degrees of coercion and the inability of many states
to manage their own affairs. He offers examples of stabilization and
destabilization efforts by the United States in the name of democracy in
regions such as the Americas and Africa.

Acts of government within states depend on other influential states
and on non-state institutions. Moreover, it is too simplistic to suggest
that one state government controls another only on the level of the state
itself. One state government also controls the populations of other
states, as do, for example, multinational corporations such as credit
card companies. While Foucault saw the remnants of the sovereign in
modern forms of governance, Hindess stresses that there is no
overarching sovereign power in these global arenas of population management, which of course is not the same as saying that these arenas are
without government.

The new regimes of global governance challenge the promise of
liberal democracy that order will be accomplished in a willed, chosen,
and self-governing way. Each relatively self-contained state government must now serve overarching regimes of trans-state and trans-
institutional population management well beyond the self-governance
aspirations of their own members. Indeed democracies themselves are
becoming increasingly dependent on the workings of undemocratic
governments.

Hindess feels that the prospects for democracy on the global landscape are limited by the system of population management that gives
states exclusive control over some areas. For example, the international
immigration and refugee regime offers the individual the liberty of
leaving an undesirable state, but not the liberty of entering a desirable
one free from the arduous process of de-selection. More generally, there
is a new global politics of nationalism that allows 'the governmental
mapping of a destructive "identity/difference" dynamic onto states
and their populations.' States retain the most substantial exclusive
control over members of their populations who are the weakest. For
example, the United States also stabilizes and de-stabilizes its own
population by leading the world league tables for rates of imprisonment. It thereby achieves global recognition for the view that 'those
who are most severely disadvantaged by the workings of the current
world order should behave as if they were ultimately responsible for
their own condition.'

Nikolas Rose works squarely within a Foucauldian framework to
understand how everyday practices in population management enable

liberty. His chapter thus contrasts with Magnusson's counsel about the limits of liberalism and a focus on the sovereign, and Hindess's counsel about the limits of Foucault's liberalism-inspired concept of govern-mentality. Rose argues that liberty requires governance, and that one outcome of the positive power of governing is liberty.

Rose begins with a review of Foucault's account of the rise of the 'social' state. Foucault saw government as a *methodology* involving sys-tematized 'conduct of conduct' of persons, populations, and things in order to achieve objectives. Power is embedded in systematic activity. It involves a system of knowledges, calculations, and goals pursued by strategies, tactics, social networks and practices. Rose argues, in con-trast to Hindess, that this conception of government does not depict the state as sovereign, but as itself being 'governmentalized' from various non-state sources into a 'social fabric' for security, order, and the man-agement of problem populations. Things are never very orderly be-cause there is always a tenuous relation between the political apparatus and the activities of governing. Anything done can be undone.

Liberalism seeks to govern by making people free, hence Rose's title 'Governing Liberty.' Freedom is pursued by imbuing the methodology of government and the populations to be governed with the norms, techniques, and values of civility. The main vehicles for this process are contestation and dialogue over these norms, techniques, and values as intrinsic practices of governing. This ongoing reflexive critique is highly organized and actively mobilized, that is, governed. It is what makes the moral territory knowable, calculable, and ultimately 'social.' Na-tional moral regularities as a dimension of national territory are what come to be understood as the realm of the social: the 'problem space' within which to pose questions of liberal government, including re-quests from the state, claims against the state, and demands for free-dom of markets and individuals.

Practices of governing determine their own objects. Therefore, there is no such thing as *the governed*, only myriad objectifications that appear in institutional classification systems. These objectifications help to constitute the self-governing individual – identities are formed through collectivization as well as individualization – resulting in what Rose terms the 'depotism of the self at the heart of liberalism.' In other words, self-governance provides a regulated liberty, a capacity for ac-tion. Self-governance as regulated liberty expresses the paradox of liberalism: having to structure liberty through micro-regimes of gov-ernance, having to discipline freedom as a relational and contextual practice. In the politics of everyday life, liberalism tries to 'assemble civility,' that is, 'to put in place arrangements that would support the subjective conditions for a liberal society of free citizens.' The less civility, the more disciplinary mechanisms are required.

Rose argues that contemporary 'advanced' liberal government is promoting new technologies of rule beyond the 'social state.' He depicts these new technologies as being in service of the 'enabling state,' a state whose mission is to foster more and more automization, rationalization, and responsibility among the governed. The new technologies include various fidelity technologies: audits, contracts, competition, quasi-markets, performance-related pay, and other forms of government by results. These fidelity technologies are augmented and refined by information technologies that allow ongoing risk assessments of who is to be included and excluded. These technologies in turn require new technicians to conduct the knowledge work entailed.

Rose considers five fundamental effects of these new technologies of advanced liberal government. First, they make economic life more like a market system. As a consequence the social recedes and is even seen as antagonistic to the economic. The social can no longer be justified in the name of economic stability. De-socialization is seen as a positive thing, part of how the enabling state can enhance entrepreneurialism, risk-taking, venture capitalism, and other means of productive growth with the promise of self-sufficiency and prosperity.

Second, social programs take on many of the characteristics of the economic because they are commoditized and fragmented into a multitude of markets. This process occurs in the interests of having the enabling state enhance entrepreneurialism. It conveys the unequivocal moral and psychological message that 'active self-advancement' is *the* obligation of economic citizenship. New markets are created in health, welfare, and security that emphasize economic over bureaucratic and social logics of judgment. These markets are underwritten by private insurance arrangements, and underpinned by the idyll of the perfect market that can coordinate the contractual decisions of individual actors in the best interest of all and each.

Third, employees in both state and non-state institutions are retooled as entrepreneurs. Each individual is to 'capitalize' himself or herself, to become his or her own political economy, to relieve both the state and the employer of some of their social- program burdens. The individual entrepreneur is to risk-manage his or her own financial capital as a capacity of his or her self and as a lifelong project. This task is underscored by the stark awareness that continuous employment is always in question, subject to perpetual audits, governance by results, downsizing, rightsizing, and insecurity. Unemployment is reformulated as part of this new employee enterprise. Unemployment is now work. The 'job seeker' is only given *employment* insurance as a short-term and contingent revenue item in his or her risk-management portfolio.

Fourth, citizens are constituted as consumers. They are to conduct their lives as a future-oriented enterprise that variously provides pleasure, prudence, lifestyle, identity, and security. In this enterprise their own 'conduct of conduct' is regulated through sophisticated technologies of surveillance and consumption: credit cards, air-miles cards, bank cards, welfare-benefit cards, and other playing cards. It is also regulated through a neo-contractualism between the consumer and each institution of consumption. All of these playing cards are subject to fine-grained contracts, as are various purchase agreements, product guarantees, and so on. The liberal language of rights, fostered by the social state, now enters the neo-liberal contractual relations between corporations and consumers, including a litigation-backed discourse of consumer rights. At the same time, the private-sector model of corporation and consumer contract seeps into social programs, which increasingly involve contractual relations not only between the professional service providers and their 'customers,' but been the state and the professionals themselves. That is, doctors, social workers, and other professional service providers do not escape the above-noted retooling of employees as entrepreneurs. They, too, are subject to fidelity and information technologies of production quantity and quality monitored by government authorities, private insurers, and 'customers' jointly and severally.

Fifth, these technologies and contractual relations design-in control. Environmental, cybernetic, insurance, and legal designs all ensure an immediate and pre-emptive calculus of risk management at both personal and collective levels.

Rose speculates whether a third way of governing, trumpeted, for example, by British prime minister Tony Blair, might offer a turn-away from the social and personal rightsizing of neo-liberalism. The third way is located somewhere between social-welfarism and free-market capitalist individualism. It still conceives state government as facilitating and enabling, albeit a little more creatively and intensively than in the recent past. State government is to create opportunities by investing in human resources through education, temporary social support, and other measures that will allow people to become better vested in themselves and their own personal political economies. It is to figure out how to include the excluded by promoting self-reliance, prudence, community, and family support mechanisms, along with non-state mutualism and insurance. It is to help constitute a new citizenship of non-state, individual civic responsibility, expressed, for example, in volunteering and charitable giving. The civic republican self is to be motivated by the common good (positive liberty), in contrast to the liberal passive self that is motivated by privatization.

One manifestation of the third way is communitarianism. In particular, there is a strong emphasis on community not as a social or geographical construct, but as a virtual space of shared cultural and moral affinities that express the *ethics* of self-governance. The ethics of self-governance is an alternative to belief in an overarching moral order. The focus is on the fair, rights-based, practical shaping of daily institutional practices in each sphere of individual life. The ethics of self-governance is to be embedded in the new technologies of governance, and expressed in public culture as investments in responsibility. As Rose states, 'Society is to be regenerated, and social justice to be maximized, through the building of responsible citizens of responsible communities, individuals and communities prepared to invest in themselves.' Personal liberty can be achieved through participation in the government of one's own affairs in a morally virtuous and self-activating manner.

Claus Offe takes up one manifestation of the new emphasis on community as a virtual space of shared cultural and moral affinities – namely, the attempt to address identity conflicts through group rights.

Offe begins with an analysis of democracy that is also germane to the chapters in Part Three. A precondition for democracy is the state form, which includes three elements: a recognized fixed territory (a country), a population forming a nation (a nation), and constituted government with sovereign authority (a regime).

Democracies help to civilize populations in four fundamental ways. They guarantee rights and procedures, thereby civilizing political conflict and fostering incremental change. They establish cooperative relations with other democracies. They serve the interests of the majority, who form the less fortunate segments of society, via positive and social rights that achieve relative prosperity and social justice. They make subjects more refined citizens, ethical agents who contribute to the public good.

On the other hand, the democratic form of government has several limits. A democracy is neither self-forming or self-enforcing. It emerges from non-democratic states, and can be terminated by social movements or anti-democratic elites who use democratic procedures to reinstall an authoritarian regime. A democratic regime cannot democratically undo the population it has inherited in its territory. Nor can it change territorial borders in obviously democratic ways: in an 'outward' case military intervention is required; in an 'inward' case of succession or separatist forces, such as Quebec in Canada, there is bound to be procedural deadlock. Finally, the citizenship of a democracy as a whole cannot decide on the issues the citizens are to decide on. Although citizens can bring collective moral pressure, issues are posed by elites and social-movement counter-elites. If any of the above limits are run up against, the democratic regime loses its viability.

Offe concludes his overview of democracy with specification of the conditions under which democracy will thrive. First, it will thrive if there is wide respect for the regime form it takes. Second, there must be respect for and among the members of the population. In particular there must be no 'desire to exclude or unilaterally include anyone beyond the existing citizenship and the rights of political participation defined by it.' Third, borders must be respected by parties within and without. Fourth, there must be respect for the right to govern, and for the competence, of political elites. Last but not least, there must be intersecting values that simultaneously enable liberty, the non-violent resolution of conflict, social justice, and republican virtue.

Offe considers how the ability to resolve conflict and achieve social justice in a virtuous manner occurs in relation to three valued things, and in terms of three kinds of differences. The valued things are resources, rights, and respect. The kinds of differences are interest-based, ideology-based, and identity-based.

Offe hypothesizes that interest-based differences are easiest to resolve, especially if they are over resources. Ideology-based differences are more difficult to resolve, in part because procedures for resolution are usually part of ideological differences. Identity-based differences are the most difficult to resolve because demands are often for assimilation or, alternatively, exclusion or denial of the right to be a different group.

These three kinds of differences interact. If interest-based differences are satisfied through compromises in a positive-sum-game, for example, economic gains recognized by all, ideological and identity antagonisms will be lessened. Offe notes that this was the promise of modernization, which has evidently not come true. Losers in the interests stakes move to the ideological level, for example, economic failure yields ideological conflict. Losers in ideological conflict move to the identity-politics level, for example, the failure of socialism yields ethnic nationalism.

Offe feels that identity politics is often organized to secure resources and rights, to make one's group the 'target of privilege.' As such, identity politics is an instrumental 'device for the protection and promotion of the interests of latecomers or prospective losers in the race for the blessings of modernity.' It is also often a residual of failed economic and political modernization and an expressive response to the frustrations of this failure.

The response of democracies to the dynamic of identity politics is to try to equalize status rights and opportunities. Equalization is attempted through various types of rights. Economic and procedural social rights are advanced on behalf of the disadvantaged. Political rights, such as freedom of expression and association, are given particular emphasis. New identity rights or group rights are formulated, for example, those dealing with special representation, polyethnicity, and self-government.

In Offe's view, there are fundamental difficulties in implementing a regime of group rights. Self-government is unlikely to work in dispora situations, where unity of the group is in question, or where several minorities of roughly equal size are involved. He points to regimes of sub-nationally based, bottom-up federalism, such as Canada, as a case in point. He notes also that such regimes can end up draining resources from social-rights programs.

Offe observes that a minority group will be given particular credence if it is a structural minority, that is, an oppressed group that deserves more recognition than it is capable of effecting by its own structurally limited means. However, such groups in turn become structured in the sense of being locked in by their constitutive characteristics and shared identity that are deemed significant in political culture. Furthermore, there is a structuration process whereby group members actively use the political-cultural framework of their constitutive characteristics and shared identity as *the* focus of self-presentation and identification.

Offe contemplates several dilemmas in the politics of identity and group rights. First, there is the elasticity of trying to determine for how long the non-minority in a society should be responsible for the negative consequences of the acts of its ancestors that oppressed minorities.

Second, in the everyday strategic politics of identity, the minority divides into subgroups for tactical purposes or, alternatively, forms coalitions with other oppressed minorities. However, success in doing so eventually removes the power of the terms 'oppressed' and 'powerless.' The acquisition of group rights signifies social and political power. Third, group rights may result in loss of freedom. Members of the group may see an identity privilege as insignificant, and at the cost of being subject to undesirable aspects of governance by the group's authorities. For example, the group's authorities may impose undesirable mechanisms to prevent religious and cultural assimilation. The study of a regional language at school may be at the cost of forgoing foreign-language training, which in turn might have a financial cost in the future by making the person less competitive in the employment market. If a group's regime of governance sees some aspects of medicine as evil, it may deny access to needed and desired medical services. Offe points to the perpetual dilemma of 'how much quid for how much quo' regarding legal privileges or exemption from duty related to language, customs, and religion.

Identity politics and the quest for group rights are subject to a dynamic of escalation. There is lack of clarity on a number of dimensions. The substance to be protected is often not clearly defined. There is typically an unclear relation to spontaneous processes of cultural change. Success is difficult to measure. All of this murkiness creates a world to be filled by moral entrepreneurs. Group demands for clarity are expressed as demands for more resources to accompany the rights granted. In turn a 'me too' sensibility emerges in which the more rights that are endowed, the more that are demanded, in an upward spiral. On the other hand, there may be a downward spiral of negative reaction and discrimination because the group and its practices may not be seen as enriching the political community or as deserving of the compensation that it is in effect taking away from others in the community.

The politics of identity and group rights is characterized by two logics of indemnification. There is a backward-looking logic of compensation for past wrongs. Offe sees this logic as a symbolic practice of recognition that is morally more demanding and honest than the second logic. The second logic is the forward-looking logic of equal opportunity. While this logic entails the positive values of sharing and redistribution, it is often ambiguous and backfires because 'positive' stigma labels are attached on the group concerned through processes of 'reverse discrimination.'

Offe ponders why group rights regarding, for example, association, and religious and cultural freedom, are preferable to a regime of individual rights for those with ascriptive identity characteristics. He feels that group rights in these areas can foster new intergroup inequalities as well as weaken civic republican loyalties and commitments. He thinks an individual-rights regime is preferable as long as governmental elites are hindered from curtailing individual rights of categories of citizens in the name of national unity. At the same time there is also a need for accompanying social rights, which of course is proving most difficult for many societies at the present time. Offe's preference is for interest- and resource-based politics around social rights. He feels such politics have much more substance than the 'symbolic politics of "recognizing" groups through the costless politics of assigning them collective rights.'

5

Divide and Govern

BARRY HINDESS

The title of the lecture series that led to this book, 'Governing Modern Societies,' brings together three contentious terms, each of which invites extended discussion. However, my contribution focuses only on the first and last of them, allowing no more than a few passing comments on the problematic character of the second. My discussion of 'governing' and of 'societies' draws, as many recent discussions have done, on Michel Foucault's studies of governmental rationalities, and especially on those relating to government of the state. The elements of his work on which I wish to build are to be found, first, in his treatment of a distinctly 'modern' (if I can use that term) art of government that Foucault describes as appearing first in sixteenth- and seventeenth-century Europe and as coming finally into its own in the course of the eighteenth century. They are to be found, second, in his treatment of the emergence of a novel understanding of 'society'– as 'a complex and independent reality that has its own laws and mechanisms of disturbance' (Foucault 1989, 261) – that Foucault presents as if it developed almost as a by-product of the liberal critique of police. I will suggest a different view of the relationship between liberalism and this particular understanding of society.

Foucault goes on to say that this image of society should be seen as 'one of the great discoveries of political thought at the end of the eighteenth century':

> From the moment that one has to manipulate a society, one cannot consider it completely penetrable by police. One must take account of what it is. It becomes necessary to reflect upon it, upon its specific characteristics, its constants and variables. (ibid.)

We might add that, in reflecting on the characteristics of their own society, liberal thinkers at this time were likely to view it as one society among a large number of others, of which the most important would be governed in similar ways to their own. Since these latter societies were ruled by states, we can reformulate this point as follows: in reflecting on the government of their society, liberal thinkers were also likely to view the world as containing a plurality of states, each of which rules over one or more societies. Rob Walker (1993) and others have noted that the system of modern states is associated with a debilitating division of intellectual labour which places the study of relations that develop between states in one category and the study of relations that develop within them in another. Foucault's discussions of the modern government of populations fall within the latter category and, in that respect at least, exhibit many of the weaknesses (as well as the strengths) of the division of labour from which it derives. I will suggest that this treatment of the government of populations as occurring largely within states represents a serious limitation, both of Foucault's own studies of government and of the more general governmentality school which has taken up and developed many of his ideas in this area[1] – and in which I include much of my own recent work. I argue, in particular, that the assignment of populations to states should itself be seen as an important governmental practice, and one on which the development of government within states clearly depends.

In his discussions of government, Foucault insists that there is a certain continuity between the government of oneself and the government of others – the government of one's wife or children, the government of a household more generally, and the government of a state or community. While they may use different instruments to work on their own specific problems, these distinct practices of government nevertheless share a concern to regulate the *conduct* of the governed. The point of this emphasis on *conduct* is to suggest that, while it will often act directly to determine the behaviour of individuals, government also aims to affect their actions indirectly by influencing the manner in which they regulate their own and others' behaviour. Government, in Foucault's view, is a special case of power: it is a matter, in other words, of acting on the actions of others (or even of oneself). But the governmental regulation of conduct also involves a significant element of calculation and a knowledge of its intended object, neither of which is necessarily present in every exercise of power.

While this overarching concern with the conduct of conduct is central to all of his discussions of government, Foucault pays particular attention to the predominant modern understanding of the term as referring to 'the particular form of governing which can be applied to the state as a whole' (Foucault 1991, 91). His aim here is to distinguish the modern government of the state both from the forms of government noted earlier (of oneself, of one or a few others, and of a household) and from the rule of the prince, feudal magnate, church, or emperor over the populations of late medieval Europe. With regard to the latter, Foucault argues that the early modern period saw the emergence of the idea of an autonomous art or rationality of government, an idea which he distinguishes both from religious conceptions of rule and from what he calls 'the problematic of the prince.' In contrast to a conception of rule which is primarily concerned with 'the prince's ability to keep his principality,' the art of government aims to rule the state 'according to rational principles which are intrinsic to it' (ibid., 90). What particularly distinguishes the modern art or rationality of government, as Foucault describes it, from other conceptions of rule is its dependence on something like the modern idea of the state – an idea which refers both to a specific institutional structure and to the population and territory which it governs.[2]

Government, in the specific sense of Foucault's discussion, is concerned not so much with the business of taking over the state, keeping it in one's possession, or subordinating it to some external principle of legitimacy, but with the work of conducting the affairs of the population and the organizations and institutions that it encompasses in the interests of the whole. On this understanding, the government of a state may be conducted by agencies of the state itself, and in particular by that group of state agencies known collectively as *the* government, but it may also involve agencies of other kinds. Rather than presenting the government of a state as emanating from a single controlling centre, Foucault's discussion suggests that it should be seen as a pervasive, complex and heterogeneous set of activities which

> has as its purpose not the act of government itself, but the welfare of the population, the improvement of its condition, the increase of its wealth, longevity, health, etc.; and the means that the government uses to attain those ends are themselves all in some sense immanent to the population. (ibid., 100)

This view of population as central to the government of the state, and the related location of the study of such government within the more general study of the conduct of conduct has been remarkably productive, generating a lively and expanding research program devoted to the study of rationalities of government in the modern West. Thus, following Foucault's lead, students of governmental rationalities have been concerned to explore the various ways in which the government of contemporary Western states has in fact been conceived, to identify the forms in which state and society, the national population and the individuals, groups, and organizations it comprises have been represented, on the one hand, as posing problems for government and, on the other, as providing resources for dealing with those problems. They have aimed, in other words, to identify the concepts, arguments, and procedures that are or have been involved both in the formulation of governmental objectives and in the consideration of ways in which those objectives could be pursued.

For the most part, these studies of governmental rationality have treated the modern government of the state in the manner that Foucault outlines in the passage just quoted, that is, as pursuing ends and adopting means to those ends, both of which are regarded as being 'in some sense immanent to the population' of the state in question. Without disputing the value of this approach, I will argue that there is nevertheless a sense in which it can be seen to be seriously incomplete. I argue, in particular, that our analysis of the government of the state should itself be located in a more general examination of the government of populations. Foucault's proposal that the ends and means of the government of the state can be treated as being 'in some sense immanent' to the state's own population raises important questions concerning the relations between government of the state and other forms of rule – some of which have been addressed by Foucault's demarcations, noted above, between the modern art of government, religious conceptions of rule, and the problematic of the prince. But it also raises questions of a very different kind concerning, on the one hand, the division of the greater part of humanity into the discrete populations of numerous individual states and, on the other, the assignment to *states* of a substantial role in the government of such populations. What is at issue in these questions is a distinctly modern view of the world as divided into a plurality of states, the more properly modern of which are also democratic. The treatment of government as something that takes place largely *within* states suggests that the realm of relations *between* states should, in contrast, be seen as

ungoverned, that is, as a kind of anarchy. I will suggest on the contrary
that we should regard the modern society of states as embodying a
dispersed regime of government that now operates over the entire
human population.

Since the populations of modern states are normally understood as
comprising one or more *societies*, these questions bring us to the second
issue noted in my opening paragraph, which concerns the emergence
of a novel understanding of society as 'a complex and independent
reality that has its own laws and mechanisms of disturbance' (Foucault
1989, 261). I consider this understanding of society and its relation to
the liberal rationality of government in the following section and then
move on to locate it in a broader perspective on the government of
populations – a perspective of which the modern project of constituting
and governing modern societies is such an influential product.

Society[3]

The term 'society' derives from the Latin 'societas,' which originally
referred to a loose federation of allies. The conception of society as an
independent reality subject to 'its own laws and mechanisms' is a
comparatively recent innovation. Up to the late eighteenth century, in
European political thought the term 'society' was used to denote a
political or governmental unity: something held together by, and therefore an artefact of, government. The term itself is still commonly used
to refer to political unities, whether these be the state societies studied
by sociologists or the stateless ones studied by anthropologists.[4]

Nevertheless, the concept of society is now often understood as
invoking a self-contained unity, a unity that is something more than a
loose federation of elements held together by government. We have
seen that Foucault presents this 'modern' concept of society as 'one of
the great discoveries of political thought at the end of the eighteenth
century' (Foucault 1989, 261), suggesting that it emerged as a by-
product of the liberal critique of police. I will argue for a different view,
which builds on Foucault's discussion of liberalism while disputing his
conclusions about the concept of society. What Foucault presents as the
discovery of 'society' does not, contrary to his own claims, account
for the emergence of an understanding of society as a *self-contained*
unity. Rather, I suggest, this understanding should be seen as reflecting
a certain kind of political fantasy, the liberal equivalent of the late-
eighteenth-century military dream of society as 'the meticulously

subordinated cogs of a machine' that Foucault describes in *Discipline and Punish*.

We begin with the liberal critique of police. Most Westerners now understand the term 'police' in a constabulary sense, as referring to the work of keeping the peace, protecting people from certain kinds of harm, and apprehending wrongdoers. Richard Ericson and Kevin Haggerty have argued (1997) that this understanding of 'police' gives a seriously misleading impression of that role in contemporary Western societies. Their analysis reminds us that the term once referred to a far more comprehensive and detailed system of government regulation. In eighteenth-century political thought, 'police' was seen as embracing all the agencies and activities in a society that had as their aim the production and maintenance of good order in a territorial community (Raeff 1983; Tribe 1995). The widespread use of police as an instrument of government required, and therefore could be expected to promote, the development of two rather different kinds of knowledge. One is a knowledge of the theory and practice of disciplinary control over the behaviour of individuals and collectivities – a form of knowledge whose development Foucault examines in *Discipline and Punish*. The other is a suitably comprehensive and detailed collection of information about members of the subject population, their forms of association and patterns of activity, much of which remained in the hands of authorities at a local level.

Liberal government involves knowledge of a different order, in part because of the liberal emphasis on individual liberty. Political theorists commonly see this emphasis as deriving from an understanding of individual liberty as an end in itself, and therefore as setting limits of principle to the objectives and means of action of government. At least as important, in Foucault's view, are the practical implications of viewing the population to be governed as consisting of individuals endowed with a more or less developed capacity for autonomous, self-directing activity. This perception suggests that, at least in cases where such a capacity appears to be reasonably well developed, detailed and comprehensive regulation of behaviour in the manner of police will be unnecessary at best and, at worst, positively damaging to social order.[5] In effect, liberalism regards the populations of modern states as encompassing a variety of self-regulating domains – the sphere of economic activity, the workings of civil society, the processes of population growth, and so on – each subject to its own laws and developmental tendencies and governed in large part by perceptions that the participants form in the course of their free interactions. One of the most important tasks of the government of the state, on this view, is to secure the forms of individual liberty required for the effective working of these domains. Thus, what is most distinctive about the liberal rationality of government, as Foucault describes it, is not so much its commitment to individual liberty as matter of principle, but the belief that individual liberty is necessary to the well-being of the state itself. Far from being opposed to the doctrine of *raison d'état*, the liberal focus on individual liberty is here presented as its most sophisticated application.

Unlike police, then, liberalism conceives of society as traversed by a variety of self-regulating domains of social interaction, that is, as substantially more than just an artefact of government. Thus, while police government aims to operate on the basis of an immanent knowledge of the subject population, liberal government aims to operate at a certain distance, making use of an abstract and theoretical knowledge of social processes.[6] However, as we have already noted, Foucault goes one step further when he maintains that the understanding of society as 'a complex and independent reality that has its own laws and mechanisms of disturbance' should be seen as 'one of the great discoveries of political thought at the end of the eighteenth century.' I argue, on the contrary, that the conception of society as traversed by a number of independent domains does not, in fact, require that it be conceived of as the self-contained unity invoked by these remarks. The claim that human interaction takes place within self-regulating domains of social interaction does not imply that the governmental unity of *society* should itself be understood as constituting an overarching domain of that kind. While such an image of society has been remarkably influential in the social sciences, it has also been widely disputed – most famously, perhaps, by Max Weber and again, from a very different perspective, by Friedrich Hayek, the twentieth- century theorist of 'classical liberalism.'

Why, then, has the idea of society or culture as precisely such a discrete, *self-contained* entity been so influential (even being taken for granted at times by Foucault himself).[7] Before attempting to answer this question, I should note that while the *discovery* of society (as Foucault describes it) clearly breaks with police thinking in certain respects, there nevertheless remains a significant element of continuity. The liberal critics of police may have rejected both the comprehensive ambitions of police and many of its methods, but they also retained its view that government should be concerned to mobilize the resources *of society* in pursuit of its welfare and security. Thus, what Foucault describes as a *discovery* is more appropriately seen as the emergence of a new perspective on a social entity whose existence and boundaries had long been taken for granted. It represents a shift from an immanent knowledge of the population of a state, collected and gathered together in the manuals of police, to a more abstract and theoretical knowledge of the kind proclaimed by the emergent social sciences – a shift, in fact, from the classical to the modern episteme of the kind that Foucault examines in *The Order of Things*.

But it is the continuity between police and liberal thinking, rather than the epistemic distance between them, which is of particular relevance to my discussion of the emergence of the idea of society as a self-contained unity. The central issue here concerns the belief that the government of the state should mobilize the resources of society in pursuit of its objectives. This shared governmental ambition is clearly reflected in Adam Smith's description of political oeconomy as 'a branch of the science of a statesman or legislator ... [which] proposes to enrich both the people and the sovereign' (Smith 1976, 428), and it has played a major part in the subsequent development of economics and the other social sciences. Since liberals see society as traversed by a variety of self-regulating domains, they also see such mobilization as requiring the harnessing of these domains to governmental objectives. It is not any conceptual necessity but rather, as we shall see in a moment, the imaginary fulfilment of this governmental ambition that presents us with the fantasy of a discrete, self-regulating society that incorporates civil society, culture, economic activity, and morality as so many interacting parts of the one political unity.

At one point in *Discipline and Punish*, Foucault refers us to an eighteenth-century 'military dream of society' which takes to a fantastic extreme the police view of the state's population as consisting of individuals, groups, and collectivities, all amenable to disciplinary control. It sees their interactions as approximating, in the limit, to those of the 'meticulously subordinated cogs of a machine' (Foucault 1979, 179). The idea of society as a self-regulating unity occupies a similar position within liberal thought as does this totalizing vision in the science of police. As Eric Wolf (1988) and others have noted, there are striking parallels between, on the one hand, the nationalistic image of the nation and, on the other, the image of society celebrated by classical French sociology from Comte to Durkheim and later by American sociological functionalism. Like the nation, 'society,' in the understanding that concerns us here, is not so much a reality waiting to be discovered by political thought as it is one that is yet to be created: it reflects a totalizing political vision that is 'incarnated in a project' (Wolf 1988, p. 755). Those of us who have reservations about the overtly political concept of the nation should be equally wary of its seemingly apolitical, social-scientific counterpart.

Both police and liberal projects of government, each of which gave rise to its own totalizing vision of society, are dependent on a view of the state as a self-contained, self-directing unity. Governmental ends and means can be seen as immanent to the population of a state only to the extent that the population in question can be regarded as being in some sense self-contained. For this reason, both police and liberal projects of government are dependent on the geopolitical conditions that fostered the territorial states within which such projects could be seriously pursued. But we should also note here that there are important senses in which these governmental projects have themselves contributed to the formation of powerful modern states with well-established systems of internal government, those same states which have developed and sustained the modern system of states and, finally, in the course of the twentieth century, imposed it on the rest of the world.

This last development has resulted in the formation of a plurality of what Jackson calls quasi-states, 'supported from above by international law and material aid' (1990, 5) but possessing poorly developed arts of government and, at best, only a limited degree of internal legitimacy. In a sense, this describes the condition of all states during the early phase of modern state development – including England and France, which, at least in retrospect, seem to have acquired the most highly developed states of this period. What particularly distinguishes the condition of 'quasi-states' today is their location within a states system dominated by states of a different kind – that is, states in which the arts of internal government have now become highly developed.

This point brings us to my final comment in this section. We have already noted that the fantastic idea of society as a self-contained unity – containing, but not constituted by, the government of the state – has been widely disputed. Nevertheless, once such an idea began to be invoked in the government of successful Western states, it could also be adapted for use in other contexts. These include, on the one hand, the government of populations not blessed with their own version of the modern state – the government, that is, of contemporary societies which are nonetheless seen in patronizing terms as 'pre-modern,' as of our time in one respect and lagging somewhere behind our time in others – and, on the other, the human sciences themselves, where notions of society and culture as shared, self-contained unities are widely used to analyse human sociality.

We can conclude this first part of this chapter, then, by observing that what particularly distinguishes the liberal project of government from that of police is not, as Foucault sometimes appears to suggest, the understanding of society as 'a complex and independent reality that has its own laws and mechanisms of disturbance' (1989, 261). Rather it is, first, the idea that society is traversed by a variety of self-regulating domains of social interaction and, second, as the practical, governmental implication of this idea, the view that prudential government should take account of the workings of these domains. That difference apart, the two projects of government share the belief noted earlier that a significant portion of the world is divided into states – and therefore into societies of a kind that make suitable objects for the government of the state.

The System of Modern Societies

Few commentators would wish to deny that geopolitical conditions have played an important role in the development of modern states. The standard view is that government operates primarily within states and, to a very limited extent, over relations between them – with treaties, a variety of less formal accommodations, and occasional wars between states serving to regulate their interactions. I will suggest that this standard view misrepresents the political character of the boundaries that divide the populations and territories of states from one another.[8]

I have already noted that the system of modern states is associated with a particular division of academic and intellectual labour between the study of international relations, on the one hand, and the study of government, politics, and political thought, on the other. One of the many unfortunate consequences of this division has been that those who work in one territory have been reluctant to trespass in the other. I use the terms 'territory' and 'trespass' here advisedly. The former derives, not from the Latin *terra*, but rather from *terreor* (to frighten) via *territoreum* (a place from which people are frightened off) (Baldwin 1992), while the latter means 'to enter a territory unlawfully.' My point, then, is not that students either of relations between states or of relations within them have failed to enter the territory of the other, but that, following an elementary principle of academic prudence, they have done so under the protection of established authorities in the territories concerned – thereby reinforcing the negative (as well as the positive) effects of the division of labour that sets their respective territories apart.

What follows is a limited act of trespass – a trespass in which I have benefited from, but not always followed, guidance both from a number of influential dissidents and others in the field and from earlier trespassers before me.[9] I begin by observing that the division of labour that is at issue here is itself predicated on a view of human history according to which the single most important political event in that history has been the constitution of political society itself – an event that secures the conditions in which both politics and government as we now understand them are able to develop. The implications of this view of history are set out with exemplary clarity in Immanuel Kant's political writings, many of which rest on the assumption that the *natural* capacities of human individuals roughly correspond to the capacities of rationality and moral autonomy that modern constitutional republics are thought to promote in their citizens. This assumption still retains considerable academic support, but, unlike more recent elaborations, Kant's treatment makes no secret of its teleological character.[10] Thus, his 'Idea for a Universal History with a Cosmopolitan Purpose' proposes to unveil the 'purpose in nature' which underlies what must otherwise seem to be the 'senseless course of human events' (Kant 1970, 42). Nature's plan, he tells us, is to use conflict between individuals and between states as instruments for the realization of these 'natural' capacities. Kant argues first that conflict between individuals has led them to form states for their own protection and, second, that, at least in the more fortunate states, conflict within them has resulted in the formation of constitutional regimes. Finally – and in part because they are seen to foster the natural abilities of their individual citizens – he suggests that constitutional republics will turn out to be more powerful than other states with similar natural endowments. For this reason, we are told, competition between states will eventually lead to the spread of constitutional regimes throughout the world.

What Kant understands by a 'constitutional republic' is a state in which individual rights are protected by law and in which government operates on the basis of the real or presumed consent of its subjects. He is not a supporter of 'democracy,' which, in a sense that was conventional in his time, he understands as referring to a system in which people govern themselves directly. Thus, rather like the American federalists, Kant argues against democracy and in favour of a constitutional republic with a system of representative government (pp. 100f). Since the term 'democracy' has now come to refer to a governmental regime of this latter type, we could insert the term 'democracy' in place of Kant's 'constitutional republic' without significant distortion of his meaning. Nature's plan, then, is to establish a world federation of democratic states

Contemporary readers will find much that is uncomfortably familiar in this Kantian story. The open invocation of nature's plan may now be relatively infrequent in academic writing, but other elements of Kant's account are the common currency of Western social and political thought in the latter part of the twentieth century. Modern representative government is now widely regarded both as the highest form of political organization and as intimately related to economic development. The related image of representative government as a practical political ideal, to be defended wherever it can be found and to be promoted everywhere else, is also a commonplace of Western (and much non-Western) political thought. Finally, the spread of the system of nominally independent states to cover almost all of the human population is seen as a sign of progress towards something like the world federation of constitutional republics envisaged in Kant's account.

This Kantian story is essentially an elaboration on what might be called the 'contractarian political fantasy,' according to which states are seen as arising out of formal or informal agreements among various groups of individuals who then become subjects of the states which these agreements have constituted. We are told, in effect, that individuals come together with the aim of maintaining order among themselves and protecting themselves against outsiders. Accordingly, they form themselves into states by appointing, or constituting themselves as, a sovereign power to perform these tasks. Once states exist, of course, they can be expected to interact with each other, but they will do so in much the same way as individuals and groups are thought to have done in the imaginary, pre-political past: that is, they acknowledge no overarching sovereign and their interactions are governed by brute force, expediency, and unstable alliances. Thus, in contrast to the order which is held to be the product of government within states, the contractarian story sees the society of states as a kind of anarchy.

Nobody, of course, believes that the contract story provides a reliable account of the actual formation of states. Indeed, Kant himself is careful to insist that no original contract

> actually exists as a *fact*, for it cannot possibly be so ... It is in fact merely an *idea* of reason, which nonetheless has undoubted practical reality; for it can oblige every legislator to ... regard each subject, in so far as he can claim citizenship, as if he had consented within the general will. (1970, 79)

The importance of the idea of an original contract, in other words, is not that it serves as an explanation of the present legal and political order, but that it functions as an injunction which requires both the state and its subjects to conduct themselves as if their interactions were in fact based on such a contract. The contractarian story has nothing of interest to say about the political conditions in which territorial states were able to develop in the first place. It simply relegates these conditions to a pre-political past – a past which may be of interest to historians but which, in the contractarian view, should have no real bearing on the modern conduct of politics.

Since the contractarian fantasy does not pretend to historical realism, it might seem that there is little point in dwelling on its historical limitations. If it is nevertheless worth insisting that the contract story presents a misleading account of conditions in the past, this is because the features it obscures are significant also for our understanding of political conditions in the present. I have noted elsewhere (Hindess 1996), for example, that the contractarian story of agreement involving autonomous agents obscures the role of government in securing such autonomy as the citizens of modern states in fact possess. What particularly concerns us here, however, is an issue of a different kind – namely, that, by presenting government as the outcome of a contract between those who are to become its subjects, the contractarian fantasy misrepresents the role of government in the constitution of states themselves. We have seen that the contractarian story draws a distinction between interstate and intrastate relations – between a sphere of governmental regulation and public order, on the one hand, and a sphere of anarchy, on the other. To describe the sphere of interstate relations in this way, as a kind of anarchy, is not to deny the possibility that interstate relations may be regulated. But it is to say that such regulation, to the extent that it develops at all, should be seen as arising after the event, that is, as a consequence of interactions between the states themselves and of developments within them.[11] In contrast to this view, I argue that the existence of a plurality of discrete territorial states is itself dependent on a regime of governmental regulation which operates not only within individual states – as the contract view maintains – but also at a suprastate level.

We can see what is at issue here by observing that the modern system of independent sovereign states has its origins in attempts to bring under control the sectarian religious slaughter which had affected Europe since the Reformation. The Treaty of Westphalia and other agreements that ended the Thirty Years War in 1648 are conventionally taken to mark the emergence of a new European order of independent sovereign states. While recognizing the existence of irreconcilable religious differences between Lutherans, Calvinists, and Catholics within political units, the treaty nevertheless granted supreme political authority to territorial rulers within their domains, leaving it to rulers and their subjects to come to an accommodation in matters of religion and restricting the rights of participating states to intervene in the religious affairs of other participants. As a result, the German Empire was redefined as a loose confederation of independent states, and the political order of the Western part of Europe became that of a plurality of sovereign, territorial powers, kept in some degree of balance by alliances formed, and occasional wars fought, between their rulers.

This conventional story suggests, as many commentators have noted, that there are external as well as internal dimensions to the development of modern states.[12] Unfortunately, in locating these external dimensions at the moment of origin, it also reinforces the contrast promulgated by the contractarian fantasy between the order established by government within states and the lack of order without – a contrast which allows the society of states established by Westphalia to be represented as a kind of anarchy. What is particularly misleading about this contrast is, first, that it ignores the governmental character of the system of states itself, and, second, that it misrepresents the sense in which states, once established, can be said to manage their own affairs. Beginning with the latter point, it is clear that the maintenance of political order within the territory of a state requires that there be no significant interference of a disruptive kind by powerful outside agencies. This is a condition which few states, if any, have ever been able to guarantee for themselves.

Throughout the second half of the twentieth century, for example, nominally independent states in sub-Saharan Africa, Central and South America, and other parts of the world have been the sites of proxy disputes between powerful outside agencies. In *Promoting Polyarchy*, William Robinson presents case studies of U.S. programs aimed at influencing the internal affairs of states in various parts of the world, both during and after the Cold War. While, in the later years of this period, many of these programs have been presented in the guise of advancing the cause of democracy, Robinson's discussion shows that they can be seen as part of a more general policy designed both to stabilize, or to promote the formation of, regimes of which America approved, and to destabilize regimes, democratic or otherwise, of which it did not approve. The U.S.S.R. similarly intervened in the internal affairs of numerous sovereign states, as did various international agencies and other leading states on both sides of the Cold War divide. Even had they wished to do so, states that were victims of such intrusions have had limited opportunities at best to develop and to maintain effective systems of administration within the territories and populations under their nominal control.

Thus, returning to the Treaty of Westphalia, one of the most important conditions required for the emergence of effective sovereign states in Germany during the early modern period was finally secured only by the agreements that brought the Thirty Years War to an end in 1648. In this case, political arrangements established in order to pacify warring populations had the novel effect of assigning to *states* the government of the populations within their territories – as opposed to those populations being subject to a variety of overlapping and sometimes conflicting sources of authority. By restricting the rights of other bodies to intervene in matters of religion, these agreements enabled the rulers of sovereign states to begin the process of bringing under control the more destructive effects of religious differences within the larger German population. This example allows us to make two points that are significant in the context of the present discussion. It shows, first, that prospects for the maintenance of order within the territory of a state – and thus the opportunity for the state to practise and to develop the modern arts of government – depend in large part on the conduct of other states and of influential non-state agencies. Effective government within states, in other words, depends on political conditions that operate above the level of the individual states in question. I have already referred to Foucault's insistence that the state is not the only agency involved in the government of its population. The dependence of government within the state on the conduct of outside agencies can be seen as another aspect of the same argument. Thus, the second point to be noted here concerns the governmental character of the international state system, initiated with the Treaty of Westphalia and later imposed more or less effectively on much of the non-European world. This should be seen not only as regulating the conduct of states, and indeed as constituting them in certain important respects, but also as a dispersed regime of governance covering the overall population of the states concerned.

Conclusions

I referred above to the contractarian political fantasy, with its distinction between the order imposed by government within the state, and the disorder, resulting from lack of government, without. Everyone, contractarians included, knows that this is too simple a portrayal. Aristotle defines a state as 'a body of citizens sufficing for the purposes of life,' but no state has managed even to approximate the self-contained condition that this formulation appears to suggest. States have to interact with states and with political unities of other kinds, while significant numbers of their inhabitants engage in social interactions that go beyond state borders. As a result, the existence of government within states can be expected to lead to the development of government also in the spaces between them. There may be a sense in which the sphere of state interaction can be seen as the anarchical society that Hedley Bull invokes in the title of his most famous book (Bull 1977), but, as Bull also insists, it is nevertheless regulated by alliances, treaties, formal and informal accommodations, stand-offs of various kinds, and, of course, the occasional war. Similarly for what has been called international civil society: it may be subject to no overarching sovereign power, but it too is clearly not without government.[13]

My concern here is not to deny the significance of such supranational and international forms of governance, but rather to dispute the contractarian framework in which they have commonly been understood. My quarrel, in other words, is with the view that such supra- and interstate forms of government can be seen as secondary developments arising out of interactions between already established states – or, for that matter, between societies. There are, of course, interactions, and forms of government arising out of them, which are of precisely that kind. My point is simply that these are dependent on the existence of a more general, dispersed regime of government that operates over the combined populations of the states concerned.

134   Barry Hindess

This point has significant implications for conventional understandings of citizenship and democracy. It poses a particularly powerful challenge, for example, to democracy's promise, as John Dunn describes it, 'to render the life of a community something willed and chosen' (1992, vi). The challenge here does not so much concern the familiar problem that the workings of democracy will often be frustrated by political and other conditions not within the control of the democratic agency in question – a problem whose very formulation suggests the equally familiar remedy of more democracy.[14] More democracy will often be eminently desirable and, in the absence of strong arguments to the contrary, I tend to prefer it to alternative political arrangements. There remains, however, a more general issue that the application of more democracy does nothing to address – namely, that the constitution of contemporary states as relatively self-contained political unities follows the imperatives of an overarching regime of population management as much as it reflects the aspirations of those who belong to such states to govern their own affairs. Thus, the more or less democratic forms of government that have emerged within some of these states and the forms of government that arise in the interactions between them should both be seen as operating within the constraints of a more general regime of government which now covers the whole of humanity. In this respect, as in many others, democracy is dependent on the workings of other forms of government.

Neither citizenship nor democracy in the modern world is quite what it seems, but, rather than pursue these issues further here,[15] let me conclude my contribution to this volume by compounding my earlier trespass, this time by way of a few brief comments on two other cherished features of the modern world order: the principles of human rights and non-interference. In the first part of this chapter, I referred to Foucault's treatment of the liberal rationality of government as organized around the view that, other things being equal, the existence of certain forms of relatively free interaction should be seen as making a positive contribution to the well-being of the state itself. On this view, the liberal commitment to individual liberty should be seen not simply – and perhaps not even primarily – as a matter of principle, but as the most sophisticated elaboration to date of the doctrine of *raison d'état*. There is a similar point to be made about the protection of human rights and non-interference. At first sight these seem to be among those principles that, like so many principles of public life *within* states, are honoured more in their flagrant and persistent breach than in their routine observance. Rather than present them entirely in such cynical colours, I suggest that we should regard these principles as distinct but related aspects of a form of government which operates through the particularistic allocation of populations to states. Like the liberal commitment to the protection of liberty within states, they reflect a fundamentally prudential concern with the effective management of populations and, most especially, with containing the effects of conflicts that arise within the territorially bounded populations of particular states.

The international human rights regime is clearly predicated on a teleological vision of world history of the kind noted at the beginning of the second part of this chapter. On this view, the division of the greater part of humanity into citizens of one or another independent sovereign state can itself be seen as a step towards the realization of democracy, development, and human rights for all. All, or almost all, people now have a state of their own which, so the Kantian story tells us, can be expected to move, in the fullness of time, towards a modern representative and constitutional form – and it is within these states that the human rights of citizens are expected to be developed. The Universal Declaration of Human Rights proclaims the right of everyone 'to take part in the government of his country' (Article 21), and again that 'everyone has the right to leave any country, including his own' (Article 13). What should be noted here is that everyone's right to leave any country is not matched by a correspondingly general right to enter any country or to remain within it. In effect, the 1948 Universal Declaration and the later treaties, declarations, and protocols of the U.N. human-rights regime are all predicated on the assumption that for each individual there is or should normally be a country to which that individual belongs. Refugees and other individuals who are lawfully present in countries to which they do not belong are also accorded various rights, but without the right to enter or to remain in these countries such rights as they in fact possess will always be significantly less than the rights of those who do belong.

Thus, while the international human-rights regime proclaims the universality of the rights in question, it also suggests that ultimate responsibility for the implementation of the full range of these rights should be assigned on a particularistic basis to the states in which the individual or individuals in question are thought to belong. The suggestion is, in other words, that human rights should normally become available to individuals by virtue of their status as citizens of one or other of the many states into which the world is now divided – which is also to say that those rights cannot all be expected to apply in states where the individuals in question are not in fact citizens. Thus, while democratic states have generally been the strongest supporters of the treaties, declarations, and protocols that make up the U.N. human-rights regime, they have also felt free to discriminate against foreigners in their midst and at their borders, often subjecting them to arbitrary action by immigration officials, restricting their access to the courts and to the welfare protection accorded other residents, and incarcerating many would-be refugees and illegal immigrants. The apparent contradiction here – between, on the one hand, the endorsement of human rights by democratic states and, on the other, the brutal and inhumane treatment of many poor foreigners by these same states – is resolved once we recognize that the limited promotion of human rights in the states to which the affected individuals are said to belong has developed within and as part of an overarching regime of government that operates through the allocation of individuals to populations, each of which is governed by its own particular state. Where the latter proposes to contain conflict within these populations by restricting external interference, the former aims to ensure that such conflicts as do arise within them will take a legal and peaceful form – a form, in other words, that is least likely to have disruptive effects elsewhere.

As for non-interference, this should not be seen merely as a symbolic injunction calling, somewhat plaintively, on states to refrain from practices of a kind that must surely be endemic to any international order. It is more appropriate for it to be seen now, as it was seen at the time of the Westphalian settlement, as a set of prudential constraints, designed to limit the spread of conflict. Thus, states are enjoined to refrain from interference in another state of a kind that is likely to provoke retaliation from the state directly affected or to threaten the interests of influential third parties. They are enjoined to refrain from supporting one party to an internal conflict if such support entails a significant risk that the conflict might then spread to other populations. These constraints apart, state interference in the internal affairs of other states is the order of the day – as, of course, it has been whenever and wherever there have been internal affairs in which others might wish to interfere.

Perhaps I should conclude by noting that the system of modern societies, which is also the modern system of states, is not to be condemned simply on the grounds that it functions as a system of population management. Effective population management can deliver indisputable benefits – as can be seen in the condition of what used to be Yugoslavia and other cases where government by states has broken down, and especially in the strenuous efforts of numerous governmental and intergovernmental agencies to contain (but rarely to terminate) the resulting conflicts. But we should also remember, as Foucault observed in another context (1986, 343), that everything is dangerous – the management of populations included. Alongside the benefits that the system of modern societies delivers to a great many inhabitants of the more successful states and to influential minorities elsewhere, there are also substantial costs to be considered. Thus, a system of population management that operates through the allocation to states of exclusive control over their own populations and territories also provides conditions for the emergence of governmental projects making use of particularistic nationalism – and, more generally, for the governmental mapping of a destructive 'identity/difference' dynamic onto states and their populations (Connolly 1991; Shapiro 1997; Shapiro and Alker 1995).

Finally, while the modern system of states may be a dispersed regime of government, a regime that operates with no controlling centre, this is not to say that the participating states (or the populations they are supposed to govern and whose interests they are supposed to represent) engage with each other as equals. As with other dispersed regimes of government – the interactions, for example, of civil society in a constitutional republic or of an established and well-ordered market – it is clear that the actions of some players carry considerably more weight than do the actions of others. Here it is important to consider not only the overall balance of costs and benefits (assuming that such a thing could be defined), but also the matter of distribution: who benefits and who pays? At this level, the contemporary supranational regime of population management has much to answer for. Apart from serving the interests of the stronger players, as forms of government commonly do, this regime imposes territorial self-government on the weakest. Now that the inhabitants of almost every region have been allocated to states of their own, it insists that those who are most severely disadvantaged by the workings of the current world order should behave as if they were ultimately responsible for their own condition.

Notes

1 Barry, Osborne, and Rose 1996; Dean and Hindess 1998. See the closely related critique of Foucault's treatment of sovereignty in Lui-Bright 1997.
2 There are interesting parallels with, and also striking differences between,

Foucault's argument here and Quentin Skinner's treatment of the importance for modern political thought of the emergence of the modern idea of
the state. See, especially, Skinner 1978, 1989, and the discussion in Hindess
1998b.

3 This section adapts an argument developed elsewhere in connection with
Christine Helliwell. Several passages are taken from Helliwell and Hindess
1999.

4 Cf. Michael Mann's comment that sociologists commonly 'take polities, or
states as their "society", their total unit for analysis' (1986, 2).

5 See, especially, Foucault 1991, 1997, and the discussions in Burchell's and
Gordon's contributions to Burchell, Gordon, and Miller 1991, and Barry,
Osborne, and Rose 1996.

6 The contrast is discussed at greater length in the introduction to Dean and
Hindess 1998 and in Hindess 1998b.

7 For example, in the treatment of 'culture' in *The Order of Things* . See
Helliwell and Hindess 1999.

8 For related arguments see Bierstecker and Weber 1996; Hirst 1998; Ruggie
1993; Shapiro 1997; Shapiro and Alker 1995; Spruyt 1994; and Walker 1993.

9 See n. 7, above. Other notable trespassers include William Connolly and
Gilles Deleuze.

10 Cf. my 'Cosmopolitan Democracy,' chap. 6 in Hindess 2000.

11 Jackson's discussion of the development of sovereignty regimes is a good
example of such an approach.

12 There are useful discussions of this extensive literature in Spruyt 1994 and
Walker 1993.

13 See Held 1995, chaps. 5 and 6, and Jackson 1990 for useful discussions of
this point.

14 As has been variously suggested by Archibugi and Held 1995; Barber 1984;
Cohen and Rogers 1982; Dryzek 1990; Held 1986; Hirst 1990, 1993; Mouffe
1992. See my sceptical discussion in Hindess 1997.

15 See Hindess 2000, 1998a.

References

Archibugi, D., and D. Held. 1995. *Cosmopolitan Democracy: An Agenda for a
New World Order*. Cambridge: Polity.
Baldwin, T. 1992. 'The Territorial State.' Pp. 207–30 in H. Gross and R.
Harrison, eds., *Jurisprudence: Cambridge Essays*. Oxford: Clarendon Press.
Barber, B. 1984. *Strong Democracy* . Berkeley: University of California Press.
Barry, A., T. Osborne, and N. Rose. 1996. *Foucault and Political Reason: Liberal-*

ism, Neo-liberalism and Rationalities of Government. Chicago: University of Chicago Press.

Biersteker, T.J., and C. Weber. 1996. *State Sovereignty as Social Construct.* Cambridge: Cambridge University Press,

Bull, H. 1977. *The Anarchical Society.* London: Macmillan.

Burchell, G., C. Gordon, and P. Miller. 1991. *The Foucault Effect: Studies in Governmentality.* Chicago: University of Chicago Press.

Connolly, W.E. 1991. *Identity/Difference: Democratic Negotiations of Political Paradox.* Ithaca, NY: Cornell University Press.

Dean, M., and B. Hindess. 1998. *Governing Australia.* Melbourne: Cambridge University Press,

Dryzek, J.S. 1990. *Discursive Democracy: Polities, Policy, and Political Science.* Cambridge: Cambridge University Press.

Dunn, J. 1992. *Democracy. The Unfinished Journey 508 BC to AD 1993.* Oxford: Oxford University Press.

Ericson, R.V., and K.D. Haggerty. 1997. *Policing the Risk Society.* Toronto: University of Toronto Press.

Foucault, M. 1979. *Discipline & Punish.* Harmondsworth: Penguin.

– 1986. 'On the Genealogy of Ethics: An Overview of Work in Progress.' pp. 340–72 in P. Rabinow, ed., *The Foucault Reader.* Harmondsworth: Penguin.

– 1989. 'An Ethics of Pleasure.' Pp. 257–76 in S. Lotringer, ed., *Foucault Live.* New York: Semiotext.

– 1991. 'Governmentality.' Pp. 87–104 in G. Burchell, C. Gordon, and P. Miller, eds., *The Foucault Effect.* Chicago: University of Chicago Press.

– 1997. *Ethics: Subjectivity and Truth.* Edited by Paul Rabinow. New York: The New Press.

Held, D. 1986. *Models of Democracy.* Cambridge: Polity.

– 1995. *Democracy and the Global Order. From the Modern State to Cosmopolitan Governance.* Cambridge: Polity.

Helliwell, C., and B. Hindess. 1999. '"Culture", "Society" and the Figure of Man.' *History of the Human Sciences* 12/4 (in press).

Hindess, B. 1996. 'Liberalism, Socialism and Democracy: Variations on a Governmental Theme.' Pp. 65–80 in A. Barry, T. Osborne, and N. Rose, eds., *Foucault and Political Reason: Liberalism, Neo-liberalism and Rationalities of Government.* London: University College London Press.

– 1997. 'Democracy and Disenchantment.' *Australian Journal of Political Science* 32/1: 79–92.

– 1998a. 'Divide and Rule: The International Character of Modern Citizenship.' *European Journal of Social Theory* 1/1: 57–70.

– 1998b. 'Knowledge and Political Reason.' *Critical Review of International Social and Political Philosophy* 1: 63–82.

140   Barry Hindess

– 2000. *Democracy* . London: Routledge.

Hirst, P. 1990. *Representative Democracy and Its Limits* . Cambridge: Polity.

– 1993. *Associative Democracy: New Forms of Social and Economic Governance* . Cambridge: Polity.

– 1998. 'The International Origins of National Sovereignty.' Pp. 216–35 in his *From Statism to Pluralism*. London: University College London Press.

Jackson, R.H. 1990. *Quasi-States: Sovereignty, International Relations and the Third World*. Cambridge: Cambridge University Press.

Kant, I. 1970. *Political Writings*. Edited by Hans Reiss. Cambridge: Cambridge University Press.

Lui-Bright, R. 1997. 'International/National: Sovereignty, Governmentality and International Relations.' *Australasian Political Studies* 2: 581–97.

Mann, M. 1986. *The Sources of Social Power*. Vol. 1: *A History of Power to A.D. 1760*. Cambridge: Cambridge University Press.

Mouffe, C. 1992. *Dimensions of Radical Democracy: Pluralism, Citizenship, Community*. London: Verso.

Raeff, M. 1983. *The Well-Ordered Police State: Social and Institutional Change through Law in the Germanies and Russia, 1699–1800* . New Haven and London: Yale University Press.

Ruggie, J.G. 1993. 'Territoriality and Beyond: Problematising Modernity in International Relations.' *International Organisation* 47/1: 139–72.

Shapiro, M.J. 1997. *Violent Cartographies* . Minneapolis: University of Minnesota Press.

Shapiro, M.J., and H. Alker. 1995. *Challenging Boundaries: Global Flows, Territorial Identities*. Minneapolis: University of Minnesota Press.

Skinner, Q. 1978. *The Foundations of Modern Political Thought*. Vol. 1: *The Reformation*. Cambridge: Cambridge University Press

– 1989. 'The State.' Pp. 90–131 in T. Ball, J. Farr, and R.L. Hansen, eds., *Political Innovation and Conceptual Change*. Cambridge: Cambridge University Press

Smith, A. 1976. *An Inquiry into the Nature and Causes of the Wealth of Nations*. Edited by R.H. Campbell and A.S. Skinner. Oxford: Clarendon Press.

Spruyt, H. 1994. *The Sovereign State and Its Competitors: An Analysis of Systems Change*. Princeton, NJ: Princeton University Press.

Tribe, K. 1995. *Strategies of Economic Order: German Economic Discourse, 1750–1950*. Cambridge: Cambridge University Press.

Walker, R.B.J. 1993. *Inside/Outside: International Relations as Political Theory*. Cambridge: Cambridge University Press.

6

Governing Liberty

NIKOLAS ROSE

In 1936, Luther Gullick, director of the Institute of Public Administration, contributed an introduction to a study of liquor control in the United States.[1] In it he wrote:

> With few exceptions all governmental work involves the performance of a service, the exercise of a control, or the execution of a task, not at the center of government, but at thousands of points scattered more or less evenly throughout the country or wherever the citizens or their interests may be. The real work of government is not to be found behind the Greek columns of public buildings. It is rather on the land, among the people. It is the postman delivering mail, the policeman walking his beat, the teacher hearing Johnny read, the whitewing sweeping the street, the inspectors – dairy, food, health, tenement, factory – on the farm, in the laboratory, the slaughterhouse, the slum, the mill; it is the playground full of children, the library with its readers, the reservoirs of pure water flowing to the cities; it is street lights at night; it is thousands and thousands of miles of pavements and sidewalks; it is the nurse beside the free bed, the doctor administering serum, and the food, raiment and shelter given to those who have nothing; it is the standard of weight and measure and value in every hamlet. All this *is* government, and not what men call 'government' in great buildings and capitols; and its symbol is found not in the great flag flown from the dome of the capitol but in the twenty-five million flags in the homes of the people. (Gullick, in Harrison and Laine 1936, xiv)

Gullick was a significant participant in the policies of the New Deal in the United States, and the liquor control study was funded by John D.

142   Nikolas Rose

Rockefeller Jr, whose foundation played a key role in this period in articulating and disseminating a new 'social' but anti-socialist mentality of government, which would apply science and expertise to the rational administration of human affairs.

In this chapter, I would like to set out an approach to political power that might help us understand this strategy of government, and indeed of the other rationalities and technologies of government that have been invented in 'liberal' societies since the mid-nineteenth century.[2] By 'government' I mean that zone of thought and action comprising all more or less systematized ways of thinking about and acting upon the conduct of persons, the capacities of populations, and the disposition of things in order to achieve certain objectives. In particular, I want to examine some significant innovations in styles of governing that occurred over the last quarter of the twentieth century. I term these 'advanced' liberal ways of governing. And, in conclusion, I would like to comment, in a preliminary way, upon a new style of governmental thought that is coming to the fore in the United States and in Britain. This seeks to identify a manner of governing, one that operates neither through 'the state' nor 'the market,' but in what its proponents, notably the current British prime minister, describe as a 'third way.'

Governing

Over recent years, political analysis has largely shifted its focus. It is now less concerned with 'who holds power' than with the means, techniques, and relations though which power is exercised. The question of who holds power was linked to a nineteenth-century philosophical and juridical image of the state later incorporated into social theory – the state imagined as sovereign, unified actor – and therefore with its capacities, its degree of autonomy from other actors, its strength or weakness (cf. Evans, Rueschmeyer, and Skocpol 1985). As this image of the state has been called into question, attention has shifted to the ways in which powers swarm through the territories of existence, flowing around circuits, through networks, devices, techniques – power, not as possession, but as activity. The perspective of government addresses itself to power as it inheres in practices, calculations, strategies, tactics, technologies, relations, goals.

This does not mean that the state ceases to be significant. On the contrary, the key characteristic of 'actually existing liberalism,' as it developed over the second half of the nineteenth century and the first seven decades of our own, was what Michel Foucault terms 'the governmentalization of the state.' That is to say, the invention and assembly of a whole array of technologies that connected up calculations and strategies developed in political centres to those thousands of points that use the constitutional, fiscal, organizational, and judicial powers of the state in endeavours to manage economic life, the health and habits of the population, the civility of the masses, and so forth. This created a 'social fabric' within which economic activity could be secured; security and order enhanced; and problematic persons contained, pacified, or reformed. This was not, as Habermassian analysts tend to suggest, a coherent process in which 'the state' colonized 'the lifeworld,' not least because the very nature and meaning of state, government, and lifeworld were transformed in the process. It was a complex, contested, and contingent set of problematizations, strategies, technical inventions, alliances, and trade-offs between different forces. The links between the political apparatus and the activities of governing are tenuous, heterogeneous, and dependent upon a range of 'relatively autonomous' knowledges, knowledgeable persons, and technical possibilities: they are intrinsically mobile and reversible.

Governing should be understood nominalistically. It is neither a concept nor a theory. Rather, it is a perspective that brings into view a heterogeneous field of more or less calculated attempts to shape the conduct of persons, populations, and things towards desired ends. Governing does not seek to describe a field of institutions, of structures, of functional patterns (cf., for example, Kooiman, 1993): it addresses an array of lines of thought, of will, of invention, of programs and failures, of acts and counter-acts. Some attempts at governing are formally rationalized, especially those which address a totalized space such as a nation: Keynesian economic management, social insurance, risk management, scientific pedagogy, child-rearing advice, and so forth. Others exist in the form of practical rationalities within particular types of practice – for example, much of social work or police work is of this type. The many words we have for the activity of governing indicate the genuine heterogeneity of this field of thought and action: tutelage, education, control, influence, regulation, administration, management, therapy, reformation, guidance.

Writing in the mid-nineteenth century, Pierre-Joseph Proudhon captured some of the fears around the expanding scope of government that were shared by many:

> Being governed means being under police supervision, being inspected, spied upon, directed, buried under laws, regulated, hemmed in, indoctri-

nated, preached at, controlled, assessed, censored, commanded ... noted, registered, captured, appraised, stamped, surveyed, evaluated, taxed, patented, licensed, authorized, recommended, admonished, prevented, reformed, aligned, and punished in every action, every transaction, every movement. (P.-J. Proudhon, in Oestreich 1982, 7)

But Proudhon thinks of government as the antithesis of freedom. My argument is different. The achievement of liberalism as an art of government that took shape in the second half of the nineteenth century was that it began to govern by making people free, yet inextricably linking them to the norms, techniques, and values of civility. Further, Proudhon suggests that all attempts at governing are different realization of a single will: a kind of early version of sociological conceptions of social control. But I think we really are dealing with a multitude.

Analysing Government

1. Intelligibility

All acts of governing take place within particular regimes of intelligibility. Governing, like other actions, is only possible and intelligible 'under a certain description.' Language is not secondary to government, it is constitutive of it. It not only makes acts of government describable, but also makes them possible. This emphasis on language is not at all novel (see, for example, Shapiro 1984; Tully 1995). But language here is not to be regarded merely as a field of meaning or shared conventions. It is significant to the extent that it participates in regimes of truth. Analysis is thus a matter of 'historical epistemology': the reconstruction of 'the epistemological field that allows for the production of what counts for knowledge at any given moment, and which accords salience to particular categories, divisions, classifications, relations and identities' (Poovey 1995, 3; cf. Daston 1994; Canguilhem 1994). We are concerned here not just with words, or even with concepts, but with a whole 'regime of enunciation.' Who can authorize concepts, who can put words into circulation, from what places, according to what criteria of truth, through what techniques of dissemination and communications, utilizing what forms of rhetoric, symbolism, persuasion, sanction or seduction? It is not a question of analysing what a word, concept, or statement means – of the meanings of terms such as community, culture, risk, social, civility, citizen, and the like – but of the way a word functions in connection with other things; what it makes possible; the surfaces, networks, and circuits around which it flows; the affects and passions that it mobilizes and through which it mobilizes. It is the truth value of language that makes acts of governing possible, and hence analysis must examine what counts as truth; who has the power to define truth; the role of different authorities of truth; and the epistemological, institutional, and technical conditions for the production and circulation of truths. In our own times, the arts of government have become inextricably linked with the regimes of truth concerning the objects, processes, and persons governed – economy, society, morality, psychology, pathology. Hence they have been intrinsically linked to the vocation of 'experts of truth' and the functioning of their concepts of normality and pathology, danger and risk, social order and social control, and the judgments and devices that such concepts have inhabited. So while historians of ideas tend to focus on the grand and canonical texts of philosophy or science, analyses of government focus upon the minor and the mundane: pamphlets of the alcohol reformers, social hygienists, philanthropists, and social reformers; manuals of asylum management; architectural plans; bureaucratic rules and guidelines; and the like.

2. Objects

Governing does not just act on pre-existing objects – economy, civil society, poverty, insecurity, risk, the popular classes, unemployables, defectives, schoolchildren, mothers do not lie passively awaiting their discovery and annexation by power. Rather, acts of governing actually constitute or make up the zones on which they act and the entities upon which they act. One can speak therefore of the constitution of governable spaces and governable subjects. I will return to this issue in detail later.

3. Interventions

Governing does not only entail certain ways of shaping truthful experiences of the world and the objects or zones that constitute it. It also entails certain ways of intervening within these constituted domains, ways of making them up practically through these practices of intervention. Thought becomes governmental to the extent that it becomes technical. It must connect itself to a technology for its realization: audits, budgets, tests, examinations, assessments, dossiers, types of inscription and calculation, forms of practical know-how and so forth. Not, of course, that thought is ever merely 'realized.' The process of invention of a technique or a technology – a form of budgeting, for example, a method of training, a practice of confession, a type of census, the architecture of a schoolroom, the mechanisms of social insurance, the mathematization of risk – is neither simple nor automatic. It often relies upon the re-utilization of technical devices that are already present at hand or are imported from other spheres. It is thus a question of examining the composition of what Foucault called 'dispositifs' and what Deleuze calls 'assemblages': lines of connection among thought, technique, judgment, persons, forces, actions. These assemblages make it possible for centres of calculation and deliberation to translate themselves into places and activities far distant in space and time, to events in thousands of operating theatres, case conferences, bedrooms, classrooms, prison cells, workplaces, and homes. These translation processes make possible what I have termed 'government at a distance.' Distance both in the spatial sense – something translated from one place to another. And distance in a semantic sense: something translated from one scale to another, from one idiom to another, from one field of concerns to another.

4. Powers

Analysing governing is analysing power. But it does not proceed by decoding strategies of government to discover hidden motives, by critiquing programs of government to identify class interests, or by interpreting languages of government as ideologies concealing hidden real objectives. Rationalities of government are analysed in their own terms, in terms of the identities and identifications that they themselves construct, objectives they set themselves, the enemies they identified, the alliances they sought, the languages and categories they used to describe themselves, the forms of collectivization and division that they enacted. Of course, many regulatory strategies are articulated, developed, and justified explicitly by bosses in the interests of increased productivity and docility of their workers. And of course class is significant, but the development of a language of class by socialist activists in the nineteenth century is itself a historical phenomenon worthy of investigation, seeking as it did to obliterate existing identifications in terms of radicalism, Chartism, Owenites, solidarities to particular trades, and so forth (cf. Stedman-Jones 1983). But the power relations and ethical imperatives put in play by strategies such as the social purity movement at the end of the nineteenth century or feminist mobilizations for birth control – some emancipatory, some eugenic, some moralistic – need to be examined in their own terms. Similarly, it is not only bosses and imperialists who have developed racist strategies of segregation, exclusion, or exploitation of immigrant labour – organized labour, too, has engaged in many racist tactics for the protection of white workers against interlopers seen as racially inferior and politically dangerous. Rather than interpret, then, analyses of government are superficial and empirical, and the powers they identify are multiple, heterogeneous, not amenable to a zero-sum calculus.

Objects, problems, techniques, spaces, and subjects of government are intrinsically historical. But history is heterogeneous; it does not march to a single step orchestrated by chronological time. There are multiple histories of knowledge, truths, techniques, authorities, objects, spaces, and subjects, and hence of the arts of governing. Each attempt at governing produces its own forms of subjectification, classification, identification, and hence the formation of counter-classifications, counter-identities, counter-subjectivities. Governing is a matter neither of functional patterns nor of institutional stability: it is complex, open, contested. Contestation is not extrinsic to government in the form of resistance: it is an intrinsic part of the processes through which practices of government are assembled and mobilized.

Governable Spaces

Governing is always spatialized: it maps out spaces, not quite real, not quite imagined – what I term 'irreal spaces'– within which it is to be exercised. The government of a population, a national economy, an enterprise, a family, a child, or even oneself becomes possible only through discursive mechanisms that represent the domain to be governed as an intelligible field with its limits, characteristics whose component parts are linked together in some more or less systematic manner (I am drawing here on Miller and Rose 1990). This is a matter of defining boundaries, rendering that within them visible, assembling information about that which is included, and devising techniques to mobilize the forces and entities thus revealed. For example, before one can seek to manage a domain such as an economy, it is first necessary to conceptualize a set of processes and relations as an economy that is amenable to management. The birth of a language of national economy as a domain with its own characteristics that could be spoken about and about which knowledge could be gained enabled it to become an element in programs that could seek to evaluate and increase the power of nations by governing and managing 'the economy.' And we are not merely talking about theories: for example, the strategies of national economic management that were invented in the mid-twentieth century were made possible not by theories alone, not merely by the installation of new sets of concepts to think about 'the economy,' but also though the construction of a vast statistical apparatus through with this domain could be inscribed, tabulated, calculated, national economies compared, indicators like 'rate of growth' devised, and so forth. Current debates about 'globalization,' whatever their basis in real economic transformations, indicate the de-territorialization and re-territorialization of economic government and the emergence of a novel conception of economic space.

Let me illustrate by considering one example: the formation of 'the social.' It was in the nineteenth century that the modern sense of 'social' started to take shape. This was itself a mutation of an early field, which is best termed 'moral.' The moral domain was a plane understood in terms of conscience, character, and conduct. It was not primarily geographical, but it did inhabit the space of the nation, and it could be acted upon in space and through space. Indeed the moral technologies invented by philanthropists and reformers in the first half of the nineteenth century – pauper schools, reformatory prisons, lunatic asylums, public baths and washhouses – used the organization of space to shape the character and conscience of those who were to be moral subjects, and hence to mould their conduct (Rose 1992, 1996a; see also Riley 1988; Joyce 1995, 1996). And it was in terms of conscience, character, and conduct that the subjects of moral reform enacted their own strategies: the working poor demanding education and housing, married women demanding property rights as a counterbalance to the power of their husbands, families seeking moral instruction for their children. This moral domain was the substantive counterpart to liberal political thought in the late eighteenth and early nineteenth centuries. Liberalism, as Foucault has argued, is less a formula of government than a constant suspicion about the powers, scope, necessity, economy, legitimacy, and effectiveness of government. Here, this criticism is couched in terms of individual liberty and the inviolability of the moral person: governing risks destroying the very moral domain that it seeks to defend.

Over the course of the nineteenth century, the moral territory was made social. Urbanization and immigration into the town, crime, war, disease, and so forth, played a role here. The status of these events was focal rather than causal (Osborne and Rose 1997). Events themselves do not determine how they are to be understood and responded to. Poverty and pauperism, illness, crime, suicide, and so forth, were the subject of a whole labour of documentation. Statistics, censuses, surveys, and a new genre of explorations of the lives of the poor attempted to render moral events knowable and calculable (Osborne and Rose 1997; Hacking 1991; Poovey 1995). The moral order was inscribed into thought: it was written down in evidence, counted, tabulated, graphed, drawn. Theorists of the moral order sought to delineate regularities in conduct that would enable it to be understood in the same way as the natural world, and argued that the moral domain, like nature itself, was governed by its own intrinsic laws. The moral order, once a zone where diverse opinions competed and contested, justified by reference to extrinsic ethical or theological principles, came to be accorded a specific 'positivity': a reality with its own regularities, laws, and characteristics territorialized across the geographical space of a nation. It was these national moral regularities that gradually came to be termed 'social.'

A new 'social' language was formulated: the social body, the social question, 'social' novels, the 'social evil,' the National Association for the Promotion of Social Science. A new breed of experts of the social was born – the doctors, the charity workers, the investigators of the 'dark continent of the poor'– who spoke 'in the name of the social.' This social gaze focused, in particular, upon the conditions of life of the labouring poor and paupers, with a particular eye for issues of domestic squalor, immorality, child mortality, household budgeting, and the conditions and actions of the working-class woman (Riley 1988, 49). Gradually 'social' comes to be accorded something like the sense it was to have for the next hundred years. It was a plane or dimension of a national territory, which formed and shaped the characteristics and character of the individual. It was a set of causes, determinations, consequences. And it was the problem space within which one must pose questions and struggles about government.

The social was not to remain a mere empirical amalgam of these investigations of the lives, labours, crimes, diseases, madness, and domestic habits of the poor. It was to be formalized, to become the domain that sociology, from Comte through Spencer to Durkheim, defined as a reality *sui generis*: hence, one that could be known by a social science. The social question became a conceptual question. By the end of the century, Durkheim was deploring the fact that

> the designation 'social' is used with little precision. It is currently em-
> ployed for practically all phenomena generally diffused within society,
> however small their significance. But in reality there is in every society a
> certain group of phenomena which may be differentiated from those
> studied by the other natural sciences ... They constitute, thus, a new
> variety of phenomena; and it is to them that the term 'social' ought to be
> applied.' (Durkheim 1964, 1–3)

The unruly complex of the social was to be organized and disciplined in the form of 'society.' Sociologists and other 'social scientists' would stake their claim as experts of the social, uniquely able to speak and act in its name. They would be engineers of society itself.

In the mid-nineteenth century, political parties started identifying themselves through the term 'social.' The word 'socialism' was first used in France and Britain in the 1820s. It was adopted by workers' movements on both sides of the Channel in the 1830s. By the middle decades of the nineteenth century, the social question and the political question existed in an uneasy relation. In Germany at the time of the Revolution of 1848, Prince Metternich acknowledged despairingly that the crisis 'was no longer about politics (*Politik*) but the social question.' In Berlin, the radical republican Rudolf Virchow concurred: 'This revolution is not simply political: it is at heart social in character' (Melton 1995, 199; cf. Schwartz 1997). By 1877, the German Social Democratic Party could poll nearly half a million votes in 1877 and win thirteen seats in the Reichstag; in 1881 the Social Democratic Federation was formed in England (it added the 'social' to its title in 1884) (Pelling 1965). Alongside the designation 'socialist'– indeed often opposing it – the term 'social' became the indicator of a certain kind of politics: one that could be directed against the claims of the state, on the one hand, and demands for the freedom of the market and the autonomy of the individual, on the other. The social question referred to all that had to do with this 'social order': a sphere of the collective activities and arrangements of the lives of individuals, families, and groups within an nation.

By the early decades of the twentieth century, politicians in Europe and North America had been forced to accept that it was not merely legitimate but necessary for the political apparatus and its officials to seek to govern at least some aspects of this social domain (cf. Polanyi

1957). Political economy alone could not prescribe and delimit the political government of economic life. Law alone could not be sufficient for achieving order and security. One must govern in the name of society: the question of how to govern must be posed from 'the social point of view' (cf. Procacci 1989; for France: Donzelot 1984; for England: Collini 1979 and Clarke 1978).

Some argued that to govern from the social point of view was to govern too much. If society had its own natural laws, government overrode or ignored these at the cost of the health of society itself (Spencer 1884). But whatever their disagreements, most agreed that politics would have to become social if political order was to be maintained. In France, Durkheim was intimately involved in the French politics of solidarism. In England, the political struggles were not fought in terms of social right; rather, they were debated in terms of the rights and obligations of the state to extend itself into zones outside those marked out by the rule of law (Clarke 1978; Collini 1979). Nineteenth-century conceptions of a single overarching 'social problem'– linked to the opposition between Labour and Capital, the One and the Many, Freedom and Cooperation – fragmented into distinct 'social problems'– the health and safety of workers, the education of paupers, the regulation of hygiene – each of which could be addressed and ameliorated discretely, administratively, technically (Schwartz 1997). And at least some aspects of the economy required to be politically governed in the name of the social, in order to dispel a whole range of conflicts – between the rights of property and those of the property-less, between liberals and communists, between revolutionists and reformists – and to ensure social order, social tranquillity, perhaps even social justice.

Governable Subjects

All political rationalities embody some account of the governed, of the persons over whom government is to be exercised: as members of a flock to be led, children to be coddled and educated, a resource to be exploited, members of a population to be managed, legal subjects with rights, citizens of society, individuals with aspirations, members of a moral community. As Paul Veyne has pointed out, there is no universal object, the governed, in relation to which a body of governors proceeds to act (1997). There is no such thing as 'the governed,' only multiple objectifications. Practices of governing are not determined by the nature of those who they govern: practices determine their own objects and these have a history – a little, variegated, multiple history, not a grand universal history.

Subjects of liberalism were thought to be capable of a certain kind of moral relation to themselves. Here, for example is Adam Smith in the *Theory of Moral Sentiments* in 1759:

> When I endeavour to examine my own conduct, when I endeavour to pass sentence upon it, and either to approve or condemn it, it is evident that, in all such cases, I divide myself, as it were, into two persons; and that I, the examiner and judge, represent a different character from that other I, the person whose conduct is examined into and judged of. The first is the spectator, whose sentiments with regard to my own conduct I endeavour to enter into by placing myself in his situation, and by considering how it would appear to me, when seen from that particular point of view. The second is the agent, the person whom I properly call myself, and of whose conduct, under the character of a spectator, I was endeavouring to form some opinion. (Smith [1759] 1982: 3, 1, 6: 113; I owe this quote to Mary Poovey [1995, 33])

As Charles Taylor has pointed out, this way of understanding the self is only possible within a particular social and cultural field (Taylor 1994, 200). But the subject is less the outcome of cultural history than of a history of what Foucault terms 'techniques of the self,' and Greenblatt has termed 'self fashioning' (a self-conscious fashioning of human identity as a manipulable, artful process, embodied in practices of parents, teachers, priests, textbooks of manners, and so on): 'a set of control mechanisms – plans, recipes, rules, instructions ... for the governing of behavior' (Geertz 1973, 49; quoted in Greenblatt 1980, 3). The arts of self-reflection of the moral individual described by Smith were not to remain at the level of philosophy. They were to be fleshed out in a whole variety of mundane texts of social reformers, campaigners for domestic hygiene, for urban planning and the like, which each embodied certain presuppositions about what human subjects were, what mobilized them in different ways, and how they could be brought to govern themselves morally. They were to be made technical, embodied in a whole series of interventions aimed at producing the human being as a moral creature capable of exercising responsible stewardship and judgment over its own conduct in terms of certain externally prescribed moral principles. Forms of moral government formulated largely in terms of self-control were instantiated in architecture, guidance to parents, in the work of pauper schools – embodied in language, in knowledge, in technique, in the fabrication of spaces and of repertoires of conduct within them: an exercise of inhibition of the self by the self, a kind of despotism of the self at the heart of liberalism (cf. Smith 1992; Valverde 1996).

Subjectification operated through collectivization as much as through individualization. That is to say that the kinds of relations to the self envisaged, the kinds of dispositions and habits inculcated, the very inscription of governmentality into the body and the affects of the governed, was differentiated in collective ways. A language of Britishness was formulated, for example, and a set of self techniques were articulated in terms of the distinctive British character, bearing, affective economy, and the like (cf. Colley 1996). Collectivized identities of class, status, gender, and gentility can be analysed in similar ways: the formation of identifications through the inscription of particular ethical formation, vocabularies of self-description and self-mastery, forms of conduct and body techniques. There is no simple evolution or succession in knowledges and practices of subjectification. Many specifications of subjectivity coexist. They are deployed in diverse practices at similar times, sometimes without being troubled by their discrepancies. At other times they are set off against one another, for example, claims as to the necessity of authenticity are used to dispute regimes of manners and civility. Our present problems of governing virtue in a free society do not arise out of a history of the evolution of subjectivity: they are the current form taken by 'wars of subjectivity'.

Liberty

Liberalism, as Barry Hindess has pointed, 'is commonly understood as a political doctrine or ideology concerned with the maximization of individual liberty and, in particular, with the defense of that liberty against the state' (1996, 65). But the perspective of government sees things differently: it treats liberty as a structuring theme of certain styles of government. Take, for example, a passage from a recent text by Frances Fukuyama. In *Trust: The Social Virtues and the Creation of Prosperity*, Fukuyama writes:

> A liberal state is ultimately a limited state, with governmental activity strictly bounded by a sphere of individual liberty. If society is not to

become anarchic or otherwise ungovernable, then it must be capable of self-government at levels of organization below the state. Such a system depends ultimately not just on law but on the self-restraint of individuals. If they are not tolerant and respectful of each other, or do not abide by the laws they set for themselves, they will require a strong and coercive state to keep each other in line. If they cannot cohere for common purposes, then they will need an intrusive state to provide the organization they cannot provide for themselves. (Fukuyama 1996, 357–8)

Only a certain kind of regulated liberty is compatible with liberal arts of rule. The subject of liberty does not enact an essential or timeless freedom, but an historically varying practice of self-government. The relation of the self to others is shaped indirectly through shaping the relations that the individual has to him or herself. This paradox of liberty within liberalism is illustrated rather nicely in the writings of Friedrich von Hayek (cf. Rose 1993). Towards the end of *Law, Legislation and Liberty*, in the third book, entitled 'The Political Order of a Free People,' Hayek writes as follows:

The only moral principle which has ever made the growth of an advanced civilization possible was the principle of individual freedom … No principles of collective conduct which bind the individual can exist in a society of free men. What we have achieved we owe to securing to the individuals the chance of creating for themselves a protected domain … within which they can use their abilities for their own purposes … We ought to have learnt enough to avoid destroying our civilization by smothering the spontaneous process of the interaction of the individuals by placing its direction in the hands of any authority. But to avoid this we must shed the illusion that we can deliberately create 'the future of mankind' … (Hayek 1979, 152–3)

Yet Hayek also realizes that certain subjective conditions, or conditions of subjects, must be met if such a form of government, a political order of a free people, is to be realized. He terms this 'the discipline of civilization.' A few pages on from the passage quoted above, he writes:

Man has not developed in freedom … Freedom is an artifact of civilization … Freedom was made possible by the gradual evolution of *the discipline of civilization which is at the same time the discipline of freedom.* (emphasis in original; ibid., 163)

It was this double-edged character of liberalism that disturbed liberal thinkers such as Herbert Spencer in the nineteenth century, and twentieth-century political philosophers like Isaiah Berlin. For those who fail to distinguish negative from positive liberty, argued Berlin, all kinds of despotism – from compulsory education, public health, and moral policing – turn out to be identical with freedom. But the link between liberty and discipline was not the outcome of philosophical confusion. Both then and now, philosophical reflections on freedom were linked to the invention of certain ways of trying to govern persons in accordance with freedom. Hayek, characteristically, ascribes the inculcation of the subjective conditions of freedom, not to government, but to tradition. Fukuyama asserts that 'a thriving civil society depends on a people's habits, customs, and ethics – attributes that can be shaped only indirectly through conscious political action and must otherwise be nourished through an increased awareness and respect for culture' (1996, 5). But both are mistaken or disingenuous. In the nineteenth century, a whole variety of political, philanthropic, and religious strategies sought, consciously and explicitly, to put in place arrangements that would support the subjective conditions for a liberal society of free citizens. These were designed to assemble civility, through enwrapping human beings in norms, visibilities, judgments, embedded in the very structuring of space, time, and bodily organization. They sought to instantiate the very divisions between politics and freedom, between public and private, between state and civil society, that they themselves seemed to violate.

Thus, from the perspective of government, the importance of liberalism is not that it first recognized, defined, or defended freedom as a right of all citizens. Rather, its significance is that for the first time the arts of government were systematically linked to the practice of freedom. From this point on, the self-government of individuals would be central to the 'games of rule' that would define them and set the terms for their own normality and their limits (cf. Rajchman 1991, 101). A multiplicity of little tactics and techniques of government were concerned with the need for individuals to relate to themselves simultaneously as creatures of freedom and of responsibility, as beings of liberty and members of society. Hence the inherent riskiness of liberal government, for what individuals are required to give, they may also refuse.

As Wendy Brown argues,

> freedom is neither a philosophical absolute nor a tangible entity but a relational and contextual practice that takes shape in opposition to what-

ever is locally and ideologically conceived as unfreedom... Rendering either the ancient or liberal formations of freedom as 'concepts' abstracts them from the historical practices in which they are rooted, the institutions against which they are oriented, the domination they are designed to contest, the privileges they are designed to protect [and] ... preempts perception of what is denied and suppressed by them, of what kinds of dominations are enacted by particular practices of freedom. (Brown 1995, 6)

Liberal freedom, today, is understood as freedom of individual right, freedom of employment, freedom of expression, freedom of consumption. Such freedoms are not so much ideas or concepts, but operative terms constitutively linked to the four main assemblages of contemporary freedom: the legal complex; the productive machine; the circuits of culture, image, and meaning; and the apparatus for promoting and shaping forms of life through relations with the world of goods. But the fact that freedom is technical, infused with relations of power, entails specific modes of subjectification and is necessarily a thing of this world, inescapably sullied by the marks of the mundane, does not make freedom a sham or liberty an illusion; rather it opens up the possibility of freedom neither as a state of being or a constitutional form, but as a politics of life.

'Advanced' Liberal Government

Robert Castel has pointed out that the idea of the social state was grounded in the presupposition that government could achieve the gradual and simultaneous betterment of the conditions of all forces and blocs within society – employers, labourers, managers, professionals (Castel 1995, 387). Political strategies could ameliorate the hardship of the worst off without destroying the principle of productive labour: they could cushion its harshness within the workplace and lessen the fear of unemployment by supporting those outside the labour market. This would contain the dangers posed by the worst off and reinforce the security and individual freedoms of the better off. It would also make it legitimate to confine and reform those who refused this social contract or were unable to give assent to it – the mad, the criminals, the delinquent, the workshy, socially inadequate. It appeared that all strata and classes could be bound into an agreement for social progress of which the State was, to a greater or less extent, the guarantor. This image of social progress through gradual amelioration of hardship and improvement of conditions of life won out over the image of social revolution, on the one hand, and the image of unfettered competition, on the other. The social state would have the role of shaping and coordinating the strategies that would oblige all sectors and social interests, no longer antagonists, to work towards and facilitate social progress. Over the last two decades, this 'social' mentality of government has come under challenge from all sides of the political spectrum. Those on the left doubted the efficacy of the social state in maximizing equality and minimizing poverty, insecurity, and ill health. Civil libertarians questioned the extent to which the discretionary powers and professional authority of social government were compatible with rights. Neo-liberals in Europe argued for the need to return from the excessive government that characterized state socialism, national socialism, and social welfare to frugal government, which safeguarded the market mechanisms that would allow the natural operation of economic processes within the rule of law. In the United States, criticisms mounted of the excessive government that had been developing since the New Deal and through the Great Society and the War on Poverty, with its large bureaucracies, its welfare programs, its interventionist social engineering, and the like. This not only interfered with the market, produced expensive and inefficient bureaucracies, led to excessive taxes, and produced a bloated and corrupt political class and political apparatus: it actually exacerbated the very problems of poverty, dependency, crime, ill health, and family breakdown that it sought to ameliorate. For these American critics, it was not merely that government must withdraw to allow the market to operate: government must actually intervene to create the institutional and subjective conditions for market relations, and must reshape all sorts of other areas and policies along market lines. Whatever their other differences, all agreed that the image of steady and incremental social progress guaranteed by a social state must be rejected.

A reanimated liberal scepticism of government has infused a whole range of attempts to regulate this or that aspect of our experience. Neo-liberal arguments were particularly significant in relation to this scepticism over the powers of 'political government' to know, plan, calculate, and steer from the centre. This was less because of their intellectual attractiveness, than because they managed to link themselves up to new technologies of rule. The image of the 'social state' began to give way to that of the 'enabling state.' The state is no longer to be required to answer all societies' needs for order, security, health, and productivity. Individuals, firms, organizations, localities, schools, parents, hospitals, housing estates must take on themselves – as 'partners'– a portion of the responsibility for resolving these issues – whether this be by permanent retraining for the worker or Neighbourhood Watch for the community. This involves a double movement of autonomization and responsibilization. Organizations, actors, and others that were once enmeshed in the complex and bureaucratic lines of force of the social state are to be set free to find their own destiny. Yet, at the same time, they are to be steered politically 'at a distance' through the invention and deployment of a whole range of new 'fidelity techniques' which can shape their actions while apparently enhancing their independence. Neo-liberal governments, such as those of Ronald Reagan and Margaret Thatcher, were particularly inventive in the take-up of such fidelity techniques as audits, budgets, contracts, performance-related pay, competition, quasi markets, and end-user empowerment in technologies of government (cf. Power 1994).

Knowledge workers have a new role in these assemblages. They no longer merely manage individualization or act as state functionaries. They provide information that enables these quasi-autonomous entities to steer themselves (for example, risk assessments). They tutor them in the techniques of self-government (as in the burgeoning of private consultancies and training operations). They provide the information that will allow the state, the consumer, or other parties (such as regulatory agencies) to assess the performance of these quasi-autonomous agencies, and hence to govern them (evaluation, audit). They identify those individuals unable to self-govern, and attempt either to reattach them (training, welfare-to-work) or to manage their exclusion (incarceration, residualization of welfare). In short, 'free individuals,' 'partners,' and stakeholders are enwrapped in webs of knowledge and circuits of communication through which their actions can be shaped and steered, and by means of which they can steer themselves.

1. Making Economic Life More Like a Market

A privileged site of these refigurations concerned the government of economic life. The social state was grounded in the belief that, through calculated strategies of government, politicians could act upon their own 'national economy' in order to jointly optimize the economic and

the social. Without destroying the freedom of action of private enterprise, they could mitigate the worst effects of capitalism – unemployment, poor working conditions, job insecurity, and the like – upon the
individual and thus earn political consent to the legitimacy of the state.
Today, however, the economy is no longer to be governed in the name
of the social. Nor is economic stability a justification for the government
of a whole range of other sectors in a social form. The social and the
economic are now seen as antagonistic: the social is to be fragmented in
order to transform the moral and psychological obligations of economic citizenship in the direction of active self-advancement. Economic government is to be de-socialized in the name of maximizing the
entrepreneurial comportment of the individual and the firm. No longer
is there a conflict between the self-interest of the employer and the
patriotic duty of the citizen (cf. Procacci 1991): it now appears that one
can best fulfil one's obligations to one's nation by most effectively
pursuing the enhancement of the economic well-being of oneself and
one's firm, business, or organization.

2. Fragmenting the Social into a Multitude of Markets

By the 1970s, neo-liberalism took as its target not just an economy, but
society itself. All kinds of practices – health, security, welfare, and more –
were to be restructured according to a particular image of the economic
– the market. Markets were seen as the ideal mechanisms for the automatic coordination of the decisions of a multitude of individual actors
in the best interest of all. Hence these styles of governing sought to
create simulacra of markets governed by economic or para-economic
criteria of judgment in arenas previously governed by bureaucratic and
social logics. For example, in the United Kingdom, social services were
restructured to split 'purchasers' of services from 'providers' of services. Responsibility for the identification of need and the working-out
of a care plan lay with the social worker. But the care itself was to be
purchased in a quasi market within which different 'providers' competed: state-funded operations, not-for-profit organizations, and private profit-making enterprises. Other welfare provision was restructured
in the form of quasi-autonomous 'agencies': the child-support agency
to chase errant fathers for contributions to their children's upkeep, the
pensions agency, even a 'prison service agency' to take on a function
which Althusserian Marxists had considered essential to the Repressive
State Apparatus.

This field was not governed by intervening directly in organizational processes or by constraining the decision making of professional or bureaucratic experts. It was to be governed by results: through the setting of targets, the promulgation of standards, the monitoring of outputs, the regulation of budgets, and the use of audits (Power 1994). Of course, these mechanisms for 'governing at a distance' were central in the social state – one thinks of Keynesian demand management and of the 'floatation' of the norms of family life (Donzelot 1979). But these new techniques worked rather differently. Agencies were set targets – numbers of errant fathers to catch each week, number of fraudulent claims to detect, and so forth – and their payment by government depended upon their meeting these targets. In the case of private prisons, the Prison Service acted as a customer, buying a certain number of daily places from suppliers, with places defined not merely as cells, but in terms of a standard of staffing levels, health care, catering, and so forth – a whole 'custodial service package' managed by making the supplier accountable for performance and delivery (cf. Tonkiss forthcoming). At one and the same time, this autonomized and responsibilized these quasi-political organizations and individuals, and enhanced the possibilities for political centres of calculation to exercise control over them. Audits, budgets, standards, performance evaluations, and the like, when assembled into simulacra of markets, provide versatile, mobile, and highly transferable, mechanisms for exercising 'government at a distance' over previously 'social' functions. Such fidelity techniques are not neutral. For example, audit reshapes that which is audited, setting objectives, proliferating standardized forms, generating new systems of record keeping and accounting, governing paper trails. These new forms of 'government at a distance' actually strengthen the powers of centres of calculation who set the budgetary regimes, the output targets, and the like, reinstating the state in the collective body in a new way and limiting the forms and possibilities of resistance.

3. Making Employees into Entrepreneurs

New linkages have been forged between the government of economic life and the self-government of the individual. Personal employment and macro-economic health is to be ensured by encouraging each individual to 'capitalize' themselves, to invest in the management, presentation, promotion, and enhancement of their own economic capital as a capacity of their selves and as a lifelong project. 'Work' becomes a switch point of the economic and the psychological: a way of earning not merely subsistence, but independence and self-respect, while simultaneously being tied into the circuits of control that employment entails. Yet this goes along with a transformation of work. The workplace once functioned as a secure site for inclusion, in the form of the lifelong career, the permanent job, and so forth. But work itself has now become a precarious activity, in which continued employment must ceaselessly be earned, the employment of each individual constantly assessed in the light of evaluations, appraisals, achievement of targets, and so forth – under the constant threat of 'downsizing,' efficiency gains, and the like. Simultaneously, we have seen the establishment of a more-or-less permanently casualized workforce. Full-time, permanent work was always, perhaps, a norm and ideal rather than the most common form of labour, in any event restricted, by and large, to adult males. But one has seen the rise of increasing numbers of persons half in and half out of work, the growth of a 'black economy,' the proliferation of part-time work, fixed-term contracts, and the like. Perpetual insecurity becomes the normal form of labour.

The new 'active' unemployment policies being developed in Britain, Europe, and the United States are consistent with these transformations. These seek to govern unemployment, not through acting on levels of demand or by creating and protecting employment, but through acting on the conduct of the unemployed person, now renamed a 'job-seeker.' The job-seeker is obliged to improve his or her 'employability' by acquiring both substantive skills and skills in job search – writing curriculum vitae, presentation at interviews, and the like. The unemployed individual must engage in a constant and active search for employment, and unemployment must become as much like work as possible if it, too, is to connect the excluded individual with the modalities of control that have come to be termed freedom and choice. It would not be too much to claim that, in the countries of the European Union at least, 'social' policy is no longer about family security or the alleviation of poverty. It has become policy around work: the regulation of working hours and working conditions, the rights and responsibilities of workers and employers, the creation of work, and the promotion of policies of inclusion through work. Assistance, in the form of unemployment benefit, was perhaps the central 'right' of welfare states; now it is no longer a right of citizenship, but an allowance that must be earned by the performance of certain duties. Work is to be the sole means by which the poor can acquire the status of citizen.

4. Making Citizens Consumers

The contemporary citizen is to be an entrepreneur of him- or herself. This is not simply a reactivation of the nineteenth-century 'characterological' values of self-reliance, autonomy, and independence as the underpinning of self-respect, self-esteem, self-worth, and self-advancement. Entrepreneurialism is now a psychologically healthy aspect or force in human self-actualizing personality, which makes it both natural and desirable for each person to conduct his or her life, and that of his or her family, as a kind of enterprise, seeking to enhance and capitalize on existence itself through considered acts of initiative, and through investments – of time, money, emotion, energy – that are calculated to bring future returns. These acts of the entrepreneurial self are now increasingly regulated not by social devices, but through consumption, in which habits, dispositions, and styles of existence are shaped by the images and fantasies of identity, lifestyle, and pleasure.

This entrepreneurialism of the person, as an individual with a right to self-identity and satisfaction, has been embodied in reshaped relations between experts and clients. If contracts governed relations of authority in early liberalism, and discretion characterized authority in social rule, in the 'advanced' forms of government that are taking shape the contract is reactivated and its scope is expanded. In these new forms of contractualism, the subject of the contract is not a patient or a case, but a customer or consumer. Parents (or children, the issue is contested) are consumers of education, patients are consumers of health care, residents of old people's homes are in a contractual relation with those who provide care, and even those occupying demeaned categories (discharged prisoners shifted to halfway houses, drug users in rehabilitation centres) have their expectations, rights, and responsibilities contractualized. Of course, these contracts are of many different types. Few are like the contracts between buyer and seller in the market. But, in their different ways, they shift the power relations inscribed in relations of expertise. This is especially so when they are accompanied by new methods of regulation and control such as audit and evaluation. Some contractualization enhances the possibilities of political control over activities previously insulated by claims to professional autonomy and the necessity of trust – as, for example, when contracts specify the delivery of a certain quantum of medical care or a certain volume of completed cases. Some contractual forms provide new opportunities for users and clients of professionals who are able to contest 'patrimonial powers' by insisting on specified services and agreed-upon standards, and having new sanctions if they are not provided (Yeatman 1995). Some, like the contracts used for clients in psychiatric wards and other residential establishments, shift responsibilities to users for their own condition and for the personal comportment and behaviour necessary to receive care, and thus bind them into professional powers and expert norms in new ways. The politics of the contract becomes central to contests between political strategies concerning the 'reform of welfare,' and to strategies of user demand and user resistance to professional powers.

5. 'Designing in' Control

The social state subsumed earlier practices of normalization and disciplinary individualization within a set of novel assemblages that sought to avoid or mitigate the sources of conflict through the collectivization of risk. As Jacques Donzelot pointed out, such techniques de-dramatized conflicts between workers and bosses, shifting disputes about the organization of work, the ownership of the product, and the rights over profit to technical questions of the levels and mechanisms of benefits and allowances (Donzelot 1991). As such bureaucratic social practices and techniques are dismantled, new ways have been invented for the management of individual, community, economic, and political risks. These new actuarial or risk-based ways of thinking and acting seek to act upon territories and fields pre-emptively, to structure them in such a way as to reduce the likelihood of undesirable events or conduct occurring, and to increase the likelihood of those types of events and activities that are desired. These try to de-dramatize conflict by minimizing the likelihood of disruption in a whole range of arenas, and hence reducing or modulating the aggregate levels of pathology. Control is 'designed in' to activity itself, though the layout of streets, housing estates, shops and shopping malls, factories, hospitals. Control is also designed in to the fabric of our forms of life, regulating acts of consumption through the provision of credit and private insurance, the use of credit cards, personal identification numbers, passwords, the routine use of databases containing personal information on previous infractions, and so forth. These produce novel open circuits of risk management, which install a kind of cybernetics of control. In these control regimes, risk information, risk calculation, risk management, and risk reduction are intrinsic to all decisions and actions, whether these concern investment, building design, organizational structure, educational practice, the purchase of goods and services, the renting of property, the conduct of health. Political authorities are only one of the nodes in these circuits of risk control: the managers of shops and enterprises, local community groups, families, and individuals are all now required to engage in control through the pre-emptive calculation and management of personal and collective risk.

Within these circuits, risky individuals become visible in new ways and subject to forms of stigmatization, exclusion, and treatment that are often harsher than those they replace. Work is made an imperative for those seeking assistance, not only in the name of self-reliance and ending dependency, but also to reattach problematic persons – such as young people who have never been in regular employment – to the circuits of control. Those who cannot manage their own risks are subject to incarceration in prisons or psychiatric hospitals not as a means of reformation, but as a mode of containment (for example, in the policy of 'three strikes and you're out' or in the re-emergence of an archipelago of institutions for the secure confinement of individuals who have committed no crime but are considered to present severe risks to the community). An image takes shape – often racialized and biologized – of a permanent underclass of risky persons who exist outside the normal circuits of civility and control and will therefore require permanent and authoritarian management in the name of securing a community against risks to its contentment and its pursuit of self-actualization.

A Third Way of Governing?

Despite all these innovations in governmental technologies, political debate in the 1980s, in the English speaking world at least, seemed limited to two options: governing through the market – free-market capitalist individualism – or governing through the state – perpetual bureaucratic reform, refinement, and technical tinkering with the mechanisms of welfare. But as we enter the twenty-first century, a new rationality for politics is beginning to take shape: 'the third way.' In fact, over this century there have been many proposals for a third way, and the contemporary political meaning of the phrase is currently the subject of much debate, especially among supporters of the New Democrats in the United States and New Labour in the United Kingdom. British prime minister Tony Blair, whose New Labour Party swept to power in Britain in 1997, is one of the most prolific users of the slogan. His 'third

way,' as set out in a number of speeches and expert seminars, rationalizes many of the arts of governing described earlier in terms of an
'enabling government.' It envisages governing economic life not through
intervention and nationalization, but through promoting 'opportunity,'
acting on the macro-economic environment, investing in education and
training which will provide the capacities and aspirations to enable
individuals and communities to advance their own economic interests.
It envisages governing security not through an all-embracing welfare
system encouraging 'dependency,' but through strategies that will 'include' the 'excluded' through promoting self-reliance by shifting people from welfare to work; through encouraging individual prudence by
means of the private provision of insurance, pensions, and the like;
through strengthening the support mechanisms imagined to inhere in
community and family bonds, and exploring non-state based forms of
mutualism. And it envisages a new politics of citizenship, in which
citizens recognize the limits of what the state can do for them, which
stresses, and even enforces, individual civic responsibility rather than
an idea of citizens as merely the bearers of entitlements to support from
others, and in which a voluntary or third sector takes an increasingly
active role.

These kinds of argument draw upon the support of a whole raft of
'policy wonks' and 'think-tanks,' and on some more dispersed muta-
tions in the intellectual machinery provided to politics by economics
and political philosophy. Thus economic discourse is turning away
from neo-classical and neo-liberal models of the market as a zone of free
competition among rational economic actors to emphasize the economic significance of gift relations, trust, networks, and regional
economic collaboration (Piore and Sabel 1984; Hirst and Zeitlin 1988;
Fukuyama 1996; Thompson 1997). Debates about the end of work highlight the significance of a 'third sector' between markets and government: community activity, community service, volunteers, from foster
parents to hospital work to local choirs and volunteer fire-fighters
(Rifkin 1995). Left political thought, prompted by the crisis and collapse
of state socialism, turns away from themes of central planning and
the authority of the party to stress the significance of 'civil society'
(Keane 1988). Within political discourse, 'anti-political motifs' are on
the rise, not only stressing the corruption and ineffectiveness of the
political classes, but, more fundamentally, asserting limits of any politics that sees itself as omni-competent and articulates itself in terms of
overarching political programs (Hindess 1994).

These are mirrored in the rise of civic republicanism in political philosophy, which counterposes the passive, privatized, individuated citizen of contemporary liberal democracies underpinned by theorists of 'negative liberty' and individual rights, to the active republican citizen, guided by common virtues and a commitment to the common good, whose active engagement in the life of the *polis* and affairs of the community would revitalize civil society. Liberty here entails the active exercise of rights in the name of the good within a political community; citizenship must continually be exercised in defense of freedom (see, e.g., MacIntyre 1981; cf. Burchell 1995). Sharing many of these principles, communitarian and associationalist arguments have proposed strategies that affirm the rights of a whole variety of communities of identification and allegiance, operating around a core of shared values, which can be re-empowered and reinvigorated within a common constitutional framework (Etzioni 1993, 1997; Fukuyama 1996; Hirst 1994).

In the politics of the 'third way' that is beginning to take shape, government is to territorialize itself in a new way: it valorizes an ethico-spatial field it terms 'community.' At the turn of the nineteenth and twentieth centuries, the social appeared both as the territory that had been brought into existence by industrialization and urbanization and as an antidote to the fragmentation and individualization these events had brought in their wake. In a similar way, community appears to emerge like a phoenix out of the fragmentation of social and political space generated in the course of commodification, marketization, and the like. And community appears as an antidote to this fragmentation. For the politics of the third way, 'community' is the 'anti-political' space in which powers and responsibilities previously allocated to politicians might be relocated. As the current British prime minister put it a year before his election victory, 'the search is on to reinvent community for a modern age, true to core values of fairness, cooperation and responsibility' (Blair 1996).

Of course, there is nothing new about the resort to 'community': communitarianism is one of the traditional themes of constitutional thought (Tully 1995). But there are different communities, differently spatialized and differently temporalized. Thus the shift from community to society detected by nineteenth-century theorists was located in a dimension of time, within a metaphysics of history. The community of which Durkheim and the English social liberals and social democrats spoke, at the turn of the nineteenth and twentieth centuries, as that set of moral bonds among individuals fragmented by the division of labour and capitalist production, to be reassembled in a 'social' form. The community that formed the focus of 'community studies' in the United Kingdom in the period after the Second World War was associated with the apparent anomie created by the disturbance of 'settled' working-class urban communities, it was community as the 'traditional' order of neighbourhood – a localized space of habitation – eroded by the bureaucratic ham-fistedness of well-intentioned but patronizing planners, the bonds of mutuality destroyed by the very welfare regime that sought to support them. The community of welfare reformers of the 1960s and 1970s was a network of psychiatric and correctional services not confined by the walls of the institution but coextensive with the plane of everyday life. Today, however, community is a kind of virtual space, not geographical, not a social space or a space of services, but a field of cultural and moral forces among persons in durable relations. 'Community,' says Etzioni, 'is defined by two characteristics: first, a web of affect-laden relationships among a group of individuals, relationships that often criss-cross and reinforce one another ... and second, a measure of commitment to a set of shared values, norms, and meanings, and a shared history and identity – in short, to a particular culture' (1997, 127). And it is through *this* community, its culture, its forms of identification, that government is to be reinvented.

Authors from Etzioni to Fukuyama seek to document a significant deterioration of social order in America in the period from 1960 to 1990 leading to problems ranging from crime, drugs, and social pathology, through democratic deficit and political alienation, to economic competitiveness in a globalized economy. And they ascribe this breakdown to the destruction of the collective moral values and moral bonds that held society together: through the rise of the counter-culture; through the promotion of a climate of individualism, self-interest, and the 'me generation'; through the increase of permissiveness, moral relativism, toleration of deviance, and the ascription of blame to 'the system' rather than to the individual; through political action itself encouraging dependency and damaging the sense of shared but personal responsibility for one's fate and that of one's family and community.

Hence the task for politics is not so much to govern morality, but to reinvent the forms of community that will re-establish the ethical basis for a self-governing polity. Robert Bellah and his colleagues identify the task as one of combating isolation and individualism through encouraging the citizen to actively involve him- or herself in associational life (Bellah 1985). James Coleman develops the notion of social capital and considers its diminution to be the cause of all manner of social ills and its re-creation to be an urgent task (Coleman 1990). Robert Putnam calls on social science to demonstrate that 'the quality of public life and the performance of social institutions (and not only in America) are indeed powerfully influenced by norms and networks of civic engagement,' and that 'successful outcomes in education, urban poverty, unemployment, the control of crime and drug abuse, and even health ... are more likely in civically engaged communities,' as indeed is the attainment of ethnic groups related to the strength of social bonds, the success of capitalism dependent upon networks of collaboration among workers and entrepreneurs, the performance of representative government determined by traditions of civic engagement and much more (Putnam 1995, 66). And Amitai Etzioni quotes approvingly from Gertrude Himmelfarb's article 'Beyond Social Policy: Remoralizing America': 'It is not enough, then, to revitalize civil society. The more urgent and difficult task is to remoralize civil society' (Himmelfarb 1995; quoted in Etzioni 1997, 96). While the religious right in the United States called for a return to tradition, communitarianism calls for a regeneration of virtue and argues that 'strong individual rights (autonomy) presumed strong personal and social responsibilities' rather than a return to an order based upon imposed duties (Etzioni 1997, 74). Moral order does not rest on laws enforced and upheld by guardians: 'community provides [individuals] with history, traditions, culture, all deeply imbued with values,' and the moral voice of the community 'is the main way that individuals and groups in a good society encourage one another to adhere to behavior that reflects shared values and to avoid behavior that offends or violates them' (ibid., 124). Etzioni refers to Tony Blair's speeches on 'the stakeholder society' to support his view that 'for a society to be communitarian, much of the social conduct must be "regulated" by reliance on the moral voice rather than on the law' (ibid., 139).

In the political rationality of the third way, the subjects of government are not isolated atomic and autonomous subjects of choice and freedom. They are individuals with 'identities' which not only identify them, but do so through their allegiance to a particular set of community values, beliefs, and commitments. Government through identity can be seen as an application to the political sphere of contemporary commercial rationalities for governing conduct through consumption in the name of culture and lifestyle, together with a much more widespread emphasis on the significance of autonomy and freedom of individuals in the shaping of their forms of life. This has had a kind of multiplier effect on an already plural moral order, and has contributed to the shift from morality, as obedience to an externally imposed moral code, towards ethics, as the practical shaping by the individual of the daily practices of his or her own form of life. The fragmentation of the social by the new technologies of images and identities, of lifestyles and choices, of consumption, marketing, and the mass media, has produced new collectivizations of 'habitus' outside the control of coherent discourses of civility or the technologies of political government – schooling, public service broadcasting, municipal architecture, and the like. The consumerization and commercialization of strategies and technologies of lifestyle formation has allowed the possibility of 'other subjectivities'– novel modes of individuality and allegiance and their public legitimation. Spaces of lifestyle and culture, as Cindy Patten has suggested, are no longer integrated in a total governmental field: heterogeneous and competing spaces challenge the capacities of social techniques for the government of conduct. Enwrapped within the cohesive discourses and strategies of the social state, subjects have nonetheless translated these to invent themselves, individually and collectively, as new kinds of political actors (Patten 1995, 226).

Community thus indicates a complex and agonistic space. In the name of community, a whole variety of groups and forces make their demands, wage their campaigns, stand up for their rights and enact their resistances. And in the name of 'becoming community,' radicals such as Jean-Luc Nancy, Giorgio Agamben, and various movements of hybridized, queer, subaltern, and non-essentialized communities seek to form new collectivizations of subjectivity and identity. Yet for proponents of the 'third way,' community is to be the site of reterritorialization of government, the ideal territory for the administration of individual and collective existence, the plane or surface upon which micro-moral relations among persons are conceptualized and administered. Conduct is problematized *in terms of* the relations of individual ethical comportment to pathologies of community values and cultures. Strategies and programs address such problems by seeking to *act upon* the dynamics of communities, enhancing the bonds that link individuals to their community, rebuilding shattered communities, and so forth. One sees the emergence of political programs, both at the micro-level and at the macro-level, for *government through community*. The moral injunctions of this community based ethico-politics are embedded in the technologies for the government of individuals, both at the individual level, in the terms and classifications used by the new agencies for ensuring job-readiness and moving people from welfare to work, and at the collective level, in the implicit explanations that inform the narratives of pathology played out in the mass media. In such programs 'society' still exists but not in a 'social' form: society is to be regenerated, and social justice to be maximized, through the building of responsible citizens of responsible communities, individuals, and communities prepared to invest in themselves (cf. Commission on Social Justice 1994).

Conclusions

Reading this diverse literature on new ways of governing, I am reminded of Jeremy Bentham's Preface to *Panopticon*, and the list of benefits to be obtained from his 'inspection house':

> *Morals reformed – health preserved – industry invigorated – instruction diffused – public burthens lightened* – Economy seated, as it were, upon a rock – the Gordian knot of the Poor-Laws not cut, but untied – all by a simple idea in architecture! (emphasis in original; Bentham 1843, 39 quoted in Foucault 1977, 207)

Now perhaps, one would write:

> virtue regenerated – crime reduced – public safety enhanced – institutionalization banished – dependency transformed to activity – underclass included – democratic deficit overcome – idle set to work – political alienation reduced – responsive services assured – economy reinvigorated by seating it, as it were, within networks of trust and honour – the Gordian knot of state versus individual not cut but untied, all by a simple idea in politics: community.

Almost a quarter of a century ago, Michel Foucault notoriously took Bentham's inspection house as the model for a certain type of power which he termed 'discipline': a versatile and productive micro-physics of power 'comprising a whole set of instruments, techniques, procedures, levels of application, targets' (Foucault 1977, 215). The Panopticon was the diagram of a political technology, one that was individualizing, normalizing, based on perpetual surveillance, classification, a kind of uninterrupted and continuous judgment enabling the government of multiplicities, reducing the resistant powers of human bodies at the same time as it maximized their economic and social utility. Discipline was destined to spread throughout the collective body, Foucault argued, and the forms of individual civility and docile citizenship set in place by the minute web of panoptic techniques and disciplinary norms was to be the real foundation of the formal political liberties of the abstract juridical subject of law and the rational economic individual of contract and exchange.

Can one conclude that these accounts of communities, associations, and so forth are related to a new diagram of power? This would be a diffuse power. It would no longer be structured by the division of the normal and the pathological. It would not be marked by the walls of the disciplinary institution. It would take the form of networks of 'control' that were disseminated throughout the very fabric of existence itself. These networks would not operate by deduction and the levy. They would not operate by normalizing individuals and rendering them docile. They would be assemblages that would shape the practices of everyday life, embodying within themselves a kind of cybernetics of control. They would be mechanisms to fabricate a kind of moral virtuous, self-activating citizen committed to the upholding of order – a person that would participate in the government of their affairs as a matter of their own personal liberty (cf. Deleuze 1995).

Far-fetched? Paranoid? Perhaps. But, to paraphrase Wendy Brown, we need to ask when certain political solutions actually codify and entrench power relations, when they mask such relations and when, alternatively, they contest or transform them (Brown 1995, 12).

Notes

1 Thanks to Mariana Valverde for advice and discussion which enabled me to write this paper; to Richard Ericson, who invited me to give it in his series 'Governing Modern Societies,' Green College, University of British Columbia, 16 September 1997, and for comments on an earlier draft; and to those who discussed it with me at the University of British Columbia, and at the Faculty of Law, University of Victoria.

2 In this paper I have drawn directly on a number of earlier published and unpublished papers: Miller and Rose 1990; Rose and Miller 1992; Rose 1992, 1996, 1997.

172   Nikolas Rose

References

Anderson, Benedict. 1991. *Imagined Communities*. London: Verso.
Baudrillard, Jean. 1983. *In the Shadow of the Silent Majorities or 'The Death of the Social.'* New York: Semiotexte.
Beck, Ulrich. 1992. *Risk Society: Towards a New Modernity*. London: Sage.
Bellah, Robert, Richard Madsen, William M. Sullivan, Ann Swidler, and Steven M. Tipton. 1985. *Habits of the Heart: Middle America Observed*. Berkeley: University of California Press.
Bentham, Jeremy. 1843. *Works*, vol. 4. Edited by John Bowring. London: Tait.
Blair, Tony. 1996. 'Battle for Britain.' *The Guardian*, 29 February.
Brown, Wendy. 1995. *States of Injury: Power and Freedom in Late Modernity*. Princeton, NJ: Princeton University Press.
Burchell, David. 1995. 'Genealogies of the Citizen: Virtue, Manners and the Modern Activity of Citizenship.' *Economy and Society* 24/4: 540–58.
Canguilhem, Georges. 1994. *A Vital Rationalist*. Edited by F. Delaporte. New York: Zone.
Castel, Robert. 1994. *Les métamorphoses de la question sociale*. Paris: Fayard.
Clarke, Peter. 1978. *Liberals and Social Democrats*. Cambridge: Cambridge University Press.
Colley, Linda. 1996. *Britons: Forging the Nation 1707–1837*. London: Vintage.
Collini, Stephan. 1979. *Liberalism and Sociology*. Cambridge: Cambridge University Press.
Commission on Social Justice.1994. *Social Justice: Strategies for National Renewal*. London: Vintage.
Cruikshank, Barbara. 1994. 'The Will to Empower: Technologies of Citizenship and the War on Poverty.' *Socialist Review* 23/4: 29–55.
Daston, Lorraine. 1994. 'Historical Epistemology.' Pp. 282–9 in J. Chandler, A.I. Davidson, and H. Harootunian, eds., *Questions of Evidence: Proof, Practice and Persuasion across the Disciplines*. Chicago: University of Chicago Press.
Dean, Mitchell.1991. *The Constitution of Poverty*. London: Routledge.
– 1995. 'Governing the Unemployed Self in an Active Society.' *Economy and Society* 24/4: 559–83.
Deleuze, Gilles. 1979. 'Introduction.' In Jacques Donzelot, *The Policing of Families: Welfare versus the State*. London: Hutchinson.
– 1995. 'Postscript on Control Societies.' Pp. 177–82 in *Negotiations*. New York: Columbia University Press.
Donzelot, Jacques. 1979. *The Policing of Families: Welfare versus the State*. London: Hutchinson.
– 1984. *L'Invention du Social*. Paris: Vrin.

– 1991. 'The Mobilisation of Society.' Pp. 169–80 in G. Burchell, C. Gordon, and P. Miller, eds., *The Foucault Effect: Studies in Governmentality.* Hemel Hempstead: Harvester, 1991.

Durkheim, Emile. 1964. *The Rules of Sociological Method.* New York: Free Press.

Etzioni, Amitai. 1993. *The Spirit of Community.* New York: Crown.

– 1997. *The New Golden Rule: Community and Morality in a Democratic Society.* London: Profile.

Evans, Peter, Dietrich Rueschmeyer, and Theda Skocpol.1985. *Bringing the State Back In.* Cambridge: Cambridge University Press.

Foucault, Michel.1977. *Discipline and Punish: The Birth of the Prison.* London: Allen Lane.

Fukuyama, Francis.1989. *The End of History and the Last Man.* New York: Avon.

– 1996. *Trust: The Social Virtues and the Creation of Prosperity.* Harmondsworth: Penguin.

Geertz, Clifford. 1973. *The Interpretation of Cultures.* New York: Basic.

Gilbert, Bentley. 1966. *The Evolution of National Insurance in Great Britain.* London: Joseph.

Gordon, Linda. 1989. *Heroes of Their Own Lives: The Politics and History of Family Violence.* London: Virago.

Greenblatt, Steven. 1980. *Renaissance Self-Fashioning: From More to Shakespeare.* Chicago: Chicago University Press.

Gullick, Luther. 1936. 'Introduction.' In Leonard Harrison and Elizabeth Lane, *After Repeal: A Study of Liquor Control Legislation.* New York: Harper.

Hacking, Ian. 1991. *The Taming of Chance.* Cambridge: Cambridge University Press.

Hayek, Frederick von. 1979. *Law, Legislation and Liberty.* Vol. 3: *The Political Order of a Free People.* London: Routledge and Kegan Paul.

Himmelfarb, Gertrude. 1995. 'Beyond Social Policy: Remoralizing America.' *Wall Street Journal,* 7 February.

Hindess, Barry. 1994. 'Politics without Politics: Anti-political Motifs in Western Political Discourse.' Paper delivered to Vienna Dialogue on Democracy, July.

– 1996. 'Liberalism, Socialism and Democracy: Variations on a Governmental Theme.' Pp. 65–80 in Andrew Barry, Thomas Osborne, and Nikolas Rose, eds., *Foucault and Political Reason.* London: UCL Press.

Hirst, Paul. 1994. *Associative Democracy.* Cambridge: Polity.

Hirst, Paul, and Jonathon Zeitlin, eds. 1988. *Reversing Industrial Decline: Industrial Structure and Policy in Britain and Her Competitors.* Oxford: Berg.

Joyce, Patrick. 1995. *Democratic Subjects: The Self and the Social in the Nineteenth Century.* Cambridge: Cambridge University Press.

Joyce, Patrick, ed. 1996. *Class: A Reader.* Oxford: Oxford University Press.

Keane, John. 1988. *Democracy and Civil Society.* London: Verso.

Kooiman, Jan, ed. 1993. *Modern Governance: New Government–Society Interactions*. London: Sage.

MacIntyre, Alistair. 1981. *After Virtue: A Study in Moral Theory*. London: Duckworth.

Melton, J. van Hoorn. 1995. '"Society" and "The Public Sphere" in Eighteenth- and Nineteenth-Century Germany.' Pp. 192–201 in Patrick Joyce, ed., *Class*. Oxford: Oxford University Press.

Miller, Peter, and Nikolas Rose.1990. 'Governing Economic Life.' *Economy and Society* 19/1: 1–31.

Mouffe, Chantal. 1992. 'Democratic Citizenship and the Political Community.' Pp. 225–39 in Chantal Mouffe, ed., *Dimensions of Radical Democracy*. London: Verso.

Oestreich, Gerhard. 1982. *Neostoicism and the Early Modern State*. Cambridge: Cambridge University Press.

O'Malley, Pat. 1996. 'Risk and Responsibility.' Pp. 189–208 in Andrew Barry, Thomas Osborne, and Nikolas Rose, eds., *Foucault and Political Reason*.London: UCL Press.

Organization for Economic Cooperation and Development. 1990. *Labor Market Policies for the 1990s*, Paris: OECD.

Osborne, Thomas, and Nikolas Rose. 1997. 'In the Name of Society, Or Three Theses on the History of Social Thought.' *History of the Human Sciences* 10/3: 87–104.

Patten, Cindy. 1995. 'Refiguring Social Space.' Pp. 216–49 in Linda Nicholson and Steven Seidman, eds., *Social Postmodernism: Beyond Identity Politics*. Cambridge: Cambridge University Press.

Pelling, Henry. 1965. *Origins of the Labor Party*, 2d ed. Oxford: Oxford University Press.

Piore, Michel, and Charles Sabel. 1984. *The Second Industrial Divide*. New York: Basic.

Polanyi, Karl. 1957. *The Great Transformation: The Political and Economic Origins of Our Time*. Boston: Beacon.

Poovey, Mary. 1995. *Making a Social Body*. Chicago: Chicago University Press.

Power, Michael.1994. *The Audit Explosion*. London: Demos.

Procacci, Giovanna. 1989. 'Sociology and Its Poor.' *Politics and Society* 17: 163–87.

Procacci, Giovanna. 1991. 'Social Economy and the Government of Poverty.' pp. 151–68 in Graham Burchell, Colin Gordon, and Peter Miller, eds., *The Foucault Effect: Studies in Governmentality*. Hemel Hempstead: Harvester Wheatsheaf.

Putnam, Robert. 1995. 'Bowling Alone: America's Declining Social Capital.' *Journal of Democracy* 6/1: 65–78.

Rajchman, John. 1991. *Truth and Eros*. New York: Routledge.

Rifkin, Jeremy. 1995. *The End of Work: The Decline of the Global Labor Force and the Dawn of the Post-Market Era*. New York: Tarcher/Putnam.

Riley, Denise. 1988. *Am I That Name: Feminism and the Category of 'Women' in History*. London: Macmillan.

Rose, Nikolas. 1990. *Governing the Soul: The Shaping of the Private Self*. London: Routledge.

– 1992. 'Governing the Enterprising Self.' Pp. 141–64 in Paul Heelas and Paul Morris, eds., *The Values of the Enterprise Culture: The Moral Debate*. London: Routledge.

– 1993. *Towards a Critical Sociology of Freedom*. London: Goldsmiths College.

– 1996a. 'The death of the social? Refiguring the Territory of Government.' *Economy and Society* 25/3: 327–56.

– 1996b. *Inventing Our Selves: Psychology, Power and Personhood*. New York: Cambridge University Press.

– 1997. 'The Crisis Of 'The Social': Beyond the Social Question.' Paper given at a symposium titled 'The Displacement of Social Policies,' Jyvaskyla, Finland, January.

Rose, Nikolas, and Peter Miller. 1992. 'Political Power beyond the State: Problematics Of Government.' *British Journal of Sociology* 43/2: 172–205.

Schwartz, Hillel. 1997. 'On the Origin of the Phrase "Social Problems".' *Social Problems* 44/2: 276–96.

Shapiro, Michael, ed. 1984. *Language and Politics*. London: Blackwell.

Smith, Adam. 1982. *The Theory of Moral Sentiments*. Edited by D.D. Raphael and A.L. Macfie. Indianapolis: Liberty Press.

Smith, Roger. 1992. *Inhibition*. Berkeley: University of California Press.

Spencer, Herbert.1884. *The Man vs. the State*. London/Edinburgh: Williams and Norgate.

Stedman-Jones, Gareth. 1983. 'Working-Class Culture and Working-Class Politics in London, 1870–1900.' Pp. 179–238 in *Languages of Class: Studies in English Working-Class History, 1832–1982*. Cambridge: Cambridge University Press.

Taylor, Charles. 1994. *Philosophy and the Human Sciences*. Cambridge: Cambridge University Press.

Tonkiss, Fran. Forthcoming. 'Corporations and Economic Governance: The Use of "Publicly-Sponsored Capital" in British Economic Management.' Unpublished manuscript.

Thompson, Grahame.1997. 'Where Goes Economics and the Economies?' *Economy and Society* 26/4: 599–610.

Tocqueville, Alexis de. 1969. *Democracy in America*. Edited by J.P. Maier and translated by G. Lawrence. Garden City, NY: Anchor.

Tully, James. 1995. *Strange Multiplicity: Constitutionalism in an Age of Diversity.*
    Cambridge: Cambridge University Press.
Valverde, Mariana. 1996a. 'Despotism and Ethical Liberal Government.'
    Economy and Society 25/3: 357–72.
– 1996b. 'Governing Out of Habit: From "Habitual Inebriates" to "Addictive
    Personalities".' Paper delivered to London *History of the Present* Research
    Network, May.
Veyne, Paul. 1997. 'The Final Foucault and His Ethics.' Pp. 225–33 in Arnold
    Davidson, ed., *Foucault and His Interlocutors.* Chicago: Chicago University
    Press.
Walters, William. 1994. 'Social Technologies after the Welfare State.' Paper
    delivered to London *History of the Present* Conference, Goldsmiths College,
    April.
– 1995. 'The Demise of Unemployment.' Paper presented at the 1995 Annual
    Meeting of the American Political Science Association, Chicago, August/
    September.
Wuthnow, Robert. 1994. *Sharing the Journey: Support Groups and America's New
    Quest for Community.* New York: Free Press.
Yeatman, Anna. 1995. 'Interpreting Contemporary Contractualism.' Pp. 124–
    39 in J. Boston, ed., *The State under Contract.* Wellington, NZ: Bridget
    Williams.

7

'Homogeneity' and Constitutional Democracy: Can We Cope with Identity Conflicts through Group Rights?

CLAUS OFFE

In this chapter I explore some ancient issues of political theory in the light of some social and cultural issues of the contemporary world. More specifically, I develop a checklist of the virtues and vulnerabilities of constitutional democracy (Part I); discuss some types and symptoms of difference, conflict, fragmentation, and heterogeneity (Part II); and end with a critical review of a particular type of strategies and institutional solutions – namely, political group rights – that are often thought of as promising devices to strengthen the virtues and overcome the vulnerabilities of the regime form of constitutional democracy (Part III). Much of the contemporary philosophical and political discussion of these issues is enchanted by the post-modern spirit of 'multiculturalism,' 'diversity,' and 'identity,' and tends to neglect issues of citizenship and social justice; it is also fixated on North American examples, neglecting some of the less benign west European and, in particular, central east European varieties of identity politics. The discussion here, while mostly raising questions rather than claiming to provide valid answers, still tries to overcome some of these biases.

I

A state, to start with some basics, is the coincidence of three things. First, the concept of a state (or 'country') refers to a fixed territory. This territory is defined by borders recognized by neighbouring states, as well as other members of the international community. A special case are island states, where borders are defined by (salt) water. Nevertheless, these borders need also to be recognized by other states or, failing that, the island state must be able to defend its territorial integrity against attempted moves by other states to occupy or conquer it (cf. the conflict between the People's Republic of China and Taiwan in 1996). Thus, territories, in order to serve as the material foundation of statehood, must be based upon agreements and the internationally mutually binding recognition of borders.

Second, the concept of a state presupposes that the territory is inhabited by a population, the state's 'people' forming a nation. Largely empty land, such as Antarctica, is not suitable for supporting a state, if only because there is nobody to defend it and nobody who is to be defended.

Third, the concept of the state presupposes a constituted government, or sovereign authority. Such authority is supposed to be superior to any other political authorities or social powers within the territory, as well as capable to assert itself against foreign interference. In short, a state is the coincidence of a country, a nation, and a regime.

The problem with these three constituent elements of a state is that they are, in a specific sense, 'contingent.' That is to say, they are the outcome of historical events and developmental trends. They originate from, among other things, climatic and physical features of the territory that make it inhabitable and resourceful, migration and other demographic trends, wars, dynastic politics, military occupation, conquest, revolutions, contracts of international law, and the like. States, in other words, are, in all three of their aspects, the accumulated sediment of history. That means, in negative terms, that democratic politics – that is, politics determined by egalitarian mass participation and elite accountability within the framework of constitutionally fixed rights and procedures – cannot determine the constituent features of a state; all three components of a state must be in place before a specific form of regime, the democratic one, can possibly begin to operate.

Next, constitutional democracy. There are a number of valuable accomplishments that constitutional democracies are often credited with. If we ask the (uncommon; cf. Schmitter and Karl 1991) question of what democracy is good for and makes it preferable to other regime forms, we would come up with four cumulative answers. First, there is the 'liberal' accomplishment of rights and liberties being guaranteed and a clear demarcating line being drawn between what can be contingent upon the outcome of the political process and the conflicts of interest entering into it, and what cannot be the object of such conflict because it is constitutionally entrenched. As a consequence of both rights and procedures being thus guaranteed, democracies make for a non-violent, limited, and civilized character of political conflict and incremental change. Second, the 'international' accomplishment, normally expressed in the 'democratic peace' hypothesis. It posits that democracies will not wage war against other democracies. Third, the 'social progress' accomplishment. As democracies rest upon majority rule, and as majorities are typically made up of those who do not share in economic privilege and social power, and as democratic state power is in fact able to affect the size and distribution of economic resources (e.g., through the promotion of growth, taxation, and social security) in more than marginal ways, democracies will normally work to serve the interests of the less fortunate segments of the population, thereby promoting 'positive' or 'social' rights and, more generally, prosperity and social justice. Finally, the 'republican' accomplishment of transforming 'subjects' into 'citizens,' that is, a kind of agents committed to and capable of employing their cognitive and moral resources in deliberative and intelligent ways so as to solve political problems, according to a logic of collective learning, and eventually striving to serve the 'public good.'

It is well known (and therefore will not be of any further concern in the present context) that a number of conditions must be fulfilled in order to enable democracies to do all those good things – at least, do them more consistently and reliably than any alternative regime form. For instance, there must be a solid and widely shared support for the democratic regime form, emanating from a democratic political culture. Also, there must be the actual possibility of controlling, through the means of democratic politics, those parameters and conditions of social life (such as the means of production and the means of violence) which are relevant for the protection of liberty and the promotion of social progress, with no 'reserved domains' standing in the way of such political control (Linz and Stepan 1996). Finally, there must be a judiciary and an administrative system that actually implements democratically legitimated laws and policies without either violating the rights of citizens or being overly 'sensitive' (i.e., corrupt) to some economic or military 'factual powers' or subservient to the corporate self-interest of the state bureaucracy itself.

If these are the (evidently, I submit, highly desirable) accomplishments that we have come to associate with and expect from the democratic form of government, at least as a realistic possibility, there are also, on the other hand, a number of democratic impossibilities, or matters that, by their very logic, cannot be resolved in democratic ways. If we ask what democracies can not do – and what hence, in case it needs to be done, must be done by methods other than democratic procedures, four things come to mind.

First, the democratic form of government (this applies almost as a matter of logic) cannot be brought into being by democratic means – although, as a rule, it is brought into being by democrats. The *pouvoir constituant* is prior to and unconstrained by the democratic principles which govern in a democratic regime once it is established, although the agents governing that *pouvoir constituant* may well be – and are as a rule – inspired by democratic beliefs and intentions. The 'initial framework in which democratically legitimated power is to be created is not enacted democratically' (Linz 1996, 10). Moreover, all democracies appear to have non-democratic roots – be it a *coup d'état*, a democratic popular movement, round-table talks, a regime breakdown, an occupation regime, a war of independence, or whatever. This observation is less trivial than it may seem, as this feature of non-democratic origin may later be held, as an alleged 'birth defect' or self-contradiction, against the democratic regime itself. It can be denounced, as has been fashionable within the ranks of the far Right of the Weimar Republic, as owing its existence not to its inherent qualities, but to a 'stab in the back' of the old regime or the exploitation of its condition of weakness or defeat, thus being a coup as much as any other imposition of a regime form. Also, nascent democracies are not state-founding, but merely regime transforming, a limiting case being the transformation of a former colony into an independent democratic state. Democracies cannot establish states, but they impose new forms upon pre-existing non-democratic states on the previous existence of which they are parasitic – also in the sense that the experience of authoritarian rule, with its systematic denial of liberties, may nurture the aspirations and resolve for a transition to democracy.[1] In these two senses, democracies are by necessity heirs to non-democracies; they owe their existence to an antecedent non-democratic state and, as I just pointed out, a non-democratic process of overthrowing the regime form of this non-democratic state.

Furthermore, not only are democracies unable to put themselves into being; they are also well able to undo themselves. That is to say, democracies are ultimately defenceless against movements and anti-democratic elites that use democratic procedures for the reinstallation of an authoritarian regime. Taken together, these considerations lead us to conclude that democracies are unable to either create or reliably preserve themselves. Democracies are neither self-founding nor self-enforcing.[2] Both their origin and their continued existence are a matter of favourable circumstances which are out of the reach of what can be done through democratic procedures proper.

A second democratic impossibility concerns the scope of the political community over which the democratic regime governs. The people cannot decide or (re)define who belongs to the people (as opposed to who is to be enfranchised within an existing people), neither by excluding parts of the population from the citizenship (e.g., through ethnic cleansing) nor by unilaterally incorporating collectivities that are outside the 'given' political community.[3] Democratic theory or constitutionalist doctrine do not provide us with good reasons as to why the social extension of the people should be what it empirically is (cf. Habermas 1996, 139f.). But neither are there good reasons to undo the 'arbitrariness' of history that has brought together a number of individuals in a certain territory under a shared regime of citizenship by claiming that 'in some cases there are two or more "peoples" in a single country,' as Kymlicka (1996, 11) puts it.

Third, and closely related to the previous point, territorial borders cannot be changed in obviously democratic ways. Again, this applies to the 'inward' direction of such a move (i.e., creating borders where there were none before) as much as to the 'outward' direction (i.e., eliminating pre-existing borders at the expense of the territorial base of some other state). The 'inward' case is equivalent to secession or separation, while the 'outward' case is the military conquest of the territory controlled by other states. Any inward move is bound to lead to procedural deadlock. After all, which constituency is to decide on secession: the majority of the separatist part, the whole, or concurrent majorities of either constituency? And which constituency is to decide in the most likely case of a second-order conflict over these procedural alternatives? A democracy cannot provide a formula for this kind of conflict, and a broad popular consensus to disunite (and where exactly to draw the line)[4] is highly unlikely to emerge, though not logically to be excluded. If the constitutionally unpaved road to an accord reached through intergroup negotiations fails, the most likely outcome is secessionist ambitions and possibly civil war. Conversely, it is international war in the 'outward' case of territorial change, as there are no populated stateless territories in the modern world. To be sure, international law provides the instrumentalities that can lead to the fusion of two states (as in the case of German unification); but that is not a matter of democratic decision of the constituency of one state, but a matter of an international treaty between two states by which one or both of them renounce(s) sovereignty. Incidentally, an attempt to 'conquer' the territory of another state by unilateral 'democratic' decision would be a blatantly self-contradictory act, as it would be based on the claim that the people of state A have the right to decide that the people of state B have no right to decide whether or not B-land should become integral part of A-land. This logic would clearly amount to denying prospective fellow citizens equal political rights.

Finally, the citizenry of a democracy cannot decide on the issues the citizens are to decide on. This is the problem of democratic agenda-setting. The role of the citizens in a democracy is to answer questions, not to formulate and ask the questions that are to be answered by the people. The latter task resides with elites (e.g., political parties nominating candidates and proposing alternative policy platforms) or, for that matter, nascent counter-elites (such as the activists of social movements introducing hitherto ignored issues into the arena of politics) or elites of other institutional sectors (such as science, the arts, or religion). One may consider this problem to be mitigated by the fact that (at least part of the) elites involved in agenda-setting have themselves been elected and thus mandated with the role of asking questions and proposing alternatives. But these elites, before being confirmed in their elite role through a democratic vote, have themselves been nominated and promoted to the role of candidacy through forces that are not democratically accountable. Note that this problem cannot be made to disappear through any dose of plebiscitary or 'direct democratic' procedural innovations, which in turn would strengthen rather than weaken the role of elitist agenda-setters and issue-raisers. To be sure, a strong public sphere within civil society can impose moral pressures upon elite members that they cannot afford to ignore or escape. But even given such pressures, nominating candidates and proposing platforms is not a matter of popular (but at best a matter of intraparty) democracy. Nor can the people decide upon when the people should decide, because that (often highly consequential) decision must be made through either elite initiative or a 'procedural clock' (such as the statutory periodicity of elections).

I have highlighted these four impossibilities and apparent deficiencies of the democratic regime form – the things democracies cannot do – not in order to put in doubt the value and virtue of democracy, but in order to derive the following thesis. The democratic regime form is a viable arrangement (and a promising vehicle for the four accomplishments stated at the beginning) only if, and only as long as, the four things that democracies cannot accomplish do not need to be accomplished. As long as democracies can live and prosper with their inherent deficiencies, these are at best of theoretical concern and without widely perceived practical significance. That is to say: As long as

- the regime form, in spite of its two non-democratic birth defects and its incapacity to effectively foreclose alternative regime forms, is widely accepted and unchallenged; and
- the people of a political community recognize each other as legitimately belonging to that political community without any relevant desire to exclude or unilaterally include anyone beyond the existing citizenship and the rights of political participation defined by it; and
- borders are accepted as given and lasting (or changes of borders are pursued within the procedural limitations prescribed by international law) because they are being recognized from within as well as by neighbors and the wider international community; and
- the right and competence of political elites to ask the 'right' questions at institutionally determined times, to integrate different cleavages into reasonably coherent platforms, and to respond to agenda innovations originating with counter-elites remains unchallenged,

we need not be concerned with the viability of the democratic regime form. This applies all the more if, in addition, this regime form demonstrably excels in doing what it supposedly is uniquely capable of doing – namely, in the simultaneous promotion of liberty, the non-violent resolution of both domestic and international conflict, social justice, and republican virtue. A political community within which all of these positive conditions are fulfilled, and, at the same time, none of the negative conditions is fulfilled, can be called a stable constitutional democracy. Its stability rests on the reflexive homogeneity of the political community.[5] It is homogeneous, or synonymously 'politically integrated,' because all (or at any rate the vast majority) of the people share a commitment to the state and its democratic regime form, are tied to their fellow citizens through an understanding of the communality of their fate and the recognition of equal liberties, and rank these commitments and loyalties higher than the various cleavages that divide the national society.

II

But, needless to say, there are such cleavages and differences, all of which can potentially undermine the coherence and integration of the political community. In fact, there are three different kinds of differences: interest-based, ideology-based, and identity-based – the three I's. The 'valued things' that are contested in these conflicts can be categorized, respectively, in terms of three R's: resources, rights, recognition (or respect). These types of difference and conflict can be ranked according to the ease with which conflict can be resolved and civilized (cf. Hirschman 1994). Pure interest-driven conflicts concerning control over and distribution of resources (more traditionally known as 'class conflict,' carried out among representative collective actors under the governance of mutually agreed-upon procedures) are most easily resolved – provided, of course, that the procedures are in fact recognized by all sides as impartial; failing that, the conflict of interest is nested within a conflict of ideology. Why should a pure conflict of interest be so easy to resolve? Because in the conduct of conflicts of interest the people involved (i.e., workers versus employers, manufacturers versus consumers, landlords versus tenants, etc.) learn that they depend upon those on the other side of the interest divide with whom they are, at the same time, in conflict. The awareness of this interdependence provides a strong incentive to compromise and to prevent the situation from spiralling into a negative-sum-game. Ideological conflict, in contrast, is more difficult to resolve. For proponents of ideologies, or comprehensive doctrines concerning the right and desirable pattern of rights and duties pertaining to the polity, society, and economy, often insist upon uprooting the 'wrong' ideas of opposing ideologies, which are branded as hostile, dangerous, or pernicious. Moreover, in an ideologically polarized field it is often next to impossible for the proponents to agree upon a method of conflict settlement and reconciliation, as any procedural rule, such as free and contested elections, will be suspected as biased and unfair. It is exactly these procedures to which the conflict pertains, and any argument advanced by one side is denounced by the other side as being an argument not for a point of view, but from a point of view. Thus people are seen to be tainted by 'bad' ideas, and these ideas must be uprooted, or prevented from circulation through repression.

Finally, identity conflict poses the most difficult type of conflict in that the bearers and proponents of one identity make the absence (or non-interference, non-participation within identity communities) of the bearers of other identities the benchmark of their well-being (as in 'ethnic cleansing') or demand the full assimilation of (linguistic, religious, ethnic) minorities. If the targets of such politics of identity discrimination refuse to go way, to assimilate and to hide, and in particular, if they respond by using their political rights for the assertion of cultural, ethnic, and linguistic difference and the struggle for its public recognition, the universe of the political community itself is put into question without recognized procedures being easily made available to reconcile mobilized groups involved in the politics of identity and difference. Typical demands in identity conflicts are claims for collective rights attached to the bearers of certain identities that serve to express their 'distinctiveness' and secure its recognition, to which claims the holders of other identities often respond by aggressively denying the recognition, toleration, and ultimately the right to exist of a group as a 'different' group. And both sides tend to insist on both the non-negotiable and the non-arguable (that is, the absence of the possibility of intergroup rational debates) nature of their respective claims, while proponents of ideological conflict, at least in their rhetoric, try to convince others and pretend to be themselves open to rational argument.[6]

The rough typology of differences (of interest, ideology, identity) that can give rise to conflict (over resources and their control, over rights, and over recognition) and the suggested hierarchy of potential disruptiveness of the dynamics of conflict (increasing from interest to identity conflicts) can also be put to use for understanding the dynamics of the transformation of conflict and the energies that drive it. Let me discuss in passing three hypotheses concerning the dynamic interconnectedness of the three levels (cf. Connor 1994; Gitlin 1995). First, the satisfaction of interest through ongoing compromises within a robust positive-sum-game will reduce the significance of ideological causes and identity antagonisms. Identity conflicts will be most effectively dissolved if they are superseded by economic conflict and competition, more specifically by the effects of successful industrialization, urbanization, and secularization, all of which tend to emphasize categories of 'having' while de-emphasizing and reducing to virtual insignificance those of 'believing' or 'being.' These are the optimistic messages of the modernization theory of the 1950s, with their visions of the 'end of ideology' and the 'melting pot.'

A second hypothesis concerns a displacement of the energies of conflict in the opposite direction. Losers move 'one level up.' The failure to acquire what is considered a fair share in the fruits of economic output gives rise, among the losers, to the resort to militant ideological mobilization. Similarly, the breakdown of the ideological hegemony of state socialism is followed by the resurgence of violent forms of ethnic nationalism in the region where state socialism once prevailed. In other regions, we see the failure of an industrial modernization generate fundamentalist theocratic backlashes. Similarly, the failure of political elites within the OECD world to come up with economic and social policies that have a credible chance to accomplish both economic efficiency and social cohesion under the new competitive conditions of the global economy leads these elites to replace political and economic issues with moral and religious ones, and masses often to resort to xenophobic excesses. Inversely, societies in which identity conflicts have become dominant are not likely to recuperate the dynamism of economic and political modernization. Instead, they lock themselves into the vicious cycle of fundamentalist backwardness.

Third, identity politics can also be strategically put in the service of winning or defending rights and resources. The drumming up of sub-nationalist secessionist threats can be a powerful device to extract subsidies from the centre or to enforce – from Katanga to 'Padania'– the protection of (e.g., regional) economic privilege. The instrumental use of identity symbols can also be a device to protect, as the secession of Slovakia suggests, regional political elites from post-communist purges. The mobilization along lines of ethnicity, gender, and 'race' can be used as an instrument to acquire access and improve group-specific protection in increasingly precarious labour markets. It can also be employed to promote the acquisition of rights and the exemption from duties.[7] In this sense, the instrumental use of identity politics can be seen as a device for the protection and promotion of the interests of latecomers or prospective losers in the race for the blessings of modernity.

Whether identity politics is the residual of failed economic and political modernization and an expressive response to the frustrations over this failure (hypothesis 2) or whether it is, and at least partly inauthentically, employed as a pretext for strategies of acquisition and protection (hypothesis 3), the promise of the universalist implications of modernization (as well as modernization theory) (hypothesis 1) has evidently not come true. Instead, the politics of identity-based difference is an increasingly prominent feature of increasing segments of the contemporary world, developed and developing alike.

How can a democracy cope with these potentially disruptive politics of difference? To be sure, all types of conflicts, not just identity conflicts, harbour the potential for tearing up the political community. But democracies are not defenceless. Through the allocation of rights and resources, they can contain the explosive potential of conflict, thereby reconciling the divided citizenship and strengthening the foundations of a liberal political community that is based upon individual and equal rights (recognized in spite of the vast variety of individual life plans and preferences), as well as the republican self-recognition of the political community and the commitment of its members to the principles of fairness embodied in the constitution. In other words, the democratic legislative process can yield results which have the potential of homogenizing and reconciling the citizenry, thus validating the conditions of democracy in a circular process of democratic self-consolidation, or fostering democracy through democratic means. The basic idea here is that of equalizing status rights and opportunities so that no party involved in any of the three types of conflict is left with rational reasons to disrupt the political community or disregard the rules on which it is based.

More specifically, there are three measures by which such self-consolidation can be accomplished. While citizenship accords one single legal status for all – namely, that of equal liberty – it does not effectively reconcile conflict, but sets the stage on which socio-economic, political, and identity conflicts are carried out. Three types of rights, corresponding to the three types of difference and conflict, have been suggested – and at least in part also implemented – by which this discrepancy between formal-legal equality and actual social inequality can be mitigated or reconciled in the service of democratic self-consolidation and on the basis of equal citizenship.

This task is most easily accomplished in the case of interest-based cleavages which unfold between socio-economic categories. The formula that has been adopted in order to foreclose this source of political disintegration is social rights – in both its versions, substantive social rights and social policies (devoted to workers' protection, social security, and full employment, but also family allowances, farm subsidies, and the protection of small businesses) and procedural social rights (such as co-determination and collective wage bargaining between trade unions and employers' associations). The net result of these policies is to involve the economically less privileged categories of society in a game, which is perceived as either of the positive-sum variety ('We are all going to gain in the long run') or the *petite bourgeoisie* variety ('We have nothing to gain, but we certainly do have something to lose'). In either scenario, defection is rendered irrational, and hence widely shared support for and recognition of the political community and its order enhanced.

Perhaps less easily contained is ideological conflict. At any rate, the clash of Christian, libertarian, communist, nationalist, conservative, and socialist views of how a well-ordered society must be run and organized can be mitigated only through the granting and meticulously fair implementation of political rights, including the freedom of expression, communication, association, and participation. That may not be enough, as the very idea of procedural fairness is one that it sometimes turns out to be impossible to agree upon among the ideologically conflicting parties. If, however, such agreement and its robust implementation are both feasible, the resulting game places a premium on either of two centripetal and integrative mechanisms. First, self-blame and learning: if the rules must be recognized as unobjectionably neutral, fair, and unbiased, and if 'we' still do not win the elections, a revision of 'our' ideological stance may be called for. Second, accommodation: if marginal ideological concessions are called for in order to win representation or governing power, the *quid pro quo* speaks in favour of actually making those concessions, given the opportunity costs of intransigence. In both cases, fairness renders ideological intransigence costly and promotes convergence, again to the advantage of political integration.

Finally, identity conflicts. These are the most intractable of all. Nevertheless, the antidote that constitutional democracies have available in order to cope with this type of conflict is group rights, which come, as far as political life is concerned, in three varieties: rights to self-government, polyethnic rights, and special representation rights (cf. Kymlicka 1995).[8] The logic behind the granting of such group rights to religious, linguistic, racial, ethnic, gender, regional, and other categories of people is clear enough: Members of these groups are to be assured, through tangible guarantees and concessions, of their full inclusion into the citizenship, and feelings of alienation, resentment, and hostility are thus to be overcome and prevented from emerging in the first place. It is these political (as opposed to social and economic) group (as opposed to individual) rights that I now turn to in order to evaluate them as an instrument to enhance the homogeneity and integration of the political community that democratic theory and its core standard of a unified citizenship must presuppose.

III

Let us consider these various political group rights in turn. Rights to limited self-government apply only to multinational societies. But also their potential use is limited. First, they are clearly applicable in case the (ethnic, linguistic, religious etc.) groups in question settle in, and also hold, by virtue of the territorial concentration of their members, regional 'structural' majorities in distinctive sub-territories. The mechanism of self-government does not work in diaspora situations, nor does it work in situations where the unity of the regional group is easily drawn into question, or where several minorities of largely equal size settle in the same sub-territory. An attractive alternative to rights attached to settled groups is rights attached to geographical territories, with the intended effect of people who consider this territory their 'homeland' moving in and minorities moving out. Second, there must also be mutually recognized substantive demarcation lines concerning the policy areas for which self-government is to be applied. If the policy area for which autonomy is granted is, for instance, 'education,' self-government should not be allowed to shade from there into research, taxation, labour-market, or fiscal policies, to say nothing about border regimes or military forces. As long as these two conditions are securely satisfied (and a jurisdictional power settling likely disputes if firmly in place), the instrument of limited self-government is a potentially powerful device of democratic self-consolidation through power-sharing. The result would be a subnationally based 'bottom-up federalism' (of the kind attempted in Spain, Belgium, and Canada). Its use, however, can easily conflict with another instrument – namely, social rights, for leaving 'too much' to regional self-government is bound to constrain the resources that the nation-state has available for the promotion of social security and distributional justice. Federalism can also conflict with notions of political equality, as second chambers do not normally assign the number of seats according to the actual size of states or other regional units, but accord disproportionate advantages to small units.

Next, polyethnic rights (applying to immigrant communities) and special representation rights (applying to non-territorial minorities), which I want to discuss together. Both apply to groups which cannot be defined in territorial terms. Polyethnic rights are special legal entitlements and policy programs, including public funding, aimed at the promotion and recognition of ethnic, religious, linguistic, and other groups, and the contribution they make to the life of the political community. Such official recognition can take the form of the promotion of minority languages, public support for particular cultural practices, representation of minority cultures in the curricula of public schools, the funding of libraries, museums, research projects, and so on. In contrast, special representation rights relate to group identity more indirectly. Here, the issue is not what substantive ideas and cultural traditions should be given special status (as in polyethnic rights), but who should do the representation or whose chances to win elected office should be selectively improved, the guiding intuition being that the more people of category X are represented in Parliament or political parties, the more forcefully the specific ideas and traditions of group X will be promoted.

The issue of group rights raises at least four normative questions (cf. Bauböck 1998). First, what are normative arguments that can motivate a majority of citizens to grant such rights to groups and tolerate the exercise of these rights, even though they violate the principle of numerical equality? Second, is it actually in the best interest of members of groups to claim and use collective rights? Third, what qualifies a 'group' as a collectivity worthy and deserving of such rights? And, fourth, what determines and justifies the extent of rights accorded to the group(s) in question? I'll focus upon the latter two questions and address the former just in passing.

What Is a Group?

Before entering into a discussion of these normative-cum-sociological issues, we need a reasonably robust concept of the phenomenon in question. How do we, be it from within (the demanding side of group rights) or be it from the outside (the granting side), recognize a group if we see it? The question is less easily answered than it might appear.

Group rights, as discussed here, are minority rights.[9] Note, however, that not all kinds of minorities are (nor conceivably should be) protected by collective minority rights. For instance, employers are typically a tiny minority compared to employees. Yet their interests are not protected by 'minority rights,' but by individual (property and other) rights that provide them with considerable leverage in the defence of their interests. Similarly, no one would think of minority rights applying to the universe of those citizens who have voted for the party that lost the last elections. Again, the legitimate concerns and interests of this political minority is normally thought to be taken care of through individual rights of political participation, communication, and association which, taken together, may be seen as opening up a fair chance that the minority becomes the majority in the next elections.

What we mean by a 'minority' as a candidate for group rights is instead a 'structural' minority – a minority that by virtue of its constitutive characteristics and the shared identity resulting therefrom is bound to remain a minority even after its members have used their individual rights to a maximum extent. But the minority, in order to make a plausible moral claim to special rights, must also be seen as an (unjustly)[10] 'oppressed' group – a group, in other words, that 'deserves' to be better known and recognized than it is capable of effecting by its own structurally limited means, be it for the sake of the full self-realization of its members or be it, in addition, for the sake of its potential of 'enriching' the political community as a whole with its distinctive contributions.[11]

So far the result is that group rights are rights claimed by or granted to unjustly oppressed structural minorities. But what is the minority a minority of? Minorities may be minorities relative to the entire population resident in a territory, or they may be minorities relative to segments of that population.[12] While women are, at least in Western society, almost nowhere minorities in the first sense, they are almost everywhere minorities in the second sense - if we focus, for instance, upon the subtotal of the holders of political and other elite positions. Similarly, Albanians are a vast majority in Kosovo, but a minority in Serbia as a whole. 'Structural' minorities are groups whose members share essential characteristics that can neither be easily and quickly acquired nor given up. Structural minorities are thus 'locked into' a set of properties which are considered significant (or constitutive of a collective 'identity') by either themselves or/and by others and which can neither be acquired nor given up. These properties of individuals are normally acquired through birth (such as identity of the parents and their ethnicity and 'race'; gender; age; location; nationality) or shortly after during primary socialization (language; religious affiliation; according to some theories also sexual orientation: heterosexual versus homosexual). Some features that people are born with (such as left-handedness) are not significantly identity-forming; some identity-shaping properties can be (but are not normally) given up and exchanged for others (such as religious affiliation). Some identity-forming properties come in grades and shades (such as 'racial' phenotypes or age), others are entirely subject to an either/or logic (such as, for all practical purposes, gender). The significance of such markers does not only result from the fact that those belonging to the minority base their own sense of identity and belonging on these markers, an effect that we might term 'internal identity building.' It does also, and often to a greater extent, result from the fact that the majority of those who do not share the property in question ascribe to the property and to persons who have it legitimate access to or exclusion from social esteem and other valued resources. The logic of this 'external' construction of social identities is of the form: Property X conditions legitimate access to good Y and/or exclusion from good Z in the eyes of the holders of non-X. It is an empirical matter to what extent internal and external identity building interact according to a logic of mutual intensification, but many examples demonstrate that this is a likely event. (For instance, the immigrant Turkish minority in Germany is said to identify, perhaps in response to the majority's practices of ethnic labelling and discrimination, more strongly with the religious tradition of their country of origin than they would had they remained in that country.)

This case indicates how the 'identity' that makes up a 'group' is not just 'structural' (in the sense that it is typically not easily acquired or abandoned), but also to varying degrees 'voluntaristic,' that is, individually chosen as a focus of identification and emphasis in self-presentation. For instance, a descendent of an Irish mother and an Italian father living in the United States can identify with none of the two ethnic origins, or with both of them, or with either of them, or alternate between these identities. Moreover, choices made from an individual's 'identity portfolio' will be conditioned by perceived (dis)advantages associated with identifications, with strong anticipations of discrimination possibly leading to an active dissimulation or 'betrayal' of a person's 'true' group identity. This voluntaristic element of 'belonging' to a group sheds further light on the complexities of the practice of looking at societies as being composed of 'groups,' and of coding individuals as unequivocally 'belonging' to groups.

But highlighting such complexities is not denying the intensity of feelings of injustice, and of conflicts emerging from such feelings, that emerge from the perceived discrimination of groups and those identifying with them. Remedial action consists in providing minorities with group rights in order to compensate for the perceived injustices of exclusion and denial of recognition. Why, then, are individual rights, such as they are enjoyed by everyone else, deemed insufficient? In what sense are group rights different from individual rights? First, they do not apply to all citizens, but just to members of targeted groups. Second, members of the target groups are categorically and authoritatively made the beneficiary in question, without being able to individually 'opt out' of the reach of the benefits attached[13] and without being able to give up the (by definition: ascriptive and 'non-changeable') characteristics that make up group membership. Group rights involve a strong quasi-corporatist status order: individuals are locked into group membership (whether they want it or not), and group as a collective body becomes the target of privilege.[14]

Such granting of collective privilege may appear entirely beneficial and unproblematic. Who, after all, would object to being legally entitled to partaking in group benefits?[15] Problems arise, however, when we consider two possible and, in fact, common, implications of the granting of group rights. One implication is that groups who then become the bearers of rights must first be designated in an act of political decision that turns some alleged 'group in itself' into a legally recognized and, as it were, accredited group. Such political definition of group status may err – and subsequently become controversial – in either of two ways. First, the authoritative assignment of group quality to a collectivity may be overly encompassing, forcibly tying together people into a common membership status who had never thought of themselves as belonging to one and the same group,[16] or, for that matter, to any group at all. The other way in which group incorporation can become contested is that the groups that are made the target of privilege are too narrowly defined (cf. Glazer 1983, 254–73). This happens if some groups are granted group rights in order to compensate for their past unfair discrimination, but other groups who feel equally discriminated are being left out – with the consequence of them feeling discriminated by their exclusion from the benefits of anti-discriminatory policies. For every act of recognition of a group as the bearer of group rights is bound to divide the world into three segments: those who do not need group rights because they do not belong to an unjustly oppressed minority; those who do belong to such a minority and are henceforth recognized as such; and those who aspire to such recognition, but fail to win it, at least for the time being.[17]

It might appear that in order to find out whether a group 'is' in fact a group deserving a privileged legal status which compensates its members for the reason of injustices suffered in the past, we may want to consult history books. This is not a consistently promising path out of

our definitional dilemmas. First, history books are written 'now,' and
even to the extent they are based upon historical documents, these are
being 'discovered' now and interpreted now. All of which is to say that
groups can 'invent' and establish themselves and their claims to group
rights by invoking a history that is being written and disseminated for
the purpose of group formation and collective status politics. Second,
even in cases where such doubts do clearly not apply, the analytical and
normative issues of intertemporal justice need to be settled. For instance, to what extent can the present level of life chances and recognition enjoyed – and experienced as unfairly disadvantaged – by members
of group X be causally attributed to the fact that the ancestors of those
members, say, four generations back, were, by the standards of today,
unjustly deprived of rights and resources? And even if so: for how long
can 'we,' the non-minority, be held morally responsible for compensating for the wrongdoing of our ancestors and for the irreparable damage
they have inflicted upon the minority's ancestors as well as the de-
scendents of these ancestors? There is, after all, no such thing as the
legal entity 'Afro-Americans Inc.' the accounts of which would have to
be balanced. Instead, there are ties of historical causation and, on the
other hand, ties of recollective identification, both of which can be
weaker or stronger.

Another complication with the 'oppressed minority' criterion of
groups claiming rights is that every group can be easily subdivided into
a virtually endless number of component groups if a tactical interest
arises for doing so.[18] What is the right level of aggregation here? Why
stop at the level of 'African Americans,' rather than further dis-
aggregating this 'group' into male and female, Spanish-speaking and
English-speaking, Christian and Muslim African Americans? In the
other direction, the contours of the 'oppressed minority' are also easily
blurred, as the vast majority ('everyone but relatively well-off, relatively young, able-bodied, heterosexual white males': Kymlicka 1995,
145) can arguably be included, or in good conscience include him- or
herself, into a giant rainbow-coalition of oppressed minorities.[19] Under
the umbrella of such an alliance, and given the potential for subdivision
of every group, the potential for the proliferation of group rights claimed,
as well as group rights granted or group privileges attacked, becomes
visible, the results of which will hardly contribute to what group rights
were originally meant to achieve: the integration of the political
community.

Note that our initial question: 'What is a group worthy of special substantive and/or representation rights?' is still unanswered. One is tempted to despair about the feasibility of a normatively meaningful answer and to resort to sociological realism, with the result being something like this: A group enjoying special rights is a collectivity the elites of which have, in spite of the minority position of its constituency, managed to mobilize a sufficient amount of political resources in order to extract from the majority special concessions and privileges collectively assigned to the group's members. If that were right, however, it would make no sense anymore to describe such groups as 'oppressed' and 'powerless'; to the contrary, the very acquisition of group rights testifies to its significant control of social and political power, whereas truly disadvantaged groups, such as the European Gypsies, have hardly the organizational and political resources at their disposal that are needed in order to raise the issue of their discrimination and marginalization.

As an alternative to sociological 'realism,' and in order to stem the danger of the proliferation of ever further 'groups,' one might also try to establish criteria which a group must meet in order to qualify for special collective status rights. Three such criteria are conceivable, and they would probably have to apply cumulatively. First, the group must be 'relevant' in quantitative terms. For instance, groups that make up less than 1 per cent of the population would not qualify for any special rights. Second, the group must be 'authentic.' That is to say, there must be clear indications of a distinctive life form and the serious and lasting allegiance of most nominal members to it, without an excessive measure of fragmentation of the group into subgroups and sub-subgroups. Third, and perhaps most controversial, there must be a measure of affinity and compatibility between the group's life form and the life form of the majority. Taken together, this set of criteria would amount to the restriction of group rights to relatively large,[20] internally closely integrated, and easily compatible minorities that share many, though certainly not all, values and cultural patterns with the majority. The reader is invited to conduct a thought experiment on how many, if any, "groups" within her/his society qualify for "groupness" according to these criteria.

What Are Rights?

After having pinpointed a few of the problems associated with the deceptively simply issue of 'groups' and their cognitive as well as moral and legal recognition, let us now look at the analogous problems that emerge as we look at 'rights.'[21] Probably the most general thing one can say about rights is that the more rights a person has, the better for him or her, as rights provide the freedom to conduct one's life in preferred ways. It is far from certain that groups rights do actually perform this freedom-enhancing function for group members. The trouble with group rights is that the benefits involved may not be entirely unqualified, but must be paid for by (some) group members in terms of corresponding losses and sacrifices. This applies to cases in which the privilege granted to group members fails to be appreciated as such by individuals within the group (e.g., because their commitment to the religion, language, or other bases of collective identity is not very intense), or where members see their civil liberties violated by the group-rights regime making them subject to the regimentation by the group's authorities. Kymlicka (1996, 8) illustrates the possible antagonism between group rights and individual rights by drawing upon the rather distant case of the millet system in the Ottoman Empire. Here, according to him 'while the Muslims did not try to suppress the Jews, or vice versa, they did suppress heretics within their own community.'

The mode in which group rights operate can be of either or both of two kinds: a plus in rights enjoyed by group members (relative to the individual rights of everyone else outside the group) or a minus in duties. Thus, an ethnic minority may be endowed with publicly funded support for its specific cultural practices, say, a folk-dance academy. Alternatively or in addition, group rights can consist in the exemption from duties that everyone else must comply with, an example being the permission granted to members of religious groups to have their female children not participate in otherwise obligatory gym classes in high-school education or the exemption from military service for reasons of belonging to a religious faith. It appears that the two – legal privilege and exemption from duties – are not strictly symmetric, as they differ in the scope of the externalities they inflict upon the larger society and its cohesion. The right to be taught language X at school may be considered harmless from this point of view, as the vast majority is neither capable to speak nor interested in learning that language. As it comes to exemption from duties, however, the situation changes, as such exemption may be polemically depicted as 'free-riding,' which, if visibly permitted, undermines the general bindingness of the law and invites others to invent their reasons for claiming exemption (e.g., from military service) as well.

Political group rights can be intended to be a temporary measure or a permanent one. In the first case, the justification is analogous to protective tariffs: A 'weak' group must be encouraged to develop the resources, competence, and self-confidence in order to become capable of eventually competing on the basis of its own resources; until it is able to do so, special preferential conditions are granted to its members. For this effect to be accomplished, an expiration clause or review procedure would have to apply. In this sense, quota rules for women concerning leadership positions in political parties (as adopted so far by the Green and Social Democratic parties in Germany) could be justified as an anti-discriminatory political headstart program that generates the conditions of its justified abolition at a later point. But expiration (or even review) clauses are typically missing in such arrangements. Group rights are granted as permanent rights. This suggest a different justification of these rights – namely, the justification of enriching the life of the community (or party, as well as enhancing its electoral prospects) by the guaranteed special representation of supposedly group-specific styles, values, and concerns of women.

Another, supposedly 'liberal' argument for group rights is proposed by Kymlicka (1996, 10) for immigrant minorities in polyethnic societies: 'If we demand that immigrants integrate into the institutions [of the country they migrate to], we must ensure that their religious holidays, dietary requirements and dress codes are respected.' The argument is based on a quid-pro-quo logic. But the argument raises more questions than it explicitly addresses. Why 'must' we – given the fact that the immigrants knew or could know what was awaiting them in terms of cultural adjustment requirements and also given the fact that new (mixed, assimilated, or diasporic) cultural patterns will inevitably develop in the second and third generation? How much quid for how much quo? Why not let the general freedom of religion, diet, and dress that is (supposedly) guaranteed in the immigration country do the job of facilitating integration? Will the purposive legal engineering aiming at 'integration' actually generate 'respect'? Where is the line that is to be drawn between 'benign multiculturalism' based upon civic respect and institutionalized identities protected by and frozen into group rights (Joppke 1996)?

Also, we do not need to consult books on Ottoman history to encounter the antagonism between group and individual rights. Group rights granted to religious groups imply that spiritual leaders or parents are permitted to impose rules on members, monitor their compliance, and constrain their civil liberties. An extreme example is the religious belief that modern medicine is evil, and the ensuing practice of denying members access to medical emergency services. Such imposition may be motivated by the group leaders' desire to prevent assimilation, with the rational fear in mind that assimilation may undermine the power and privilege of leadership. 'To prevent religious or cultural assimilation, the minority must precommit itself in ways that reduce the freedom of its individual members' (Elster 1996, 53).

The granting of group rights is often justified in terms of a necessary condition of preserving the group's distinctive identity. This, again, raises the question why such identity cannot be preserved on the basis of the rights of equal citizenship alone, including, of course, the right to form associations and communities within which religious beliefs and cultural traditions can be cultivated and propagated. Even if we were to agree, in a slightly paternalist perspective (reminiscent of the protection of endangered species), that the preservation of identities must be assisted by special legal provisions (rather than through generally available liberties), we would still have to come to terms with the thorny question of what exactly the 'substance' is that is to be protected and whether such benevolent protection does not interfere with spontaneous processes of cultural change. As there is no clear-cut measure as to what kind of rights and how many of them are required for exactly that purpose to be achieved, and as there are obvious vested interests of the elites of groups (such as ethnic artists and intellectuals, movement entrepreneurs, regional politicians, and religious leaders) to expand these rights, the escalation of special rights, including representation rights, is an inherent dynamic element in the situation.

This dynamic of escalation is enforced by two factors. One is the interminority rivalry following a 'me too' logic. The more groups are endowed with group rights, the more rights they may feel to be in need of in order to preserve their identity and make their voices heard. The other is the use of group rights for the purpose of acquiring additional rights, as in the case of minority language rights, once granted, being used for mobilizing more far-reaching demands, such as minority language radio stations or minority language teachers' colleges. Once a minority culture is institutionalized through a set of protective rights, there is no obvious equilibrium or saturation point; to the contrary, the more rights are granted, the easier it becomes for the group's leadership to mobilize demand for even more rights. In principle, and from a liberal and individualistic point of view, there are two normative yardsticks by which these group rights and the built-in dynamic of their expansion can be evaluated. They can be formulated in the questions of (a) whether or not group rights do actually benefit, or protect the best interest of, the members of the group and (b) whether the non-members can be justly expected to pay the costs of group privilege. We can refer to the two standards as (a) an internal and (b) an external justification of group rights.

As to the first, increments in the rights of minorities can well go hand in hand with a decrease of the rights and actual life chances of minority members, even if such sacrifice is not imposed by the group's leaders in the interest of maintaining their power and privilege. Language acquisitions is a case in point. The opportunity costs that are involved in studying a regional language at school are often equivalent to the non-acquisition of a foreign language that may be of greater practical use. Thus students pay for the benefit of having their linguistic identity strengthened by the chance of forgoing labour-market opportunities. Another case in point is political affirmative action, or preferential representation rights. As in ordinary quota and affirmative action practices, chances are that a revengeful majority of white males tends to discredit and stigmatize resulting advantages as undeserved and illegitimate, thereby reversing the intended effects of 'reverse discrimination,'[22] without any enforceable rule being available to control such second-order hostile responses. This raises the question to what extent recognition and respect can at all be mandated and enforced by formal law, as opposed to the insistence upon informal standards of common decency and civility, which may or may not be strengthened by the law and the mechanisms of its enforcement. At any rate, group rights of minorities must be honored and redeemed by majorities, and honored as a recognized 'duty,'[23] not just as a statutory rule.

Motivating Recognition: Group Rights and Majorities

Turning to the second of the above criteria, the one concerning the sacrifices the majority can legitimately be expected to make in favour of minority rights, it is sometimes countered (cf. the discussion in Kymlicka 1995, 122–3) by the assertion that such costs are not a sacrifice, but an investment that society makes into its own multiculturalism, thereby enriching, as it were, its cultural genetic pool. In other words, it is not just the majority's moral duty, but at the same time its long-term collective self-interest to honour group rights. Now, arguments according to which self-interest and moral duty coincide are always suspicious. At any rate, the alleged collective advantage of diversity must be balanced against the collective disadvantage of increased transaction costs of communication and of the ongoing adjudication of polyethnic rights as well as the conflicts over the limits of those rights, that is, the costs of such 'investment' in diversity. Given these costs, and due to the awareness of these costs, the consequentialist argument that diversity is enriching is hard to trust in the abstract.

Proponents of this argument usually refer to some specific group or group practice (such as art form or ethnic cuisine) they happen to consider as enriching, with typically less sanguine emphasis on the potential contribution of others. And neither can such implicit ranking be avoided. If that is true, there are by implication also groups and cultural practices that do not enjoy the reputation of being 'enriching,' but are considered alien, unworthy, dangerous, and potentially hostile – and therefore not deserving any sacrifice or toleration on the part of the majority. Hence 'enrichment'-oriented multiculturalism may turn out to be not so colour-blind, but in effect strongly discriminating. On the other hand, if the argument for toleration does not start from desirable contributions and enrichment coming from the group in question, it must start from the desired consequence of enhancing democratic homogeneity by eliminating reasons for justified complaint about non-admittance to a homogeneous citizenship status. But that could also be, and in collectively less costly ways, achieved through stricter provision and enforcement of universal citizen rights and equal opportunities, which, after all, include the opportunity to pursue a great diversity of values, styles, and identities which, however, would have to be relegated to a 'sub-political' realm of the personal conduct of life. Consideration of consequences does not seem to yield a conclusive argument concerning costs and sacrifices the majority can be required to make.

Alternatively, one can (and, in fact, must) rely on the justice argument that it is the duty, whatever the costs involved, of the majority to eliminate the minority's suffering that would result from inadequate opportunities to practise its inherited life form and cultural tradition. The Achilles heel of this argument from justice is that it is so difficult to assess the amount of such suffering in unobtrusive ways, as revealed preferences for the preservation of 'identity' values must always be suspected, in either negative or positive ways, to be tainted by strategic considerations. Moreover, some cultural life forms, including languages, have disappeared as a living cultural practice even in the absence of any trace of discrimination and perhaps even painlessly so; they have simply fallen victim to the forces of cultural change, the resistance to which can hardly be postulated to be a moral duty. At any rate, any indicator as to how strongly the minority actually values and needs for its collective self-realization the protection of its life form is unlikely to be strategy-proof.

Certainly the strongest moral reason for recognizing group rights is the majority's awareness of past injustices inflicted upon a group by its predecessors. Accordingly, minorities will find it easier to extract concessions from majorities if they can invoke the logic of a fair compensation for such injustices. This applies to the cases of Afro-Americans; ex-colonial populations resident in France, Britain, or the Netherlands; aboriginal people in Canada, Australia, or the United States; the Basques in Spain; to say nothing about Jews and other Holocaust victims in Germany. Feminists have made analogous arguments in view of the injustices inflicted upon women by millennia of patriarchy. But even in these cases, and with the passing of the generations of both the immediate victims and the immediate perpetrators, it is an open question at which particular time it is appropriate to switch from a backward-looking logic of compensation to a forward-looking logic of colour-blind fairness and equal opportunity. As 'equal opportunity' involves issues of sharing and redistribution as opposed to the symbolic practice of recognition, the former is likely to be morally more, not less, demanding (as well as more honest) than the ambiguous and often backfiring practices of attaching a 'positive' stigma on groups through 'reverse discrimination.'[24]

So far we have discussed two classes of objections to group rights. First, given hostile reactions to and opportunity costs of such rights, they may not really be in the best interest of the members of the group that is seemingly favoured by such rights. This is also the case because group rights will typically empower group representatives who can use these rights in order to infringe upon individual rights or discriminate against internal heretics or others whom they consider less 'worthy' members of the group they represent. Second, the damage caused by group rights affects everyone in the political community, be it through the transaction costs caused by multilingualism or through the dynamic of demand escalation and group proliferation set in motion once the first group rights are adopted. It is unclear and cannot be discussed here whether, third, there is also a class of objections based upon the legitimate interests of the majority not to have their (linguistic, religious, etc.) life form disturbed and threatened by overly generous concessions to minorities, particularly if the majority fails to appreciate the legal foundations of polyethnicity as a unqualified 'enrichment' of their social life and national culture (which is, e.g., not the case with most Estonians regarding the Russian minority in that country).

A final objection to group rights must be mentioned. There cannot be any doubt that ascriptive groups exist in modern societies whose members attach great value and significance to the practice and preservation of group identity. Neither can there be any doubt that members of groups suffer often severe disadvantages due to the fact that they belong to and identify with the group. The denial of the right to express and practise their identity and the attachment of negative sanctions and deprivations to those who bear the marks of ascribed identity is an injustice that stands in the way of the consolidation of a homogeneous citizenship status, which, in turn, is an essential precondition for democratic stability. For if the belonging to the political community and the equal liberty it guarantees is put in question, a type of conflict arises that the highly precarious regime form of liberal democracy cannot easily cope with. What does not follow, however, from this set of considerations is that the integration of groups into civil society is best served by granting them group rights, as opposed to individual rights (including the standard rights of religious and cultural freedom and the right to form voluntary associations) and social rights.

These sceptical considerations apply all the more as there is an obvious intergroup difference in the chances of groups to acquire group rights. For the willingness of majorities to grant group rights to minorities is contingent upon both properties of the minority in question and properties, perceptions, and considerations of the majority.

As far as minorities are concerned, their struggle for rights will succeed more easily the larger the group is and the more political resources it has at its disposal due to its size and visibility. If the group in question is an ethnic group, it will also benefit from the presence of nearby ethnic patron states of the same ethnicity. Similarly, in the case of religious groups international religious organizations (such as the Roman Catholic Church or Islamic theocracies) will mobilize effective support. Moreover, international examples, policy moves, and role models can both encourage minorities and discourage their opponents in the struggle for group rights, as is indicated by the advances of feminist movements that have been a distinctively international phenomenon throughout the OECD world and beyond in the 1970s and 1980s. Inversely, if the group is relatively small or highly dispersed, if it is poorly organized, does not enjoy the patronage of transnational forces or movements, and does not enjoy the moral advantage of being able to trace its plight back to previous unfairness, now recognized as such, committed by the majority's state (all of which applies to the Romany in east central Europe), then the acquisition of minority rights will be a vastly more difficult matter. Finally, it is likely that those minorities will be given priority in the granting of group rights who are most similar and show the greatest affinity in terms of cultural (phenotypic, ethnic, linguistic, and religious) traits.[25] From the point of view of the majority which is called upon to grant group rights, all depends upon how strongly it values 'diversity.' The belief that 'interaction with different cultures, belief systems and presumptions makes us smarter'[26] is typically not shared by everyone in the majority,[27] nor does it apply to every minority. By the same logic, some groups may be branded as having no potential for 'making us smarter.' Beyond the appreciation of diversity, two additional points play a role in motivating recognition.[28] First, group rights will be conceded more easily if there is no fear of proliferation, that is, no expectation that group rights, once granted to one group, will soon be demanded by other groups as well. That is to say, the group to which rights are conceded must be in some plausible sense singular, so as to preclude proliferation of demands for rights with its incalculable implications. Second, the majority that is to grant the rights will be more forthcoming in doing so if it has reasons to expect that, once these rights are granted, a durable balance will be reached. That is to say, demands for group rights should not be seen as potentially instrumental for the acquisition of further group rights, and thus as the initial step in a process of escalation eventually leading to break-up of the political community.[29] Thus the hypothesis is that majorities tend to grant group rights most readily to minorities of which there are the least reasons for the concern that the granting of such rights will trigger the dynamics of proliferation or escalation.

Conclusion

Of the four principal strategies that democracies have available to consolidate a homogeneous *demos* and implement the ideal of citizenship – civil, social, political, and 'identity group' rights – the last one is less promising in its effects than those belonging to the previous three 'generations.' Equalizing citizenship rights by granting special group rights to minorities is at best an ambiguous formula because the questions both of what constitutes a 'group' and of what is the adequate and sufficient amount of 'rights' remain contested and tend to give rise to the dynamics of proliferation and escalation. As the number of groups, the groups' identity, the strength of the sense of group allegiance on the part of members, the durability of such allegiance, and the alleged suffering resulting from the state's policy of 'colour-blindness' all do not lend themselves to easy and unobtrusive measurement, group issues are susceptible to tribalistic political entrepreneurship. As a consequence, group rights (other than sub-territorial rights to self-government at the municipal or state level) have a strong potential for further dividing rather than unifying the encompassing political community, and of weakening civic republican loyalties and commitments. This is also the case because any recognition of political groups and their rights elevates the status of the collective recipient of these rights relative to those potential groups that are not, or not yet, considered worthy of being granted such rights, with new unfairnesses being implied by the very method of compensating for unfairness.

Individual civic, political, and social rights, including the right to form civic as well as religious associations and to mobilize for support through fair access to the media, appear fully sufficient to voice the concerns of 'ascriptive' groups (Kukathas 1991; Tamir 1993). That applies, of course, with the proviso that governments are effectively hindered (if need be, through the supervisory role performed by international juridical institutions) to curtail the individual rights of categories of their citizens for the sake of fostering 'national unity.' Moreover, social rights that can equally be claimed by all citizens will effectively compensate for categorical disadvantages suffered by groups. In fact, the implementation of social rights (to education, health, housing, labour-market access, etc.) that would redeem the liberal promise of equal opportunity are both a more demanding and more effective way to accommodate group conflict, compared to the symbolic politics of 'recognizing' groups through the costless politics of assigning them collective rights. There is neither a demonstrable need for, nor a innocuous way to create and administer, a fourth generation of rights in response to identity conflicts.

Notes

The author has received helpful comments from David Abraham, Rainer Dombois, Bob Goodin, Peter A. Kraus, Jacob T. Levy, Bernhard Peters, Ulrich K. Preuss, and Philippe C. Schmitter. They are gratefully acknowledged for helping to improve this essay, which is a modified and expanded version of the text that appears in S. Saberwal and H. Sievers, eds., *Rules, Laws, Constitutions* (New Delhi: Sage 1997). This text is reprinted by permission of the author and the publisher, from *Journal of Political Philosophy* 6 (1998).

1 'It is important to stress that democracy is a way to govern a state and that, therefore, in countries where the existence of the state is in question ... it is not possible to talk about a transition to democracy ... To put it simply, no state – no democracy. Stateness [is] a requirement for political democracy' (Linz 1996, 6–7, 9). Incidentally, it is not entirely clear what this means regarding the potential democratic quality of the European Union, which lacks not only a pre-established stateness, but also a fixed territorial extension.

2 At best, it might be said that the democratic regime form propagates itself through imitation effects – arguably in the same way as the nation-state has internationally spread itself as a political form during the 'spring of the people' throughout nineteenth-century continental Europe.

3 Note that the latter case is different from the perfectly normal democratic adoption of immigration laws, because these become effective only after a 'foreign' subject has 'voluntarily' (i.e., in ways other than through the discretion of some domestic authority) declared his or her intent to become part of the domestic citizenry.

4 It helps if at least one of the units to be separated is an island, as in the separation of Singapore and Malaysia.

5 The empirical test of homogeneity is behavioural: Will those defeated in the democratic political process, in particular 'structural' minorities, still prefer to stay part of that community? Or do they show tendencies of escaping or seceding from that community or of abandoning their role and obligations within it?

6 For a strong feminist critique of universalist citizenship and its opposition to identity group representation, see Young 1989.

7 Much of the legal and philosophical discussion of the issue of group exemption from the duties of citizenship is of course focused on the Old Order Amish and the *Yoder* v *Wisconsin* decision of the Supreme Court.

The question, again, is whether the permission granted to one group to (partially, cf. Spinner 1994) drop out of citizenship generates second-order effects of undermining civic commitments more broadly and/or of punishing the beneficiaries of exemption with hostile (though informal) exclusionary responses.

8 I disregard here and in the following those social and economic group-specific rights that are designed to compensate members of specific groups for the consequences of past and present discrimination at school, in neighbourhoods, in the media, and particularly in the job market.

9 Upon closer inspection, not even that turns out to be true. There are a number of cases in post-Communist central east Europe where majorities of the respective titular nation assign to themselves, constitutionally and through their citizenship laws, a privileged status so as to prevent the alleged danger of 'contamination' of the majority's identity with 'alien' linguistic, ethnic, and religious influences coming from internal minorities. Cases in point are Estonia, Latvia, Slovakia, and Bulgaria.

10 There are also structural minorities which are justly oppressed; most people would probably consider drug dealers or child molesters as cases in point.

11 Groups can also claim group rights that are in no way 'oppressed' or unfairly deprived of the recognition of their identity. In fact, they may be ruling minorities. But that can happen only under non-democratic regime forms, for example, South Africa under apartheid. Thus, a full account of all types of beneficiaries of group rights would have to include ruling or otherwise privileged minorities, oppressed minorities, and majorities (such as members of the 'titular' nation).

12 A dramatically extreme case is that of the Black population in South Africa. While constituting a vast majority in the general population, Blacks were until recently denied full citizen rights and, as a consequence, access to political, economic, and other elite positions.

13 This collective form of the attribution of rights is not to be confused with other forms of group privileges, such as, for instance, tax privileges granted in some countries to the publishers of academic books. While in this example no publisher is able to opt out of the privilege that is categorically accorded to the industry, he or she may well individually opt out of the industry itself – unless we deal with an authoritarian state-corporatist regime which excludes exactly this option.

14 It is worth bearing in mind the nominal nature of that 'privilege.' For, first, preferential treatment of group members can give rise to second-order effects of retaliatory discrimination and hostility, coming from the majority

or from competing groups, against which the group's members may be entirely defenceless (see below). Second, status rights for minorities can be openly double-edged, an example being provisions (granting but also) limiting the admission of Jews to a fixed percentage of the student body that used to be in force in British institutions of higher education.

15 The question is not quite as rhetorical as it sounds. An example is the 'gendering' of the German language that has been adopted as an administrative practice in a number of states and institutional sectors during the 1980s. The result is that all nominally male forms in legal texts must be complemented by the female form (like in actor/actress), for which the German language provides abundant opportunities. This grammatical advancement of the status of women must not naturally be desired by all women. Objections include that the readability of the text of legal documents and journalistic prose, for women and men alike, is highly adversely affected by this linguistic regime, as more than half of all nouns are subject to such gendering duplication; another objection is that the grammatical status advancement of women is just symbolic, not real.

16 The policy of German local governments of forming as consultative bodies *Ausländerbeiräte* (foreigners' councils) is a case in point. People represented by such councils often belong to half a dozen or more different nationalities. It would never occur to them having their identity cast in terms of being 'foreigners,' an identity label that is entirely shaped by the perceptions and preferences of the domestic majority population.

17 Soysal (1995, 8) provides the example of the Netherlands where the ethnic minority policy 'officializes' a number of ethnic immigrant groups but leaves out the Chinese and the Pakistani for the reason that, as she quotes an official, 'they are assumed to have no problems with their participation in Dutch society.' That obviously raises the question: whose problems? What pretends to be respect for the 'truly deserving' minorities may also be read as an arbitrary administrative coding practice driven by opportunistic considerations.

18 To illustrate, let me take an example from social and economic rights and a case that I have been involved in. German universities have instituted 'women's promotion plans' that provide special grants for which women at advanced stages of their academic career can apply. When applying for such a grant, one female colleague was told by administrators of the program that, although being highly qualified on the basis of her academic record, she still could not be considered as her files showed that she is, although a women, *not a mother*. This indicates how flexibly and opportunistically criteria of group membership can be handled.

19 If the group code is so widely applied, what happens to those who do not identify with any of the groups? Is there a residual 'group' of all those lacking group markers? To assume this would be following the logic of American Protestant sects who divide the universe into two major sects: their own sect of true Christians and the sect they oppose – namely, that of 'secular humanists.' Such sectarian social ontology is also evident in some feminist writings. As all women are seen as united and self-identified *as* women, there must also be a dominant conspiracy of 'malehood.'

20 Note, however, that the relationship between (relative) group size and the ease with which the group obtains collective rights may be U-shaped. Very small ethnic minorities can be granted rights by the majority because the risk that the disruptive mechanisms of escalation or proliferation will set in as a consequence is deemed negligible by the majority.

21 An elaborate classification of the very different kinds of group rights that are to be found in practice is provided in Levy 1997.

22 A blatant, though not singular, example of 'secondary discrimination on the grounds of reverse discrimination' is this. In German state universities, candidates for full professorships are short-listed and ranked by the university and appointed by the state ministry of higher education. As universities know that ministries are committed to increasing the (incredibly low) proportion of women in the professorate, they can be virtually certain that a single female name, should it appear on the short list, will very likely be chosen for appointment, and the preference order of the list will be overruled. As a consequence, hiring committees (irrespective of their gender composition) have a rational interest in keeping any female applicant (unless she is consensually ranked first) off the short list in order to preserve the university's 'autonomy' to express priorities and its chance to have its priorities respected. (Thanks to Gerd Grözinger for pointing out this mechanism to me .)

23 As shorthand for 'recognized duties,' we may think of the following subtraction formula: Duties is the amount of operative bindingness of social norms that remains in force of its nominal bindingness after (a) all opportunities for unsanctioned violation have been eliminated and (b) all excuses for non-compliance have been invalidated.

24 Bauböck (forthcoming) argues the following with respect to ethnic groups who have been subject in the past to the deprivation of the economic and political rights and 'second-class citizenship': 'These effects are so pervasive that equal individual rights are clearly insufficient. Group-differentiated programmes of community development and affirmative action are needed to overcome them.' I disagree on both counts. If individual rights,

including 'positive' rights, are deemed to be 'insufficient,' they need to be augmented (in courts and legislatures) rather than supplemented, particularly as group rights are unlikely to do the job except under the most favourable of circumstances (under which they appear least needed).

25 Note, however, that 'similarity' is itself a social construct that would have to be validated by both sides involved. For instance, for the outside observer Roman Catholicism and Orthodoxy may not appear a matter of significant divergence of religious identities. That, however, is not the view taken by either the Serbs or the Croats.

26 As stated in an Op-Ed comment in the *New York Times*, 2 April 1996.

27 Bauböck (forthcoming) persuasively asks the question: 'What could convince a true believer that it is better for her to live in a society together with people of other faiths, agnostics and atheists rather than in a society where her religion is shared by all?' Only religiously unaffiliated actors are likely to develop a preference for institutionalized religious diversity through group rights, if only for the (slightly cynical) reason that that arrangement would maximize her or his chance to be left alone by any of them. A more respectable argument for the intrinsic value of diversity is that it affords 'the reflexivity that results from experiencing other cultures' (ibid.) and, supposedly, the opportunity for self-scrutinizing the limitations of one's own culture; but it is not evident that this opportunity, so ubiquitous in modern society, should be contingent upon the presence of group rights.

28 In a brief filed with the U.S. Supreme Court in August 1997, the Clinton Administration elaborated an argument as to why adherence to affirmative action does not only make 'us' smarter, but, more specifically, the police more effective. 'Local law enforcement agencies can demonstrate a compelling need for a diverse work force that justifies the carefully tailored use of race in employment decisions. For instance, if an undercover officer is needed to infiltrate a racially homogeneous gang, a law enforcement agency must have the flexibility to assign an officer of the same race to that task' (quoted in the *New York Times*, 23 August 1997). It is, however, in no way evident that such flexibility could not equally well – or better – be achieved within a framework of equal opportunity (as opposed to preferential) hiring practices.

29 This fear of escalation explains the stubbornness with which governments in central east Europe have resisted the demands for ethnic minority group rights, particularly so in Slovakia, Bulgaria, and Romania. The anticipation on the part of the majority is that, once we grant the first step, we are bound to be sliding down a slippery slope: from cultural rights to

language rights, from language rights to an autonomous educational and
media regime, from there to successful mobilization for territorial self-
government, and from there to secession or fusion with some 'historically
hostile' neighbouring state, with either international or civil war as the
necessary by-product. These seemingly obsessive fears are often not entirely irrational, as both sides to the conflict know, and know that the other
side knows, that the region has a history of imperial control, with the
present minority being just a remaining residue of some former imperial
power – as are the Turks in Bulgaria, Hungarians in Slovakia and Romania, or Russians in Estonia. The result is that the constitutions of these
post-communist countries are not only weak on minority rights, but often
strongly proclaiming the cultural and ethnic majority rights of the respective titular nation (Preuss 1995).

References

Bauböck, Rainer. Forthcoming. 'Liberal Justifications for Group Rights.'In
    Christian Joppke and Steven Lukes, eds., *Multicultural Questions*. Oxford:
    Oxford University Press.
Buchanan, Allen. 1991. *Secession. The Morality of Political Divorce*. Boulder, CO:
    Westview.
Connor, Walker. 1994. *Ethnonationalism: The Quest for Understanding*. Prince-
    ton, NJ: Princeton University Press.
Elster, Jon. 1996. 'Ulysses Unbound: Studies in Rationality and Precommit-
    ment.' Unpublished manuscript.
Gitlin, Todd. 1995. *The Twilight of Common Dreams: Why America Is Wracked by
    Culture Wars*. New York: Holt
Glazer, Nathan. 1983. *Ethnic Dilemmas: 1964–1982*. Cambridge, MA: Harvard
    University Press.
Habermas, Jürgen. 1996. *Die Einbeziehung des Anderen. Studien zur politischen
    Theorie*. Frankfurt: Suhrkamp.
Hirschman, Albert O. 1994. 'Social Conflicts as Pillars of Democratic Market
    Societies.' *Political Theory* 22: 203–18.
Joppke, Christian. 1996. 'Multiculturalism and Immigration: A Comparison
    of the United States, Germany, and Great Britain.' *Theory and Society* 25:
    449–500.
Kukathas, Chandran. 1991. *The Fraternal Conceit: Liberal vs. Collectivist Ideas of
    Community*. Sidney: Centre for Independent Studies.
Kymlicka, Will. 1995. *Multicultural Citizenship*. Oxford: Clarendon Press.

– 1996. 'Interpreting Group Rights.' *The Good Society* 6/2: 8–11.

Kymlicka, Will, and Ian Shapiro, eds. 1997. *Ethnicity and Group Rights* (Nomos xxxix). New York: New York University Press.

Levy, Jacob T. 1997. 'Classifying Cultural Rights.' Pp. 22–66 in Will Kymlicka and Ian Shapiro, eds., *Ethnicity and Group Rights* (Nomos xxxix). New York: New York University Press.

Linz, Juan J. 1996. 'Democratization and Types of Democracies: New Tasks for Comparativists.' Unpublished paper, Yale University.

Linz, Juan J., and Alfred Stepan. 1996. *Problems of Democratic Transition and Consolidation. Southern Europe, South America and Post-Communist Europe.* Baltimore: Johns Hopkins University Press.

Preuss, Ulrich K. 1995. 'Patterns of Constitutional Evolution and Change in Eastern Europe.' Pp. 95–128 in J.J. Hesse and N. Johnson, eds., *Constitutional Change in Europe*. Oxford: Oxford University Press.

Schmitter, Philippe C., and Terry Lynn Karl. 1991. 'What Democracy Is ... and Is Not.' *Journal of Democracy* 3/3 (Summer): 75–88.

Soysal, Yasemin. 1995. 'Boundaries and Identity: Immigrants in Europe.' Unpublished paper, Harvard University, Sociology Department.

Spinner, Jeff. 1994. *The Boundaries of Citizenship. Race, Ethnicity, and Nationality in the Liberal State.* Baltimore: Johns Hopkins University Press.

Tamir, Yael. 1993. *Liberal Nationalism.* Princeton, NJ: Princeton University Press.

Young, Iris M. 1989. 'Polity and Group Difference: A Critique of the Ideal of Universal Citizenship.' *Ethics* 99: 250–74.

Part Three:

Prospects for Social Democracy

Introduction

In Part Three, Ronald Beiner, Dietrich Rueschemeyer, Anthony Atkinson, and Edward Broadbent focus on social rights and the prospects for greater economic equality in the context of new forms of governance. Recognizing the substantial continuing impact of economic globalization, they contemplate how social democracies can respond through social rights and welfare.

Ronald Beiner provides a normative analysis of how global capitalism is eroding the discrete decision-making powers of political communities to determine their own destinies. He fears that global capitalism is invading the political domain to the point where that domain's ability to provide for the collective determination of priorities and aspirations is seriously threatened. Against that threat, he reasserts the values of social-democratic politics, including a commitment to the modern welfare state and its redistributive mechanisms, its discourse of social justice, and its affirmation of liberal principles with respect to representative democracy and the mixed economy. The neo-liberal emphasis on individual responsibility must be shifted towards social responsibility to the less privileged, backed up by the strong agency of the state to articulate and coordinate collective responsibilities.

Beiner identifies with the social-democratic project of seeing social justice as a problem of morality, rather than as a problem of economy as Marx did. In Beiner's view, social justice can be achieved within an appropriately governed capitalism rather than beyond or in opposition to it. The social-democratic project is currently faced with the structural problem that nationalist and centralized forms of socialism have 'dropped off the political map,' and the resulting void means that social democracy is now largely unchallenged from the left. At the same time a discourse of state fiscal responsibility prevails, with a resulting emphasis on deficit reduction and balanced budgets as opposed to the challenges of social inequality. With the aid of an overarching neoliberal mentality, this discourse has become common sense to the point where social democrats themselves have become part of it. Indeed, this discourse often does make sense. For example, a higher level of public borrowing is a significant problem because the result is both greater dividends and greater leverage over government policy by the capitalist lenders.

Beiner finds bald neo-liberalism easy to criticize. For example, Hayck's view of procedural justice as simply honouring the multiplicity of discrete individual contracts is clearly not going to provide for collective responsibility, in general, and social responsibility to the less privileged, in particular. The absolutism of individual liberty expressed in neo-liberal ideology can be easily exposed as simply an apology for greed.

Beiner introduces Walzer's collectivist premises about social justice to advance his argument. Walzer's position is that social justice will not emerge from a regime of individual rights that fashion autonomy, but rather from the articulation of communal standards arising out of shared experiences. These standards will not necessarily be fully embedded in a society's social institutions, but they may be evident at the community level and put into effect to varying degrees regardless.

Beiner advances the view that social rights need to be seen not just as the rights of individuals, but also as duties connected with full membership (citizenship) in the political community. The paramount duty is to ensure that fellow citizens are not 'crushed in the marketplace of everyday life' to the point where they 'are effectively denied the conditions of meaningful citizenship.' Beiner advocates a shift from the now unrealized ideal of a general socialization of property, to the ideal of the 'socialization of perils of living in a modern society.' If humans have been collectively responsible for risks posed by the modern advance of science and technology – risks to the environment, health, and financial security – then they should also be collectively responsible for the amelioration of those risks.

Beiner turns to the theory of Rawls as an example of an approach that is unworkable. Rawls tries to undermine claims of individual desert by arguing that individual deserts are a product of social and biological forces beyond the individual's control. This move allows him to advance claims that individual assets belong to a social pool of assets that can be redistributed without significant incursions on individual rights and entitlements. However, following Nozick's critique, Beiner points out that Rawls fails to establish why individual assets should devolve to society (the nation-state) as the agency of redistribution. Rawls's analysis results in welfare liberalism, which emphasizes individual liberty and fulfilment, rather than social democracy, which emphasizes solidarity.

Beiner quarrels with Walzer's decision to take as the normative standard whatever is the prevailing standard in the political community being analysed. For example, within Walzer's framework, if a political community is especially committed to individual liberty, alternative normative conceptions are not proffered. For Beiner, the wants of socially responsible citizenship must prevail over the wants of individual consumers in the private marketplace. These social wants can be nurtured only by an egalitarian web of relationships based on moral criteria. It is this web that constitutes democracy. This is the web not only of government, but also of all aspects of social, cultural, and economic life.

Beiner sets the normative tone for the other essays in Part Three. Dietrich Rueschemeyer observes that capitalism and democracy are two sides of the same coin, and that this coinage is a currency in social inequality. In particular, class inequality, evidenced, for example, by wealth and income gaps, is central to the dynamics of democracy. Rueschemeyer proceeds to analyse these dynamics.

Rueschemeyer delineates the core features of 'real or practical democracy' as consisting of free and repeated elections of representatives by a fully enfranchised population; the accountability of those representatives to the state machinery; and rights to expression and association. In combination, these features promise to reduce inequality through power sharing, and through sustained efforts to ameliorate the starker forms of economic, cultural, social, and political inequality.

Democracy arises in the context of class inequality, and in conflicts created in the course of capitalist development. Capitalism is associated with the development of democracy because it brings about a change in the balance of class power, for example, the emergence of an organized working class. However, there is considerable variation in what transpires, depending upon the context and the class forces involved. The interests pursued by each class must articulate with the processes of organization available in the specific context, and with how those organizational processes relate to the versions of class interest that coexist and compete with each other. The process is hegemonic, with relations among classes having a fundamental influence on the chances for democracy.

Rueschemeyer argues that the strongest pro-democratic influence is from classes that are relatively deprived of power resources apart from their power of collective organization. Since organization is power, alliances are crucial. Alliances enhance the power of collective organization and augment resources. However, the capacity of alliances to enhance democracy again varies by organizational processes and context. For example, in some contexts farmers have been strong and successful allies of the working class, but in other contexts they have aligned with landlords and been an obstacle to democracy. The middle class sometimes coalesces with the working class and overlaps with it substantially in ideologies and interests. On the other hand, the middle class has sometimes aligned with anti-democratic hegemonies and served as an accomplice in the denial of democracy.

These varied processes, contexts, and outcomes of class relations and democracy indicate that wide participation in public affairs by different classes is not, in itself, a sign of better democracy. Such wide participation in a 'dense civil society' may be against democracy, as was the case in Nazi Germany. What must be fostered is autonomous self-organization of groups and strata positively disposed towards democracy, and mechanisms that protect those groups and strata against anti-democratic hegemonies and that enhance their ability to pursue their interests.

Rueschemeyer emphasizes that democratic development is better explained by class inequality as compared with other dimensions of inequality. He argues that, while gender relations are obviously important for relations of democracy – the life situations of women in some contexts have improved considerably – women's issues are typically less important than class issues in known histories of democracy. Rueschemeyer observes that fragmentation along lines of race and ethnicity is often negatively associated with democracy. Racial and ethnic divisions cut across, deepen, and weaken class differences. Racial and ethnic groups sometimes constitute their own class-like activities and identities that perpetuate divisive fragmentation.

Rueschemeyer sees cultural inequality in part as the symbolic 'politics' component of class inequality. Different cultural groups use their preferred symbols, rituals, and myths to constitute the political-culture realities of a class society. In this formulation, class conflict in political culture becomes a dominant feature of the cultural landscape.

In addressing the levelling or equalizing effects of democracy, Rueschemeyer turns to questions of economic inequality. He concludes that there is no clear statistical relation between the level of democracy and the level of social-security provision. Again democracy, including greater economic equality, depends on the correct balance of self-organization capacities and coalitions of subordinate classes and their ideological allegiances to democracy. It also depends crucially on economic growth, which makes some redistribution possible without sharply reducing the privileges of the 'haves.' Rueschemeyer feels that the current situation with respect to social-security provision is much more uneven and less unidirectional than the rhetoric of economic globalization suggests. There remains substantial democratic support for many universal programs, for example, in the areas of health, schooling, day care, and elderly care. This support is bolstered by enormous institutional and professional infrastructures of health, education, and welfare that continue to promote social-security initiatives and have iatrogenic effects. The fact that labour-market changes are affecting many former middle-class 'haves' who are now unemployed may also have a long-term sobering effect on the middle class in general, making them more sensitive to social-security needs.

Regarding communitarian solutions to problems of governance, Rueschemeyer observes that social and political participation in general grows with increasing levels of state social-security provision. As he expresses it, 'moves towards social and participatory democracy buttress each other as well as reinforce the underpinnings of elementary, formal democracy.' In contrast, neo-liberalism suffers because it remains too embedded in formal democracy. The privileged who initially experience the sweetness of neo-liberalism eventually realize that decay is setting in and that their political roots may rot because their participatory underpinnings are weakened. Rueschemeyer points to new democracies in Latin America as stark evidence of this effect. There, multinational financial institutions – underpinned by the neo-liberal ideology and financial stability of their own primary nation-state contexts – are able to leverage 'marketization, privatization, and shrinking the state' on behalf of a globally privileged few, and to the detriment of the less privileged locals.

Rueschemeyer observes that, if democracy becomes too deep and equalizing, it may be subject to increasingly intense opposition and containment, and it may even become aborted. Democracy requires class compromise. The more powerful must believe that the system of democratic governance is safely protecting their interests. The more that class interests become sharply opposed, the greater the likelihood that powerful groups will see democracy as merely at their pleasure.

Rueschemeyer worries in particular about the current reign of neo-liberalism in the United States. There are sharply widening gaps in wealth. There is direct moneyed influence on elections. This moneyed regime was recently backed up by a U.S. Supreme Court decision that declared spending money is a freedom equal to freedom of speech, and thus equally protected under the First Amendment. Such neo-liberal moves do not enhance the prospects for democracy. Democracy depends on more traditional notions of liberalism as non-partisanship and as circumscribing the 'haves' in order to open more things up for the 'have-nots.'

Anthony Atkinson contemplates how welfare states can remain vital in the context of economic globalization. He begins with examples of official and media discourse that represent the dominant view on this matter. Welfare states can no longer compete because they are far too expensive; and, because they have perverse consequences which inhibit adjustment and ultimately make them the problem rather than the solution for collective well-being. The recommended solution is to relieve state budgets of the burdens of social-security expenditures.

Atkinson provides data on the wide discrepancy among developed nations in the percentage of the GDP that goes into social security expenditures, with Japan (12 per cent) and the United States (13 per cent) at the low end, and France (23 per cent) and Sweden (25 per cent) at the high end. These data allow him to pose his question figuratively and sharply: 'Is a move in the U.S. direction being forced on us by the globalization of the economy?'

Atkinson emphasizes that there is no straightforward answer to this question. He reviews six interdependent factors in economic globalization that must be analysed. First, the nature and degree of the free movement of capital across capital markets requires examination. Second, the possible loss of export markets because of both the spread of technology and the transfer of production to newly industrializing countries is a factor. Third, analysis is required as to whether there is more competition from imports produced in these countries, in particular because of reduction in trade barriers and transportation costs. Fourth, the degree of increased competition within OECD countries themselves must be analysed, for example, within the North American Free Trade Agreement or the European internal market, because of the same factors. Fifth, there is the consideration of loss of national sovereignty because of fiscal and other policies of neighbouring states. Sixth, one can assess economic globalization in terms of homogenization of consumer tastes.

Atkinson also regards the welfare state as multifaceted with respect to fiscal matters. There are many complexities regarding social transfers, and their relation to other policies such as those governing the labour market. He illustrates with the example of a state that introduces long-term-care insurance that is to be financed by an increase in the employers' payroll tax. In this case there is a need to analyse, among other things, the balance between wage effects, higher-priced goods and services, the possibility of ensuing problems for exports, the possible resulting adjustment lower in the exchange rate which makes imports cheaper, and changing labour agreements.

Atkinson observes that the dominant discourse boils down to cost-benefit analyses, for example, regarding how the welfare state might increase costs by causing unemployment or by adversely affecting other aspects of economic performance such as the rate of growth. He feels that there is particular concern among politicians about unemployment. When political discourse is about not being competitive, the main concern is with jobs because unemployment lowers living standards and related aspects of well-being.

Atkinson focuses on unemployment to again emphasize the complex analyses required to address the question of whether welfare states can compete in a global economy. Quantitative analyses of unemployment and the economy suffer from several limitations. For example, it is difficult to establish causality; aggregate measures of the generosity of benefits are crude; there is a need for more subtle analyses of the time path of responses to unemployment; and complex systemic interrelations within a country's welfare system mean that transnational comparative evidence is very problematic. It is simply not reasonable to isolate a single element of the 'social settlement' such as unemployment and attribute it to some difference in economic performance.

The main problem of dominant discourse about the global economy, including many academic analyses, is economic reductionism. Countries are not simply driven by economic imperatives, but also by political judgment. For example, Atkinson notes that there is now a considerable history of using unemployment benefits to ease structural change. In the present conjuncture, unemployment benefits are important for people who need to change jobs more frequently, retrain, and take risks with respect to their work and need for self-sufficiency. In conjunction with political judgment about other social-security provisions, unemployment insurance provides not only compassion, but also growth in productivity.

Edward Broadbent's focus is precisely on this political judgment regarding the welfare state, which he sees as judgment about social justice and citizenship. This political judgment is heavily dependent upon the political rights of liberalism, combined with a commitment to ameliorate forms of inequality and insecurity that are endemic to capitalism. There must be a particular commitment to social rights, not just political and civil rights, if one is to have a 'sharing and caring' nation-state.

Broadbent observes that many Western countries have moved away from the relative consensus across the spectrum of political parties that gave use to the rights-based welfare state. He recalls a period when a stronger welfare state constantly articulated moralities beyond the marketplace in its everyday practical decision making, and when this decision making was more forward-looking and less ad hoc. During this period the basic question was what constitutes a dignified life, and the prevailing view was that the state should be integral to the process of not only answering this question, but putting in place citizens' rights and welfare programs that enhance human dignity. In particular, there was a commitment to making money incomes less important in their social consequences. Social justice was to be achieved with 'equal social incomes running side-by-side with unequal money incomes.'

Broadbent joins Rueschemeyer in recognizing the importance of class compromise. In the welfare-state model, the less fortunate accept a degree of economic inequality within the market system but gain equality of social rights, including some elements of economic equalization. The major holders of capital achieve social peace for relatively smooth operation of their market economy. Broadbent argues that in strong welfare states, middle-class life is the shared experience of a universal rights-based social agenda backed up by the state, not the result of individuals striving on their own initiative to be successful. He might have added that it is the retreat from this agenda, and the collective subjective reality it fosters, that is reflected in the contemporary middle-class *angst*.

Broadbent argues that there is a need to balance self-interest – which is required to produce a level of wealth that in turn ensures an adequate commitment to social rights – with altruistic collective interest and well-being. He feels that there is a major imbalance at the present time, with self-interest being turned into selfishness. He attributes this imbalance to the popularity of the view that altruism has gone too far, that it has undercut self-realization as well as the efficient production of wealth. In this view, the virtuous, civil life is achieved by acting as if the social is not significant and the individual in pursuit of personal satisfaction is the most virtuous. Welfare shifts from being a 'hurrah' word associated with the common good to become a 'boo' word, associated with the 'burden' of having to provide for the de-selected poor.

Broadbent notes the irony that this dominant view may have been fostered by the success of the welfare state. In the comfort of relative economic well-being, people come to believe that their prosperity is a result of their own efforts rather than the complex interinstitutional efforts of the welfare state. Neo-liberalism convinces people of their own virtue, and opens them 'to the lures of private solutions to what had once been seen as common problems.' This neo-liberal move to individual responsibility and private solutions has arisen in the context of increasing economic inequality.

Broadbent points to some counter-trends that he sees as hopeful for social justice and citizenship. The Conservative party in the United Kingdom was removed from office in 1997 after nineteen years largely because of its regressive health and education policies. A socialist-dominated national assembly was elected in France in 1997 in reaction to intended reductions in social benefits to meet the deficit-management criteria of the planned European currency. Broadbent also finds that there is a healthy, continuing debate about how to meld private and public desires, and personal and community responsibilities, through the political order.

Broadbent joins Atkinson in stressing that strong political decision making is required to shape the allocation of resources beyond the marketplace. This decision making must include the taking of resources from the marketplace in the interests of social, economic, and cultural rights and responsibilities. At the same time, Broadbent argues that it is not possible to go back to the welfare-state model that worked reasonably well in the past. That model is not practical in the present realities of lower rates of economic growth, greater proportional costs of social programs, the restructuring of employment markets in the context of technological change, and the globalization of markets. The reduction of deficits, bureaucratic inefficiencies, and population dependencies are a good thing, as long as they take place within a framework of social citizenship.

Broadbent concludes with six suggestions about how to produce a framework of social justice and citizenship that will make life more dignified than simply 'an incessant quest for security and consumption.' First, he calls for ideological leadership from politicians that emphasizes both the positive role of private-sector competition, efficiency, and private gain and the balancing role of state-guaranteed social and economic rights. Second, there is a need for greater recognition of how citizens' rights are related to responsibilities on each side of the class divide. Third, there is the practical requirement of a reversal in the increasingly regressive tax system as a contributor to economic inequality. Fourth, as a corollary to the previous point, there is a need to emphasize the political importance of progressive and substantial taxation for both social rights and social peace. Fifth, Broadbent encourages more informed public debate on the costs and benefits of the welfare state. Citing Atkinson, he calls for analyses of how social expenditures by the public sector relieve burdens on the private sector and contribute to competitive advantage. Sixth, he urges more informed debate on the core issues in globalization.

The effects of globalization are real, in particular their effects on nationhood, social justice, and citizenship. Nations are still needed to provide a model of citizenship and civility in a world of markets without borders. Along with Held, and against the scepticism of Magnusson, Broadbent sees some hope in new international regimes of sovereignty. Again, civilized political judgment at many levels is required. The economy must always be made political.

8

Is Social Democracy Dead?

RONALD BEINER

We live, we are told unceasingly, in an era of globalization. What globalization means, fundamentally, is the triumph of capitalism. And since this triumph is by definition global rather than local, it is a triumph from which there is no escape. Globalization means that the capacity of all states to determine their own economic and social destiny inexorably declines, and decisions about social and economic policy are increasingly dictated by imperatives of transnational markets in a way that is not likely to favour egalitarian or social-democratic outcomes. What's left of the hope for social democracy (let alone socialism) in the face of these globalizing realities? Speaking as a political philosopher, that is, as one who is concerned with how different possible social orders fare with respect to normative justification rather than with how they fare out there in the empirical world, I don't feel obliged to let the imperatives of the contemporary world dictate my reflections – however much these imperatives *do* dictate the governance of actual states.

Perhaps this is putting the point too negatively (it sounds as if it is conceded in advance that political theory is limited to idle dreaming), so let me characterize in a more positive way the role of political philosophy vis-à-vis evolving empirical social orders. If it really were true that in an era of globalization, state sovereignty – the deliberate decision making of discrete political communities – necessarily succumbs to the imperatives of transnational competition, this would mean that we live in an age in which the space of political agency necessarily shrinks. Politics is the domain of human life that provides for the collective determination of shared priorities and means of fulfilling shared aspirations. If agency is trumped by a worldwide process of the disposal of capital and the setting of levels of public services, politics itself as I have defined it becomes a dubious possibility. Here political philosophy to some extent comes to the rescue, for merely to conceive of a range of divergent social orders that can be submitted to normative reflection (with a view to ranking them normatively) is already to reassert the idea of political agency. In this sense, the idea of globalization goes with a fatalistic concession to shrinking agency, and therefore shrinking politics; correspondingly, it is the duty of the political philosopher to sustain the hope of agency by refusing to forgo the special demands of this particular intellectual enterprise: imagining different shapes of possible social order so that they can be compared and ranked normatively.

I've stated as clearly as I can that the questions that concern me are normative rather than empirical ones. But let me first say a little bit about what one associates with the idea of social democracy (most of this will be fairly obvious), and then begin to draw the discussion onto the plane of political philosophy.

We all know that social democracy is an egalitarian political commitment located somewhere along the continuum joining socialism and liberalism. The notable features of social-democratic politics include a strong commitment to the modern welfare state and to the redistributive function of the state, an affirmation of the classic liberal principles associated with representative democracy and the mixed economy, an embrace of political reformism (as opposed to the revolutionary tradition stemming from Karl Marx), and a defining allegiance to the moral ideal of social justice. Although it is impossible to situate social democracy on the liberal–socialist continuum with any precision, it suffices as a rough identification to say that social democrats stand somewhere to the left of liberals and somewhere to the right of socialists. It is considerably easier to define social democracy in relation to the more far-flung political alternatives – namely, libertarian liberalism and Marxist socialism. Libertarians uphold an uncompromising vision of the rights of individuals to resist the redistributive aspirations of the welfare state, whereas social democrats emphasize notions of social responsibility and the duty to come to the aid of less privileged members of the community, along with a firm willingness to employ the power of the state as the agent of these collective responsibilities.

Turning to the other side of the spectrum, one could offer the following characterization of the relation between Marxism and social democracy. Marxism, one might say, sought to 'economize' the idea of social justice, that is, to identify the moral claims of disadvantaged social classes with the advance of a fully rational (post-capitalist) economy. Social democrats, on the other hand, sought to 'remoralize' political economy, that is, to retrieve the question of social justice as a problem of morality rather than economy, and one that might find its solution within capitalism (suitably modified) rather than necessarily beyond and against capitalism. Historically, social democracy arose out of the acknowledgment by the German Marxist Eduard Bernstein, around the turn of the century, that what were presumed to be scientific predictions by Marx of the explosion and demise of capitalism and the consequent triumph of working-class revolutionism, were in fact little more than false prophecies. This acknowledgment of Marxism's spurious promise gave rise to Bernstein's version of revisionist socialism with its emphasis on a parliamentary and reformist pursuit of socialist aims. A comparable political development, begetting social democracy as a middle position between socialism and liberalism, took place in Britain in the late nineteenth/early twentieth century through the vehicle of the Fabian movement (in the latter, one may name as representative figures: Beatrice and Sidney Webb, Graham Wallas, George Bernard Shaw, and H.G. Wells). This Fabian revisionist-socialist tradition in Britain extends up to C.A.R. Crosland's book, *The Future of Socialism* (1956).[1] Viewing social democracy historically as a process of political accommodation with capitalism or with the quasi-capitalist mixed economy, along a course of political evolution in the twentieth century that shades off into welfarist liberalism, an unchastened Marxist would no doubt object that socialism is watered-down Marxism and social democracy is watered-down socialism: a double dilution. The implicit charge here is that social democracy retains no theoretical integrity of its own but simply defines itself by its half-heartedness in relation to the social ideals from which it borrows its real substance. To answer this kind of challenge, one would have to put to one side the question of historical genesis of the social-democratic movement and of its century-long course of development, and to inquire instead at the normative level, asking whether social democracy does indeed name a coherent set of ideas possessing a moral core with its own distinctive (non-parasitic) identity.

Indeed, there is today an even more compelling reason why social democracy must undergo normative re-examination. The 'political geography' with respect to social democracy has changed dramatically in the last decade. This is because more robust forms of socialism, involving nationalization and central control of the economy, have simply dropped off the political map, leaving social democracy more or less unchallenged from the left. (As we sketched at the beginning of this essay, this is precisely why the rhetoric of globalization has taken hold, where globalization refers more or less to the globalization of capitalist imperatives.) This means that egalitarian hopes and aspirations repose on social democracy alone: if social democracy is dead, then the left is dead.

To what extent is there still some life left in the left? It requires no more than a glance at the contemporary political scene within our own political community here in Canada to see the tenuous survival of egalitarian politics even in a country with once-strong social-democratic traditions. The federal New Democratic Party (NDP) can consider itself fortunate to have a parliamentary presence as an official party; but its restored status as a party does little to remedy its marginalization. The governing Liberal party, which used to borrow its ideas from the left, now takes its cue from the right-wing party that forms the Official Opposition. It's true that there are still two provincial NDP governments in Canada, but in Saskatchewan, the fountainhead of social-democratic traditions in this country, the government is an even more rigorous budget-balancer than the present government in Ontario. The Parti Québécois is still nominally a social-democratic party, but, again, it, too, is now as committed to program-slashing and fiscal discipline as the right-wing government in Ontario.

When one casts a glance abroad, the prospects for a viable left-wing politics look equally grim. It's true that nominally centre-left parties now hold executive office in the United States and Britain. But in both cases, these parties have made themselves electable again by forsaking any serious egalitarian commitments. Recall the egalitarian rhetoric that President Clinton permitted himself to express in his first Inaugural Address: 'We must provide for our nation the way a family provides for its children ... In serving, we recognize a simple but powerful truth – we need each other. And we must care for one another ... [in] the knowledge that, but for fate, we – the fortunate and the unfortunate – might have been each other.' But far from remaining faithful to this authentically social-democratic aspiration, Clinton's administration yielded to the anti-welfarism of the Republican party, and Clinton now congratulates himself for balancing the budget rather than for offering any kind of serious challenge to social inequality in America. In Britain, as well, the secret of electoral success consists in appropriating the ground of one's conservative adversaries rather than abiding with the traditions of the British left. Nor is this a great mystery. Britain and the United States have strong economies and (relatively) low unemployment, whereas states in Europe with stronger social programs and more robust welfare provisions suffer stagnant economies, and in some cases shockingly high unemployment.[2] Nor is it any great surprise why middle-class voters would fail to see anything attractive in chronic budget deficits, why they would prefer lower taxes to higher taxes, and why they would grow impatient with problems of welfare dependency. For that matter, even committed social democrats have good reason to favour balanced budgets since higher public borrowing means both larger dividends and vastly greater leverage over government policy for capitalist bankers. These are not, to put it mildly, propitious circumstances for an ambitious left-wing agenda. Hence the need to revisit the normative basis of egalitarian politics.

The normative challenge to the welfare state would be more manageable if the challenge came only from the libertarian right. Libertarian critiques of the welfare state are easily dismissed because they are either based on implausible absolutist conceptions of individual liberty or simply intended to perform an apologetical function on behalf of human greed. Much less easy to dismiss are challenges that come from egalitarians, for there are such challenges. I'm thinking, for instance, of thoughtful social philosophers like Christopher Lasch and Alasdair MacIntyre, both of whom have solid egalitarian credentials but who are relentlessly hostile to the modern state as the vehicle of social justice.[3] Lasch's view is that all genuine solidarities are local and community-based solidarities; therefore the attempt to advance social equality by having a remote and bureaucratic state dispense entitlements to passive individual recipients of these entitlements is bound to injure the dignity of these recipients of state charity since it is ungrounded in their own communally cultivated sense of agency. Equality must be built from the ground up, founded on community mobilization, neighbourhood self-help, and collective self-empowerment. For MacIntrye, too, all genuine solidarities are local solidarities, and for him as well, the intention of the state to promote social justice is corrupted by the incapacity of the modern state to be anything other than a mere 'bureaucratic mechanism' – 'a tree dead from half-way up.'[4] MacIntyre's view is that the fact that there is, within most liberal polities, an electoral alternation between parties with less generous and more generous welfare policies in no way redeems the liberal state from its fundamental complicity in the basic structures of capitalist modernity.[5] If, as

MacIntyre holds, the modern state is one of the monstrosities of modern life, then one is obliged to conclude that the welfare state, too, is normatively indefensible. There is no easy way to rebut these challenges; indeed, I think they have to be taken very seriously if we are serious about pursuing the task of normative justification.

The starting point for the kind of normative requestioning of social democracy that I want to pursue is an awareness of the diversity of theoretical approaches that present themselves for this purpose. Among the variety of argumentative strategies for the normative justification of social-democratic policies, let us consider a few leading candidates. One theoretical strategy is to argue that all individuals in a liberal society must receive an equitable share of overall social resources in order to explore and give play to their unique vision of individual life-purpose, or their plan of life (whatever it happens to be); that there should be no lack of moral and material encouragement for individuals to make of their lives something that confers self-respect and wins the respect of others, and to grasp the opportunities for self-development that a liberal regime puts in their hands. This is, roughly speaking, the form of social theory associated with welfarist liberals such as John Rawls and Ronald Dworkin. The authoritative statement of this liberal-individualist version of social democracy is Rawls's towering work, *A Theory of Justice*.[6] In order to unpack the idea of distributive justice that defines this kind of theory, it may be of help to contrast it with the Nozickian and Hayekan social theories (libertarian doctrines formulated by Robert Nozick and Friedrich von Hayek) that allow no legitimate place for state economic intervention or redistributive social policies. For an egalitarian liberal like Rawls, a just society must engage its citizens in an agreement, at least hypothetically, as to a fair distribution of the totality of goods and benefits that the society makes available for consumption. That is, social justice requires, and social theory attempts to clarify, what Nozick labels, in order to reject it, a 'patterned principle' of distributive justice. For a libertarian thinker like Hayek, by contrast, procedural justice extends no further than the imperative that the multiplicity of discrete contracts entered into by consenting individuals be honoured by those who have promised to do so, rather than allowing some kind of super-contract somehow negotiated by the society as a whole. For Hayek, the Rawlsian enterprise would be seen as promising something that is necessarily out of reach – namely, the vision of an overarching social order that legislates specific distributive outcomes. Therefore, from Hayek's point of view, in practice the appeal to substantive principles of macro-justice cannot help but coercively invade and overturn acts of micro-consent.[7]

Another strategy of argument in justification of social-democratic policies has a much more collectivist orientation. Here one might consider, for instance, Michael Walzer's defence of a robustly egalitarian liberal regime in his book *Spheres of Justice*.[8] Walzer argues that the standard for judging questions of distributive justice is not based on the rights individuals possess to design for themselves an autonomous plan of life, but rather, is a communal standard, arising from the shared experiences and collective self-understanding of a given society, unfolded in a unique shared history. Walzer wants to show that sometimes a society is implicitly committed, according to the logic of its shared practices and self-conception, to ideals that are insufficiently realized in its existing institutions and policies, and he believes that this is in fact the case with the American welfare state in particular. If Americans had a clearer grasp of their own narrative identity, of the underlying commitment to provide for reciprocal needs implicit in their historical togetherness, they would embrace more expansive collective provision for health care than their social and political system currently offers, would empower less privileged groups in the society to seize greater control over their own social and economic destiny (for instance, by encouraging the formation of workers' cooperatives), and would strive to lessen the domination of money and market power in shaping power and opportunities across the whole fabric of social and political life – or so Walzer tries to argue. In any case, the comparison between Rawls and Walzer proves that one can argue from either individualist or collectivist premises in the direction of more or less convergent policy commitments.

Social democracy, then, admits of alternative routes to a common destination. Yet there is an irony in appealing to American theorists in order to defend social-democratic conclusions, whether one prefers the more liberal or more socialist version, for, in an important sense, social democracy is the outgrowth of an authentically European social consciousness (and, in this sense, is remote from the categories of thought of American liberalism). The social-democratic idea is sometimes conceived in terms of 'social rights,' characteristic of twentieth-century liberal democracies, that are thought to offer a supplement to the nineteenth-century 'political rights' and eighteenth-century 'civil rights' associated with earlier instantiations of liberalism. The original, and still most famous and influential, source of this conception is T.H.

Marshall's lectures on 'citizenship and social class.'[9] The problem with this formulation is that it privileges the notion of rights held by individuals at the expense of notions of social duty and obligation, and in this regard seems alien to the collectivist traditions upon which European social democracy historically draws. As Mikhail Gorbachev rightly observed in his address to the Twenty-seventh Communist Party Congress (25 February 1986), 'the gist of socialism is that the rights of citizens do not, and cannot, exist outside their duties.' Moreover, as one commentator on Marshall's theory of citizenship has pointed out, it may well be that Marshall himself meant to affirm a reciprocity of rights and duties, rather than intending any one-sided primacy of individual rights and entitlements.[10] For these reasons, it strikes me that a more promising idiom for the exposition of the idea of social democracy is offered by the vocabulary of citizenship (where citizenship is not taken to be exhausted by a rights-based conception).

The idea here would be that social democracy specifies a certain conception of citizenship, of the social conditions that have to be met in order for individuals to consider themselves full members of the political community. Social democracy, on this understanding, presupposes affirmation of an at least minimal core of social membership: no one starves; no one goes homeless; no one lacks for essential medical needs; the elderly are cared for; no child is denied the opportunities necessary for eventual full participation in the life of the society; and so on. I think that implicit in the logic of the social-democratic idea is a further corollary: no one should lack employment and be denied the sense of dignity that goes with the knowledge that one is making a productive contribution to the needs of one's society. Of course, our society, much as it prides itself on being more egalitarian than the highly individualistic political culture to the south of us, is currently failing this test of citizenship relative to our more prosperous neighbour. Even if we weren't preoccupied with fiscal discipline, as we presently are, there is in any case today widespread scepticism about the employment-generating powers of government. In general one can observe that *all* the items on our list defining social-democratic citizenship are far from being adequately realized in contemporary liberal democracies.

Recall again the passage from Clinton's first Inaugural cited earlier. What Clinton's social idealism expressed (leaving aside the question of whether he made any serious attempt to put it into practice) is the conviction that the nation, conceived as a moral community, cannot be indifferent to whether its members, as individuals and whole classes, thrive or are crushed in the marketplace of everyday life, and that the state must assume responsibility for ensuring that the perils of life in civil society are not so overwhelming that certain inhabitants of the society are effectively denied the conditions of meaningful citizenship. As I've put the point elsewhere, even if people on the left can no longer sustain a commitment to a general socialization of property, they can at least still insist on a socialization of the perils of living in a modern society.[11]

This 'civic' conception of egalitarian politics offers, I think, an alternative to the Rawlsian and Walzerian versions of social democracy sketched earlier, and I think it remedies some of the normative defects of these two other alternatives. One relevant defect in the Rawlsian version of social democracy was brought to light in Michael Sandel's influential critique of Rawls. As Sandel showed in an important section of his book, Rawls undermines the claims of individual desert (individual assets such as energy and intelligence are the product of a biological and social lottery), and assumes that this entitles society to regard these assets as belonging to a 'social pool' from which shares and benefits can be distributed without any injury to the individual's rights and entitlements. But Sandel borrows Nozick's argument against Rawls to the effect that merely weakening the claims of individual desert fails by itself to establish why these assets automatically devolve to society as a whole as an agency of redistribution.[12] The question that Sandel drew from this argument is whether Rawls can give an account of community rich enough to explain why this should be so. Sandel's answer, of course, is that Rawl's idea of political community is too thin to supply such an account, and what is needed is what Sandel calls a 'constitutive' understanding of community that would be capable of providing a sufficient account of why unattached assets might be thought of as common assets. In this sense, we can see that the communitarian critique of Rawlsian liberalism was motivated in part by the urge to give the welfare state a 'thicker' justification than Rawls could give it, by searching for a richer understanding of the kinds of communal identity and experiences of political community necessary to generate and sustain the required social solidarity. Otherwise, egalitarian politics succumbs to the first right-wing populist who tries to incite a middle-class tax revolt.[13]

This raises the more general question of the relation between welfare liberalism of the Rawlsian variety and social democracy as we know it from various European (and Canadian) political traditions. Both, to be sure, are egalitarian philosophies. The difference, I believe, comes down to contrasting rhetorics – but when I say 'rhetoric,' this is intended not in any trivial or cynical sense, but in the sense in which one rhetoric as opposed to another defines one's fundamental vision of social and political life. The rhetoric of liberalism is a language of individual security and fulfilment. The social democrat, by contrast, is defined by a refusal to forgo the language of solidarity – even in circumstances where the solidarities one seeks to preserve are modest indeed. Therefore I think it makes sense to say that while the *content* of Rawls's social philosophy is social-democratic, the defining social vision is still (merely) liberal.[14]

Walzer's version of social democracy is certainly closer to the solidaristic rhetoric of the political traditions I have in mind, but here, too, there is a serious problem. Both the strength and the weakness of Walzer's way of doing political philosophy is its attempt to stay close to the historical self-understanding of actual political communities. Walzer thinks that the effort to search for abstract and universal normative principles on the part of mainstream Anglo-American political philosophers does violence to the shared commitments that derive from historically based communal practice. Conceptions of justice are necessarily particularistic because they relate to social goods that are a function of the collective imagination of historical communities. Accordingly, political theorists must strive to be more contextual and more historical in the ways they ply their trade. *Spheres of Justice* is a wonderful example of the rich results that can arise from this kind of approach. But the virtue of this contextualist form of political theory is simultaneously a vice: it can't legislate philosophical norms unless those norms are already rooted in the historical practices of the societies whose practices are in philosophical question. Since the ultimate standard of theoretical judgment for Walzer is fidelity to the shared understandings already inscribed in a political community's way of life, there is little place for independent philosophical norms that challenge in a radical way a society's pre-existing shared commitments. Walzer emphasizes that all legitimate social criticism (including the social criticism that issues from political philosophy) is a form of immanent critique. If, contrary to Walzer's own narrative, Americans really are more fundamentally committed to individual liberty than to social equality, Walzer's meta-theory deprives him of the philosophical wedge that would allow him to question American social priorities on the basis of conceptions of justice far removed from those already inscribed in American social practices. Perhaps Walzer thinks that such a possibility is incoherent, but if one really found oneself in a political community where libertarian notions are much more deeply entrenched historically than collectivist notions, one would be obliged (according to Walzer's meta-theory) to regard egalitarian principles as inapplicable to such a society. (Is it obvious that the United States isn't such a society?)

Basing an egalitarian social philosophy on a robust conception of the requirements of shared citizenship would, I think, yield a form of political philosophy that is richer ('meatier') than the welfare liberalism of Rawls, but also less dependent on existing social practices and their corresponding shared understanding than Walzer's social theory. The ultimate reason one has for embracing egalitarian commitments is that they embody a conception of mutual solidarity and responsibility for fellow citizens that defines a vision of political community that is normatively more attractive than rival visions. As Brian Barry, for instance, articulates his egalitarian political philosophy, 'socialism is above all a theory of citizenship: it is concerned with empowering citizens to act collectively in pursuit of the interests and ideals that they share with one another and that can be realized only by collective action.' 'The socialist principle is that what people want as citizens should prevail over what they want as private buyers or sellers.'[15] But are citizens of the modern liberal state capable of summoning up a sufficient sense of civic co-responsibility to serve this kind of purpose? Again, one can't possibly overestimate the magnitude of the political challenge that this poses.

What does it mean, then, to be a social democrat, and to embrace social-democratic commitments? One of the basic intuitions underlying any version of socialism or social democracy is that it is offensive that certain members of society earn incomes that are grossly out of relation to their real contribution to the welfare of society (because of arbitrary aspects of the social system of one sort or another). When one considers the wealth accumulated today by sports stars, celebrities in the entertainment industry, and opportunistic speculators, this intuition seems well founded. And when one adds to it a consideration of the kind of social power commanded by wealth and ownership in an even moderately or benignly capitalist society, and what this entails for the notion of common citizenship, the case mounts for social-democratic redistribution, that is, state intervention in the web of economic relationships for the direct promotion of moral purposes.

Typical of the social democrat is a sympathy for the underdogs in society, whether workers, or women, or cultural minorities, or the elderly, sick, or handicapped. Social democracy implies a principled commitment to the welfare state, as opposed to merely instrumental acceptance of it. Social democrats tend to be the ones who mobilize political support for progressive social legislation – welfare and unemployment benefits, labour legislation favourable to the trade union movement, expanded educational opportunities, provision for health care and child care, guaranteed pension plans, public housing, and so on – prodding the rest of the population to adopt creative means for the amelioration of the social condition that eventually become objects of widespread popular consensus. In this respect, the cause of social democracy has made notable advances with the postwar achievements of the welfare state in most Western democracies.

It remains to consider social democracy as a species of democracy. *Social* democracy may be construed as an ambitious interpretation of what full democracy requires. Relating the social-democratic synthesis to its two constitutive sources – namely, socialism and democracy – one might say that social democracy is more than democracy but less than socialism, in the following sense. A social democrat believes that a set of fair and reasonable mechanisms for electoral representation does not sufficiently qualify a society as a genuine democracy. Rather, a real democracy depends on shaping a more robustly egalitarian web of social relationships. As C.B. Macpherson, for instance, has argued, democratic theory falls short of its mandate if it limits itself to the question of how to democratize *government*; rather, democratic theory in its full sense must concern itself with how to democratize *society*, that is to say, how to institute a more egalitarian regime throughout economic and social life.[16] This challenge to the standard liberal understanding of democracy was quite sharply articulated (in an otherwise plodding book) by the last leader of the socialist world in the days when alternatives to capitalism were still imaginable: 'Western propaganda officials ... have skilfully played a verbal game of democracy. But we will believe in the democratic nature of Western societies when their workers and office employees start electing the owners of factories and plants, bank presidents, etc., when their media put corporations, banks and their bosses under a barrage of regular criticism and start discussing the real processes inherent in Western countries, rather than only engage in an endless and useless argument with politicians.'[17] Accordingly, efforts by various democratic theorists such as Carole Pateman and Robert Dahl to investigate possibilities of democratizing the workplace are entirely in the spirit of social-democratic ideals.[18] This is the sense in which social democracy means more democracy; but it means less socialism in so far as the social democrat does not necessarily share a faith, or perhaps has shed his or her faith, in the economic prescriptions of classical socialism (as regards, say, the nationalization of industry). When one has given up on any magic solutions supposed to be forthcoming from the economic doctrines of socialism, what remains is a demanding egalitarian morality that is common to social democrats and old-style socialists.

Social democracy, one is tempted to say, is the moral residue that is left when socialists lose their confidence about how to organize a modern economy. But even if this seems an ungenerous way of defining social democracy, the power of this moral residue should not be underestimated. The current situation with respect to egalitarian possibilities is clearly a mixed one. On the one hand, the libertarian enthusiasms of the Thatcher–Reagan years have receded, and centre-left parties are once again electable. On the other hand, popular scepticism about alternatives to capitalism makes it very difficult for anyone to summon up much confidence in an ambitious reorganization of economic life, either in regard to redistribution or in regard to workers' democracy.

The question posed in the title of this lecture naturally arouses the expectation that I intend to supply an *answer* to the question. In fact, I have a more open-ended view of history, and think it's foolhardy for intellectuals to play the prophet. In 1989, just on the threshold of the end of the Cold War, Francis Fukuyama made himself very famous by declaring that history had ended. But in no time at all, the liberated nations of the collapsed Soviet empire were back in the history-making business, rather than simply melting inconspicuously into the reign of post-historical liberalism. At the time, it was also common for people to say that these nations had been so disgusted by the socialist regimes by which they had been ruled for decades that socialism would be dead for at least a generation, if not permanently. Not so: today in Poland, where the whole anti-Communist revolution originated in the early 1980s, there is a reform-Communist president, and even in Russia itself, the refashioned Communist Party had some chance of winning the last presidential election, and might well have done so had there not been so much deception during the election campaign by the ruling regime about the true state of Yeltsin's health. The fact that I teach in a political science department hasn't blinded me to the unwarranted presumptions on the part of fellow political scientists concerning the forms of social order that history supposedly favours and those it supposedly rules out. Let me therefore conclude on a hopeful note, by reciting a poem that nicely expresses the enduring open-endedness of our historical situation. (The poem, by Artur Miedzyrzecki, was written to lampoon the failure of political scientists to perceive the fragility of Soviet-bloc regimes, but it certainly applies more generally.)

What Does the Political Scientist Know?

What does the political scientist know?
The political scientist knows the latest trends
The current states of affairs
The history of doctrines.

What does the political scientist not know?
The political scientist doesn't know about desperation.
He doesn't know the game that consists
Of renouncing the game.

It doesn't occur to him
That no one knows when
Irrevocable changes may appear
Like an ice-floe's sudden cracks

And that the natural resources
Include knowledge of the venerated laws
Ability to wonder
And a sense of humor[19]

Notes

1 For a useful survey of the idea of social democracy in its historical dimensions see Raymond Plant's article ('Social Democracy') in *The Blackwell Encyclopedia of Political Thought*, ed. David Miller (Oxford: Basil Blackwell, 1987), 481–5.
2 According to a *Globe and Mail* editorial entitled 'Which Capitalism?' (13 January 1997, p. A14), a 1996 estimate of unemployment rates in twenty-six industrialized countries showed the United States to have the sixth-lowest rate of unemployment. The rate in the United States was 5.3 per

cent; the rate in Britain was 6.9 per cent; the rate in Canada was 9.7 per cent; and the rate in the European Union as a whole was 11.4 per cent. The *Globe and Mail* editorialist, while strongly preferring the Anglo-American version of capitalism to European capitalism, conceded that 'it is indisputable that poverty and income inequality have risen under the Anglo-American system [with its lower social benefits and greater job insecurity].' It goes without saying that the choice between joblessness and minimal protection against the ravages of capitalism is not a pretty one.

3 See Christopher Lasch, *The True and Only Heaven: Progress and Its Critics* (New York: W.W. Norton, 1991); and Lasch, *The Revolt of the Elites and the Betrayal of Democracy* (New York: W.W. Norton, 1995); his hostility to the state runs through both books. For representative statements of MacIntyre's view, see Alasdair MacIntyre, 'Poetry as Political Philosophy: Notes on Burke and Yeats,' in *On Modern Poetry*, ed. Vereen Bell and Laurence Lerner (Nashville: Vanderbilt University Press, 1988), 145–57; and MacIntyre, 'A Partial Response to My Critics,' in *After MacIntyre*, ed. John Horton and Susan Mendus (Notre Dame, IN: University of Notre Dame Press, 1994), 302–3.

4 MacIntyre, 'Poetry as Political Philosophy,' 153, 156.

5 In a recent text, MacIntyre reaffirms his allegiance to the basic theses of the Marxist critique of capitalism: see '1953, 1968, 1995: Three Perspectives,' introduction to MacIntyre, *Marxism and Christianity*, 2d ed. (London: Duckworth, 1995), pp. v–xxxi. On p. xxi, he explains explicitly why social democracy represents an inadequate response to the injustices of liberal capitalism: 'it would be absurd to deny that the achievement of pensions, health services and unemployment benefits for workers under capitalism has always been a great and incontrovertible good. [Nonetheless, liberal social democracy is to be rejected for the Marxist reason that] if trade unions made it their only goal to work for betterment within the confines imposed by capitalism and parliamentary democracy, the outcome would be a movement towards, first, the domestication and, then, the destruction of effective trade-union power. Workers would so far as possible be returned to the condition of mere instruments of capital formation [... which] has of course turned out to be true.'

In a discussion on 10 May 1997, I asked MacIntyre how he squares residual Marxism with antipathy to the state, since, in our situation, in the political world in which we live, the state offers the only restraint upon the capitalist market, both in its provision of regulatory mechanisms and in its capacity as an agent of distributive justice. Here is the gist of his interesting reply. MacIntyre said that what we've had since 1945 is the state-cum-market. The welfare state was invented by Bismarck, as well as Disraeli, Lloyd George, and Balfour – that is, not social democrats but conservatives trying to preserve an orderly capitalist society. Operation of this state/market produces a certain amount of disorder, which in turn needs to be corrected by welfare-state policies. Welfare is therefore bound to a cycle: the state promotes growth, it regulates the market with welfare, then it needs to cut back. It issues promissory notes that have to be paid for by Republican policies. So Democrats and Republicans are simply occupying different positions within this cycle, yet they are bound to the same process. What MacIntyre therefore rejects is the whole package – namely, a growth economy managed by the state, with occasional corrections with welfare and so on. Consequently the welfare state is not an alternative to the state/market; it is, on the contrary, part-and-parcel of the kind of state entirely implicated in the operation of market capitalism.

6 John Rawls, *A Theory of Justice* (Oxford: Oxford University Press, 1971).

7 For a good summary of the anti–social-democratic, Hayekian view of justice, or rather the view that there is no *need* for a theory of distributive justice, see Roger Scruton, 'Contract, Consent and Exploitation,' in *Essays on Kant's Political Philosophy*, ed. Howard Williams (Chicago: University of Chicago Press, 1992), 213–27.

8 Michael Walzer, *Spheres of Justice: A Defense of Pluralism and Equality* (New York: Basic Books, 1983).

9 See T.H. Marshall, *Class, Citizenship, and Social Development* (Garden City, NY: Anchor Books, 1965).

10 Morris Janowitz, *The Reconstruction of Patriotism* (Chicago: University of Chicago Press, 1983), 5–7.

11 Ronald Beiner, *What's the Matter with Liberalism?* (Berkeley: University of California Press, 1992), 96–103.

12 Michael Sandel, *Liberalism and the Limits of Justice* (Cambridge: Cambridge University Press, 1982), 96–103.

13 In my view, Sandel's more recent explorations of 'civic-republican' possibilities continue to be motivated by the same concern. I discuss this dimension of Sandel's work in 'The Quest for a Post-Liberal Public Philosophy,' introduction to *Debating Democracy's Discontent: Essays on American Politics, Law and Public Philosophy*, ed. Anita L. Allen and Milton C. Regan, Jr, (Oxford: Oxford University Press, 1998).

14 In *Political Liberalism* (New York: Columbia University Press, 1996), p. li, Rawls appeals to the notion of civic friendship, which has a more ambitious ring to it, but the context is the idea of public reason, not the norms

of social-economic equality that (according to Rawls himself) ought to prevail in a liberal society.

15 Brian Barry, 'The Continuing Relevance of Socialism,' in *Liberty and Justice: Essays in Political Theory 2* (Oxford: Clarendon Press, 1991), 274–90; the quoted passages are from pp. 276 and 281, but cf. pp. 283 and 289. See also Michael Igantieff, 'The Myth of Citizenship,' in *Theorizing Citizenship*, ed. Ronald Beiner (Albany: State University of New York Press, 1995), 53–77, for some thoughtful reflections on the relation between the welfare state and ideals of citizenship.

16 C.B. Macpherson, *Democratic Theory: Essays in Retrieval* (Oxford: Clarendon Press, 1973).

17 Mikhail Gorbachev, *Perestroika* (New York: Harper & Row, 1987), 127–8.

18 Carole Pateman, *Participation and Democratic Theory* (Cambridge: Cambridge University Press, 1970); Robert A. Dahl, *A Preface to Economic Democracy* (Berkeley: University of California Press, 1985).

19 In this essay I have drawn freely from an article on social democracy published previously in *The Encyclopedia of Democracy*, ed. Seymour Martin Lipset (Washington, DC: Congressional Quarterly Books, 1995), vol. 4, 1139–42.

9

Democracy and Social Inequality

DIETRICH RUESCHEMEYER

These days, democracy seems to be on a roll. And it appears that it goes well with free-market economies as well as with a build-down of welfare states. In fact, many see capitalism and democracy as two sides of the same coin – capitalist democracy or democratic capitalism. This capitalist democracy, it seems, is conquering the world – except, perhaps for the time being, China and many Islamic countries.

Given this much-hailed, for some even euphoric, picture, you might think it takes a spoiler to talk about 'Democracy and Social Inequality.' It does take, perhaps, a spoiler to remind us that the heartlands of democracy, the United States and the United Kingdom, are now competing with some less-developed countries when it comes to widening the income gap between the richest and the poorest 10 or 20 per cent of the population; it may take a spoiler to point out that the new democracies in eastern Europe indeed combine free-market policies with democratic government, but also that they see only now the beginning of economic growth compensating for years of decline, and that now, with market competition and political pluralism, they are too poor to maintain the features of the old system of social provisions that many expect as their due (the poor, that is, fare worse than before); and it takes a spoiler to talk about the fate of the poor in Latin America, where democracy has made a phenomenal comeback, but social inequality has worsened at the same time.

These dark sides of the triumph of capitalist democracy are real. But while I will touch on these issues too, I will approach the issues of democracy and social inequality with a slightly more academic focus.[1] Though academic, I promise to be brief as well as plain-spoken. I want to present and defend four propositions, to wit:

- The very idea of democracy is inevitably intertwined with social inequality.
- The rise of democracy cannot be understood without looking at class inequality.
- Democracy tends to have an equalizing (or, if you prefer, a levelling) momentum.
- But, precisely because of that, if democracy has a chance of deepening – with more participation and less social and economic inequality – it may be opposed, contained, or even aborted.

The first claim to be discussed, then, is: 'The very idea of democracy is inevitably intertwined with social inequality.' The idea of democracy comes in two forms. One is the ideal – rule of the people, equality of all adults when it comes to making collective decisions, independent of family background, wealth, income, education, reputation, smarts.

For some, this was and is not an ideal but a frightful prospect. John Stuart Mill worried about the wrong kind of democracy; and Alexis de Tocqueville feared the tyranny of the majority. Still, in its basics most see it today as an ideal; an ideal grounded in reciprocity: 'Let's treat others as we would wish to be treated if we were in their shoes.' But it is also *only* an ideal – reality may approach it, but it can never be realized in full. That brings me to the other form taken by the idea of democracy.

What do we mean when we use the word about real countries? I suggest a definition of really existing democracy that comes in three parts:

1/ repeated elections of representatives that are free and fair and in which all adults can participate;
2/ accountability of the state machinery to these elected representatives; and
3/ guarantees for freedom of expression and freedom of association.

This definition sounds innocent to the point of being trite, but it should come with a warning: it is more demanding than one may think. Britain, by this definition, became a democracy only after the First World War, because all during the nineteenth century the right to vote was restricted by class (as well as gender); and the United States made the grade only by 1970, because until and through the 1960s the vote was restricted by race (or rather race and class).

In the late twentieth century, limiting democracy is not so often done any more by limiting suffrage, the right to vote. Rather, democracy can be contained more smoothly and less visibly by limiting basic civil rights; for instance, in South Korea unions were until very recently limited to one per enterprise, which often gave company unions a monopoly, and unions still are not allowed to link up with parties. Or, and this is even more important, democracy may be limited by restricting the accountability of the state to the elected representatives; for instance, Alfredo Christiani, a president of El Salvador during the 1980s, was duly elected but was unable to control the bloody civil war conducted by the very army whose commander in chief he was. Lack of full accountability of the executive branch is, of course, a common problem, even in the oldest democracies.

There are two morals to be drawn from this: First, if you think this modest, realistic definition makes sense, beware of newspapers that label a government as democratic once the Carter Center in Atlanta has certified its elections as free and fair. Second, even this modest definition involves complex judgment calls about the critical terms – about *fair* elections, about *effective* accountability, about *freedom* of speech and association.

What, then, about my first claim? Whether you take the ideal conception or a more realistic definition, democracy inevitably involves issues of social inequality. It promises – or, in the realistic version, it is a first step towards – a separation of politics from social inequality, from the systematic differences in income and wealth, status and prestige, social power and influence. If you are sceptical about whether the actual existing democracies are even a first step in this direction, look back in history a bit further: In feudalism, where economic ownership, hereditary status, and political authority were *fused*, democracy – even the modest, really existing kind – was unimaginable. And Milovan Djilas taught us that the same applied to communist state socialism.

Both the ideal of democracy and its various more limited really existing forms promise to reduce inequality in politics. This means that democracy is a matter of power and power sharing. It means also that democracy stands in tension with stark inequalities in the sources of social power – in the means of coercion, in wealth, in cultural hegemony, in collective and individual status.

In much of the discourse about democracy, this tension is systematically neglected. The discussion then proceeds as if fundamentally all citizens *were* in fact equal. This is related to the frequent neglect of universal suffrage as a criterion. Until the middle of the nineteenth century, democracy was indeed seen as playing itself out within the circle of the free and propertied, in Jefferson's ideas, within a one-class society. In this view, which takes a rough equality for granted, the critical issue for the emergence and the maintenance of democracy then becomes the tension between state and society, rather than divergent class interests.

While the threat of an overpowering state is real, it is, in the conception advanced here, only one part of the broader claim that, to repeat: 'The very idea of democracy is inevitably intertwined with social inequality.'

I now turn to my second claim: 'The rise of democracy cannot be understood without looking at class inequality.' Here I have to be brief to the point of radical simplification, because the argument rests on complex comparative historical evidence that I cannot relate here. In *Capitalist Development and Democracy,* Evelyne Huber Stephens, John Stephens, and I did a comparative historical analysis of the fate of democracy in western Europe, the former English settler colonies, South America, and finally a comparison of the Spanish-speaking countries of Central America with the English-speaking islands of the Caribbean.

Starting from the premise that democracy is a matter of power, we theoretically identified, and found empirically, three clusters of power relations as being of overwhelming importance:

1/ the balance of power between groups and classes in society;
2/ the balance of power between the state and civil society;
3/ the impact of international power relations.

I will speak here virtually exclusively about the first, the balance of power within society, primarily the balance of class power. I will be extremely brief.

The rise of capitalism and its spread around the globe are related to democratization. This has been established again and again, both by rough historical assessment and by systematic quantitative cross-national analyses. The association is far from perfect, but it represents a very sturdy finding. But statistical association and historical sequence do not reveal causation. The causal mechanisms remain in a 'black box.' What accounts for the association between capitalist development and democracy?

The main explanation of this association, compressed into a single sentence, is: a change in the balance of class power that was brought about by capitalist development. Large landlords lost power, and if they controlled a large labour force with political means, they were the classic enemies of democracy. The emerging working class of capitalist economies was the first subordinate class in history able to organize itself and acquire political power. Overall, the organized working class was a consistently pro-democratic force.[2] The bourgeoisie, the major owners of merchant and industrial capital, was soon strong enough to open up political decision making and to secure a place in the new politics for itself, but it was typically not eager to include other groups in what often remained a deliberative and electoral oligarchy.

One must not speak too simply about *the* interests of a class. In historical reality, the interests that are actually pursued, are goals developed by leaders and organizations that find a following in a given social class. Class interests that are actually pursued cannot be 'read off,' as it were, from the objective situation of a class. The actually pursued interests are socially constructed in the very process of organization and organizational growth. Such social construction is inevitable; consider a union – over time, it must be decided whether to emphasize income, job security, work safety, industrial power relations, free time, or broader political goals; it also must be decided how narrow or wide to define one's solidarity – across building electricians in one construction site, electricians as an occupation, construction workers industry-wide, the working class in a country, the 'workers of the world.'

This conception of a social construction of class goals does not mean that everything is contingent and equally likely in different historical circumstances; it is quite likely that certain interests we see as 'objective' or 'well understood interests' will typically be included in the actually pursued class goals. This conception does mean, however, that important variation will occur and that there will often be several competing versions of class interests coexisting with one another – in the case of the working-class, social-democratic, as well as Leninist versions, but also liberal, and Catholic formulations of working-class interests, and even Tory ones.

This conceptualization of class interests has another important consequence. It makes it impossible to see classes in isolation from each other. Class interests are importantly influenced: (1) by the hegemonic influence exercised by other classes; (2) by alliances with other classes; (3) by conflict with other classes and by the threat other classes pose. Relations between classes – alliances, dependencies, antagonisms – thus acquire a critical importance for the chances of democracy.

'Objectively' we might well argue that all classes that have few social-power resources other than collective organization – that is, in particular all classes devoid of significant wealth, coercive power, and cultural authority – will have an interest in advancing democracy. That includes in particular, in addition to the working class, small-holding farmers and the middle classes of craftsmen and merchants as well as white-collar employees. However, both peasants and the middle classes are often under the hegemonic spell of influence of large landlords and other interests opposed to democracy. Where this was not the case (for farmers you might think of Switzerland, Norway, or the North of the United States; for the middle classes, quite a few other countries are examples), both small-holding farmers and urban middle classes have been important pro-democratic forces. The working class was not immune to such hegemonic influence; but it was usually far more insulated from it than the peasantry and the urban middle classes.

In no country was the working class strong enough to open up liberal oligarchies for all to participate in. It needed allies. Farmers could be allies of the working class, as they were in Scandinavia, but they could also be dominated by large landlords and become an obstacle to democratization. The middle classes could be in the vanguard of democracy, but they could also fall under the spell of anti-democratic hegemonies, as they did in Germany after the First World War. Much depends on the coalitions at the top. Where the bourgeoisie allied itself with the large landlords, things did not look well for democracy, especially if large parts of the old and new middle classes were under the influence of the bourgeoisie.

These arguments and findings have implications for the current discourse on 'civil society.' Allow me a brief excursion on this. Civil society, a concept derived from Hegel's and Marx's 'bürgerliche Gesellschaft,' covers a bewildering array of meanings. Rooted in the state–society polarity common in eighteenth- and nineteenth-century thought, it had a resurgence in the context of the crumbling and the eventual fall of the state socialist, communist regimes of eastern Europe. Civil society reasserted itself and won out – even if other factors may in reality have been equally or more important in causing the collapse of the Soviet system. The concept of civil society is today invoked by post-Marxist theory as well as by right-wing opponents to the Swedish welfare state.[3]

If we pin the word down to a neutral meaning, pointing to all groupings, networks, and organizations relevant for public discussion that are *not* based in family and kin ties, in economic production and exchange, and in the organization of the state, it covers a delimited if still wide field. Is a dense civil society in this sense, is dense participation in public affairs in the widest sense, good for democracy? What I have argued so far suggests caution: not necessarily. There are groups whose interests stand against democracy. If they are well organized, so much the worse for democracy. Even more important, if these groups and the institutions they control gain hegemonic influence on the organizations of other strata, they can effectively undercut the chances of democracy. What is critical for good prospects of democracy is the *autonomous* self-organization of groups and strata positively disposed towards democracy. This protects them against anti-democratic hegemonies and it enables them to advance their own cause. There is a strict analogy here to the hypothesis of earlier theories about mass society and authoritarian or totalitarian rule: Mass organizations controlled 'from the outside' function as ideological transmission belts. Various middle class and farmers' associations as well as non-class organizations such as veterans' associations can become transmission belts for authoritarian ideologies. Pre-Nazi Germany is the paradigmatic case of a country in which a dense civil society proved to be no protection for democracy.

Things, then, were complicated and developed differently in different countries. But there remains the predominantly positive relation between capitalism and democracy in the overall picture. And this has – that is my claim – its explanation in the profound shift in the balance of class power just indicated. From this follows that democracy is not so much a direct product of capitalism, but rather the result of conflicts and antagonisms created in the course of capitalist development.

This is an explanation at odds with others that may sound more familiar:

1/ It was not the broadening of the middle class that primarily accounts for the association between capitalist development and democracy. In quite a few cases, the middle class was an accomplice in rolling back democracy.

2/ Nor was this association due to a systemic affinity between capitalism and democracy. Many think of a parallelism between an open market for goods and services and reaching political decisions in an 'open marketplace of ideas.' Others argue that modern and complex capitalist societies require a complex and flexible political order that only democracy can supply. Aside from the truism, first, that analogies do not establish causation and, second, that many countries need something, yet do not have or get what they need, aside from the flaw in the logic of these arguments, it is not so obvious that authoritarian regimes have always served capitalism ill – think of Germany in the late 1800s and the 1930s, think of Chile in the 1970s, think of South Korea and Taiwan from 1960 to the middle and late 1980s, think of China now; closer to home, you might also consider the support for capitalism offered by Britain's liberal oligarchy – before the 1830s, in the 1840s, and before the successive extensions of the suffrage in the 1860s, 1880s. and finally 1920.

Finally,

3/ neither can the relation between capitalism and democracy be explained by a claim advanced both by classic liberal and by Marxist theory – it cannot be explained as the deed of the bourgeoisie. Too often was the dominant class of modernizing societies involved in breakdowns and roll-backs of democracy, quite aside from the fact that in most countries the bourgeoisie was in no hurry to extend the vote to everybody.

This, then, is the bottom line on my second claim: Class inequality was historically at the centre of the dynamics of democracy – its origins, its obstacles, its halting development, its breakdowns.

Before I proceed to the next proposition, let me briefly comment on four objections to this class-centred account. First, isn't class a dusty concept of the nineteenth century, confined in its utility to the stark conflicts capitalist industrialization created? I believe this objection to be mistaken. Social inequality refers after all to the cumulative distribution of things that are fairly universally desired: economic resources, status or recognition and respect, and power, or at least freedom from being pushed around, and the capacity to get things done. Did the patterns of inequality change over past generations? Yes, of course; and they vary across societies as well. Perhaps you want to reserve the term 'class' for some special version of structured inequality, one that is dear to your ideological heart or one that you find especially obnoxious. But relative to the abiding reality of structured inequality in the three dimensions of wealth, status, and power, that is merely a terminological squabble.

The next two objections point to the fact that there are other forms of social inequality than class inequality. One is gender inequality. Gender relations are likely to shape future developments in democracy in a powerful way. Women's life situations have changed drastically in objective terms in all developed and many less-developed countries, while gender roles have a tremendous tenacity. This discrepancy is likely to call forth repeated and protracted political interventions.[4] Women's issues were, however, far less important in the known histories of democratization. The struggle for women's inclusion was not as fierce as the class issue in democratization. When it occurred, women's inclusion did not dramatically change the political landscape. And there are no instances of roll-backs of democracy responding to the inclusion of women.

Another objection points to race and ethnicity. Race and ethnic cleavages affect the chances of democracy in important ways. Cross-national research found that 'ethno-linguistic fragmentation' is negatively associated with democracy. However, quite a few ethnically divided societies enjoy viable democratic politics, among them the oldest democracy – Switzerland – as well as Belgium, Spain, the United States, and Canada. While ethnic and racial divisions may undermine the cohesion of a society that is minimally necessary for democracy, many of their effects are related to the dynamics of class inequality: such divisions may deepen or cut across (and thus weaken) class differences, and they may within ethnic segments increase the influence of dominant groups that harbour reservations about democracy. Often, however, racial and ethnic divisions constitute segments of society that behave much like classes except for the particular nature of their boundaries (which among other things may create a solidarity that eases the process of organization).

Finally, there is the concern that the analysis just sketched gives too little weight to cultural factors. Arguments of political culture often are circular in their logic: For instance, a liberal political culture may be invoked to explain pervasive liberal orientations among political actors. Values and beliefs are of course important. And they are not neglected in the analysis presented. The different social constructions of contrasting class interests, replete with symbols, rituals, and myths, and often complex enough to include analyses and normative visions of culture, economy, and politics in the past and in the future – these different articulations *together represent an ensemble of political culture*. This conceptualization, complemented by analyses of states and religious institutions, has the advantage of grounding culture firmly in different groups, organizations, and institutions. It thus avoids vagueness and circularity. Yet this approach is often not recognized as giving culture its due as a causal factor because it offers a very diverse and conflictual picture, while more conventional cultural analyses often conceive of culture as a unified whole.

These very brief and schematic comments must suffice to defend the second proposition, to repeat: 'The rise of democracy cannot be understood without looking at class inequality.'

My next claim is a little overstated, if taken by itself. It's limited by the next and last one. But let me stick to it first – to repeat: 'Democracy tends to have an equalizing (or, if you prefer, a levelling) momentum.'

Lenin did not believe this. He thought of democracy, 'bourgeois democracy' as he saw it, as the ideal political shell of capitalism; of a thoroughly unreformed, unmitigated capitalism, to be precise.

Yet even formal democracy – the really existing democracies of today with protection of the freedoms of speech and association, regular elections every four or five years, and at least some significant accountability of government to the elected representatives – that formal democracy may open the possibility of deepening, with more dense and active participation and with participation less associated with economic and educational privilege. And it may open the possibility of policies seeking to reduce social and economic inequality. Formal democracy, then, offers the hope that it becomes more 'substantive' by moving towards participatory and social democracy.

These possibilities seem realistic, given the role of subordinate classes in getting to (formal) democracy in the first place. It is, after all, their self-organization that accounts for the extension of deliberative and electoral politics. Some ideological support may also derive from the allegiance many feel towards the ideal of democracy.

What is the evidence? If you look at a cross-section of different countries, there is no statistical relation between level of democracy and level of social provisions. There is some evidence that over fairly long periods of time democracy tends to be associated with greater social expenditures. But that statistical relationship is not overwhelmingly strong.[5]

This is plausible on closer reflection: It takes the right coalitions to get beyond formal democracy as much as to get to democracy in the first place. And even with the right coalitions, transformation of a whole society and economy takes time. And not just time: it also takes successful policies. And it takes favourable conjunctures. A context of long-term economic growth makes redistribution possible without reducing the privileges of the haves, except in relative terms.

This is, in different ways, the story of the successful Western welfare states, of Scandinavia, the Netherlands, as well as Canada, to name a few. But systems of social provision, while politically popular and embodied in powerful institutions, are not immune to change and decay. They require again and again successful adjustments to new situations. And they may be assaulted and fairly radically revised and cut by hostile coalitions, as happened in Britain under Thatcher.[6]

Some argue that democracy was historically favourable to broad policies of social security when the majority would benefit from such provisions. With a growing standard of living, however, large majorities do not see themselves as benefiting from public provisions but rather as being burdened with high taxation. The new 'two-thirds society,' as some have called this phenomenon, is in this view unfavourable to generous welfare-state policies.

This argument does point to vulnerabilities that attacks on welfare-state systems can exploit. However, it overlooks a number of things, and it is simplistic in its assumptions about self-interest. It overlooks, for instance, that some needs are rather universal – such as the need to deal with illness, schooling and day care, and old age – and that universal provisions for these needs create powerful political constituencies; it overlooks that other risks such as unemployment are far more widespread than they appear when we just look at the 5 to 10 per cent figures at any one time: A multiple of that number experiences unemployment over time, and an even larger number has reason to fear it – with far-reaching consequences: for instance, for how one relates to one's boss. This argument also overlooks something that individualistic lenses quite easily make you overlook – that organizations, parties, coalitions, and institutions supporting welfare-state policies, once they are established and successful, play a critical role in shaping people's opinion on what is worthy of support, what is necessary, what is critical for a humane society, what is 'normal.' Finally, it is not a forgone conclusion that increased wealth makes people more self-interested; it is equally plausible to argue that increased wealth allows for more generosity. However that may be, which kinds of individual orientations enter the political arena as powerful determinants is shaped to a large extent by the 'political culture' of a place that is grounded in different organizations and institutions.

We know much less about the prospects of increased political participation. This was an end in itself, central to the human value of democracy, for political philosophers like John Stuart Mill and C.B. McPherson. It is also, as we have seen, of critical importance as a means – a means in the struggle for democracy and a means of moving from formal to social democracy – because the one resource of power available to the many is collective organization. What we do know about the conditions of active participation points to an important connection between social and participatory democracy. Across different countries, differences in politically relevant participation are largely the consequence of differences in the participation of different class and status groups.[7] Countries with strong social policies have higher and more even rates of political participation. This contradicts views that see welfare states choking off participation as they meet people's needs 'from cradle to grave.' Quite the contrary: social participation of various kinds grows as social provisions offered by the state grow. This finding is not confined to a country like Norway. A study of the third-sector history in the United States came to the same conclusion.[8]

For democratic outcomes it is equally important that higher levels of political participation tend to be associated with fewer disparities in participation across different social classes. It is at least plausible to argue that participation is in part a function of success. More privileged groups everywhere participate more, because they have a better chance of getting what they want. Subordinate groups participate more in welfare states for the same reason. Politics is more fun when you win, or have a chance to do so. That suggests that moves towards social and participatory democracy buttress each other as well as reinforce the underpinnings of elementary, formal democracy.

What, then, is the verdict on the claim under discussion, my third proposition? The picture I offered is a complex and only moderately progressive one. Moving from formal democracy to a social and more deeply participatory democracy is a possibility. In the long run, some social progress is even a likely outcome of democratic politics. And the safeguards of social security (in the original, broad sense of the word) seem to buttress social and political participation, while more even participation, more participation of the less privileged strata, supports both formal and social democracy.

But formal democracies may also stay formal. This was in line with the aspirations of classic liberalism in the nineteenth century; and that outcome would be embraced as desirable also by many neo-liberals of today.

And formal democracies may decay as their participatory underpinnings are weakened. This appears to be a special problem in today's new democracies, which also happen to be the countries under special pressure from international competition and debt regimes – a topic I can only allude to here. This seems to be the heart of the matter in Latin America's current dual and paradoxical developments – a spread of formal democracy and a weakening of social policy impulses. In many Latin American countries, initially high levels of grass-roots participation have died down in the absence of a strong organizational infrastructure, while the leverage of lender countries and multilateral financial institutions effectively imposed the medicine of marketization, privatization, and shrinking the state.[9]

Before I turn to the next and last claim, let me be clear on one point: Formal democracy may be just formal, but it has a value of its own; it is in fact something to be treasured, even if it does not turn out to have transformative levelling powers. It not only keeps the door open for a more just future. It delivers results that are valuable even if inequality is not further reduced: it offers the elimination or control of brutality by police or military; it offers the opportunity to voice opposition and discontent, and on occasion it leads to the creation of public goods that would not have come about without broad-based input; and it offers a restraint of abuses of power through public accountability.

My last claim is (yet) a little darker: 'Precisely because democracy may have an equalizing momentum, if democracy has a chance of deepening – with more participation and less social and economic inequality – it may be opposed, contained, or even aborted.'

From our Latin American studies (where the working class was much smaller and weaker than in western Europe) but also from examining interwar Europe, we learned that democracy is only secure where powerful groups see their interests more or less safely protected. These may be threatened by vigorous and radical subordinate-class movements, unless the dominant classes have at their disposal large and effective popular or clientelistic parties. In the extreme, democracy may be rolled back. One way of putting this is to say that a viable democracy rests on a class compromise. Another, less polite, way is to argue that, where class interests are sharply opposed to each other, democracy exists at the pleasure of dominant groups. This is the story behind the breakdown of democracy in Chile, Argentina, and Brazil in the 1970s. Such a rollback of democracy must not necessarily be seen as intentional action, as the result of a conspiracy. It may well involve as much not-objecting, taking advantage of tendencies and constraints that arose otherwise and earlier.

The fact that many new democracies, many instances of the current 'triumph of democracy,' are rather defective, even on the standard criteria for formal democracy, may be relevant here as well. They may be tolerated precisely because they have only a weak foundation in broad-based and stable participation, and thus can mount no threat to the interests of economically and socially dominant groups. At the same time, these democracies may be in danger of decay precisely because of the vicious circle of weak participation, low results, and even weaker participation.

Let me conclude with the discussion of a question that you may have asked yourselves already: 'Is all of this about other countries? Is democracy, at least formal democracy, safe in the places where we live, in the United States, in the United Kingdom, in Canada, as well as other Western countries?'

One might indeed think so. Class antagonisms are moderated. The lower and working classes have their organizations and often sympathetic parties.

Furthermore, much of what constitutes the essence of democracy is firmly institutionalized: Governments that lose elections do not try to stay on. The armed forces and the police hardly dream of taking over politics. Civil liberties are rather well protected, with vigorous skirmishes where they are threatened at the margins. Such a settling of democratic practice into unquestioned institutional patterns is important. A joke has it that stable democracy is like an English lawn: You set it up and then cut and roll it for a couple of hundred years. And there is some truth in the joke.

However, it is useful to remember that things social are never set forever. They must not just be taken care of, but they must be adjusted to new situations, defended against new threats.

If we look at developments in the United States, we find an ominous combination of developments: a decline of participation, particularly in political and quasi-political organizations, and especially among lower-class groups and Blacks;[10] a tremendous rise in moneyed influence on politics, both before and after elections, an influence that is virtually crowding out the voters' voice; and this latter development protected by an outrageous Supreme Court decision that equated spending one's money with speech: both, the Court said, are equally protected by the First Amendment.

When Skelley Wright, then a justice on the Court of Appeals in Washington, DC, criticized this decision in one of the splendid Civil Rights lectures that Brown University sponsors every year, I remember talking to the head of Rhode Island's Civil Liberties Union. He was critical of Wright and supportive of the Supreme Court: 'Whatever enlarges the scope of the First Amendment is good, whatever diminishes it is bad.' I have since taken to think of him and others like him as the 'Ayatollahs of the First Amendment.'[11]

Considering these developments perilous is not to make a partisan judgment. Sure, the losers are disadvantaged groups; thus my judgment may sound liberal and rather not conservative, in the political sense of these labels. Yet it is both liberal and conservative in the non-partisan meaning of the words. That the two meanings of 'liberal' coincide when it comes to democracy is no accident. That a functioning democracy limits the power of the haves and opens space for the power of the have-nots is in fact the central point of this essay.

What is at stake in the United States is indeed democracy, even formal democracy. If we set aside the axiom that the democratic character of the United States is beyond question, that in effect the United States, together with a few other countries, defines what it is we mean by democracy, we can reasonably ask whether elections as they come to be taken for granted in the United States are indeed still free and fair elections.

Notes

1   This essay was presented at Green College, University of British Columbia, Vancouver, on 18 November 1997. Rather than rewriting it, I have retained the style of the talk and kept references and notes to a minimum. The paper relies strongly on joint work I did with Evelyne Huber Stephens and John D. Stephens. See Dietrich Rueschemeyer, Evelyne Huber Stephens, and John D. Stephens, *Capitalist Development and Democracy* (Cambridge: Polity Press, and Chicago: University of Chicago Press 1992), and Evelyne Huber, Dietrich Rueschemeyer, and John D. Stephens, 'The Paradoxes of Contemporary Democracy,' *Comparative Politics* 29/3 (April 1997): 323–42.

2   This is a claim that must be maintained and defended against the thesis of an inherent 'working-class authoritarianism.' This thesis, put forth with some ambivalence by Seymour Martin Lipset in 1955, relies on too direct inferences from generalizations about the social psychology of lower-class life and gives too little weight to fundamental interests as recognized and worked out in working-class organizations. It also reflects the disillusionment of radical idealizations of the working class in the old left (as expressed, for instance, by Ignacio Silone, whose words open Lipset's essay). And finally, it fits into the atmosphere of the Cold War. (It's at least sym-

bolically remarkable that Lipset's paper was first presented at a conference sponsored by the Congress for Cultural Freedom.) See Seymour M. Lipset, 'Working-Class Authoritarianism,' in *Political Man*, expanded ed. (Baltimore, MD: Johns Hopkins University Press 1981), 87–126.

3 See for instance Jean L. Cohen and Andrew Arato, *Civil Society and Political Theory* (Cambridge, MA: MIT Press, 1993). Hans Zetterberg, a prominent Swedish publicist, claims the idea of civil society as legitimating a builddown of the social-welfare state. The concept owes its recent revival to the self-understanding of oppositional groups in Communist eastern Europe. For an excellent account of its historical origins see Charles Taylor, 'Invoking Civil Society,' Working Paper 21 (Chicago: Center for Psychosocial Studies, 1990), also in Charles Taylor, *Philosophical Arguments* (Cambridge, MA: Harvard University Press, 1995), 204–24.

4 See Dietrich Rueschemeyer and Marilyn Rueschemeyer, 'Progress in the Distribution of Power: Gender Relations and Women's Movements as a Source of Change,' pp. 106–22 in Jeffrey C. Alexander and Piotr Sztomka, eds., *Rethinking Progress: Movements Forces and Ideas at the End of the Twentieth Century* (Boston: Unwin Hyman, 1990).

5 See Kenneth A. Bollen and Robert Jackman, 'Political Democracy and the Size Distribution of Income,' *American Sociological Review* 50 (1985):438–57; Edward N.Muller, 'Democracy, Economic Development, and Income Inequality,' *American Sociological Review* 53 (1988): 50–68; Erich Weede, 'Democracy and Income Inequality Reconsidered: Comment on Muller,' *American Sociological Review* 54 (1989): 865–8; Edward N. Muller, 'Democracy and Inequality: Reply to Weede,' *American Sociological Review* 54 (1989): 868–71.

6 See Gosta Esping-Andersen, *Three Worlds of Welfare Capitalism* (Princeton, NJ: Princeton University Press, 1990), and Paul Pierson, *Dismantling the Welfare State: Reagan, Thatcher and the Politics of Retrenchment* (Princeton,NJ: Princeton University Press, 1994)

7 See Sidney Verba, Norman Nie, and Jae-on Kim, *Participation and Political Equality* (New York: Cambridge University Press, 1978); Russell J. Dalton, *Citizen Politics: Public Opinion and Political Parties in Advanced Western Democracies*(Chatham, NJ: Chatham House, 1996).

8 See Per Selle, 'The Norwegian Voluntary Sector and Civil Society in Transition,' pp. 157–202 in Dietrich Rueschemeyer, Marilyn Rueschemeyer, and Björn Wittrock, eds., *Participation and Democracy East and West: Comparisons and Interpretations* (Armonk,NY: M.E.Sharpe, 1998), and Lester M. Salaman, *Partners in Public Service* (Baltimore, MD: Johns Hopkins University Press, 1995).

9 See Evelyne Huber, Dietrich Rueschemeyer, and John D. Stephens, 'The Paradoxes of Contemporary Democracy,' *Comparative Politics* 29/3 (April 1997): 323–42.

10 See Robert Putnam, 'Bowling Alone,' *Journal of Democracy* 6/1 (1995): 65–78; Robert Putnam, 'Tuning In, Tuning Out: The Strange Disappearance of Social Capital in America,' in *PS: Political Science and Politics* 28/4 (1995): 664–83; Pippa Norris, 'Does Television Erode Social Capital? A Reply to Putnam,' in *PS: Political Science and Politics* 29/3 (1996): 474–80.

11 For a legal analysis of this Supreme Court decision see Ronald Dworkin, 'The Curse of American Politics,' in *New York Review of Books* 43/16 (17 October 1996): 19–24.

10

Can Welfare States Compete in a Global Economy?[1]

ANTHONY B. ATKINSON

Introduction: The Challenge to European Welfare States

In the past few years, many economists have argued that advanced economies with sizeable welfare states cannot compete in a global economy. This argument has been taken up with enthusiasm by the popular press, with such headlines as that in the *Economist* – 'Farewell, welfare'– and articles such as that in *Newsweek* –'Dismantling Europe's Welfare State'– in which they said that

> the panoply of social programs, benefits and protections designed to cushion Europeans from the harshest effects of their capitalist economies have become enormously expensive and, in some cases, their consequences extremely perverse. As a result, many people in government and private business believe the system is as much a source of Europe's problems – high unemployment, sluggish economies, lagging productivity growth – as a solace. (20 December 1993)

International organisations have expressed similar anxieties. The IMF *World Economic Outlook* for May 1994 argued that European governments 'should not allow fears about distributional consequences to prevent them from taking bold steps to implement fundamental labor market reforms' (IMF 1994, 156), including reducing the generosity of unemployment insurance, and the reform of minimum-wage laws and employment protection. At the G7 meeting in Hong Kong in September 1997, the IMF managing director, Michel Camdessus, said:

> We see it as extremely important for the future of European economic and monetary union that member countries be flexible enough, that they alle-

viate the burden on their budgets of regimes of unemployment benefits or
social security which are no longer suited to the present world, and which
are of a very high cost. (as reported in *The Observer*, 21 September 1997)

The Issues Paper prepared by the OECD for a high-level conference in
1996 opened with the statement that 'the slowdown in the growth of
OECD economies over the past twenty-five years has been accompanied by fears about the sustainability of current systems of social protection' (OECD, 1996, 2).

In all of this, a contrast is being drawn between the United States, on
the one hand, and Continental Europe, on the other. In terms of public
spending on social security, there are indeed big differences. As is
shown in figure 1, the United States spent in the early 1990s about 13
per cent of GDP on social transfers, whereas the average for the European Union was about half as much again (19 per cent). The figure for
the United Kingdom is in the middle, between these.

The question being asked in this essay is whether we have any
alternative. Is a move in the U.S. direction being forced on us by the
globalization of the economy? Or is there a choice between the U.S.
combination of labour-market flexibility and low social protection, on
the one hand, and the mainland European model of social partnership
and welfare state, on the other?

Clarifying the Question

One the most important functions of the social sciences is to clarify the
meaning of terms which are widely used in public debate, and it is here
that I begin. The title of this essay contains three elements, each of
which needs clarification: welfare state, globalization, and competitiveness.

Welfare State

We may well know a welfare state when we see one, like an elephant.
The United States is not a welfare state; Sweden is. But, like the prover-
bial elephant, the welfare state poses problems of definition. What are
the essential features? One important element is the system of social
transfers to which I have already made reference in figure 1. European
welfare states typically provide sizeable state retirement pensions, dis-
ability benefits, unemployment insurance, and child benefits, among

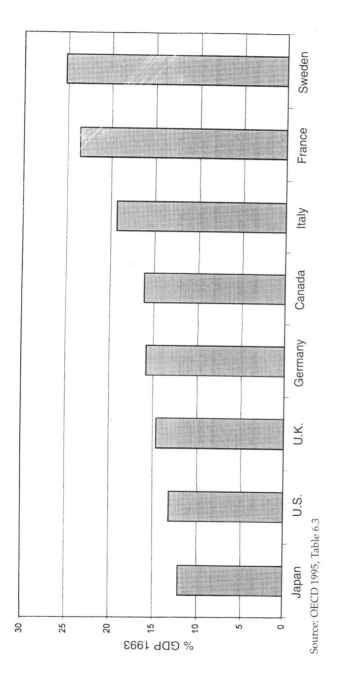

Source: OECD 1995, Table 6.3

Figure 1. Social Security as Percentage of GDP

other programs. They differ in the structure of provision, some countries having more extensive schemes in certain areas than others: for example, Sweden has about the OECD average for unemployment-insurance entitlement, whereas France has a figure about half as much higher. But the scale of overall provision, and the associated financing cost, is nonetheless higher in most EU countries than in the United States or Japan.

The budgetary cost is not, however, the only issue at stake. If it were, then all forms of government expenditure would be open to the same scrutiny. We would have to compare the merits of cuts in social protection against those in other budget headings. We might find the managing director of the IMF saying that 'European countries should alleviate the burden on their budgets of levels of military spending which are no longer suited to the present world, and which have a very high cost.' He did not say that, and one reason is that he believes that the welfare state is in itself inimical to good economic performance, preventing the necessary economic adjustments. He would presumably want to see the welfare state scaled back even if it were financed by an external donor.

We have therefore to distinguish between the argument that the cost of the welfare state is unaffordable and the argument that the welfare state has intrinsic negative economic consequences, inhibiting adjustment. The attack is two-pronged. The prongs are separate arguments, and their policy implications are different. This is illustrated by the fact that there are welfare-state provisions which may affect competitiveness without having a direct budgetary cost. In the United Kingdom, the Thatcher government reduced state spending on such programs as National Insurance Sickness benefit by transferring the obligation on to employers; state benefits were replaced by mandated benefits. Employers' costs may have been left unchanged, or increased, even though the state budgetary cost was alleviated.

More broadly, there are the institutions of the labour market. When comparing the 'American' and 'European' models, the IMF describes the former as having 'lower levels of unionization and less centralized wage bargaining; less government intervention in the wage bargaining process; fewer restrictions on hiring or firing employees' (1994, 156). It is important to see the provisions – both social transfers and labour-market protection – as forming part of a whole, an idea encapsulated in the title of a recent article by Richard Freeman: 'The Large Welfare State as a System' (1995). I shall return to this later.

Globalization

Use of the term 'globalization' seems to be growing exponentially. Recently, for example, the Economists' Bookshop in London issued a fourteen-page catalogue of new and forthcoming titles on this subject: there were sixty-six books with 'global' or 'globalization' in the title. But what does it mean?

The term seems to be applied to several different phenomena, which are related but whose implications may be quite different. In the economic sphere, we may identify at least the following interdependent factors (illustrated in each case by mock newspaper headlines):

a/ globalization of capital markets, allowing the free movement of financial capital: 'Overseas Interest Hike Leads to Capital Outflow';
b/ spreading worldwide of technology, and the transfer of production from advanced to newly industrializing countries, with resulting loss of export markets: 'U.K. Car Firm to Assemble in China';
c/ increased competition from imports from newly industrializing countries, resulting from the removal of trade barriers and reduction in transport costs: 'Asian Imports Have 50% of Market';
d/ increased competition between OECD countries, particularly within the European Internal Market and NAFTA, resulting from the same factors: 'Frankfurt Rivals Lloyds of London';
e/ greater pressure on national governments from the fiscal and other policies pursued by their neighbours, as part of a more general reduction in the autonomy of national governments: 'Canadian Voters Eye U.S. Tax Cuts';
f/ greater homogeneity of consumer tastes in different countries: 'McDonald's Opens in Tibet.'

I shall not be saying anything about (f), even if it is the aspect about which people often get most excited. I will return to (e) at the end. For the most part, I concentrate on (a)–(d). In doing so, I am not endorsing any view as to their quantitative significance. A number of economists, notably Paul Krugman (1994a), have argued that the actual impact has been exaggerated, particularly when viewed from a historical perspective. Here I am not taking sides, but simply examining what would be implied *if* there have been serious moves towards globalization of capital, production, and trade.

The different elements of globalization are interrelated, but it is important to keep them separate. Not least, we may need to use different economic models when considering different aspects of globalization. For instance, if we are concerned with increased competition within the European Union, and we move to European Monetary Union, then it is appropriate to use a model where the exchange rate is fixed. Whereas if the key issue is that of competition with Malaysia, then currencies can indeed change – as we have seen recently.

This brings me to the final clarificatory issue – what do we mean by 'compete'?

Competitiveness

I have always had difficulty understanding what it means and what is implied by the different measures of national competitiveness that are published by international organizations. I was therefore relieved to read Paul Krugman saying that 'competitiveness is a meaningless word when applied to national economies' (1994a, 44), and that 'economists, in general, do not use the word ... Not one of the textbooks in international economics I have on my shelves contains the word in its index' (1996, 24).

This may surprise non-economists. To take a concrete example, suppose that the United Kingdom were to introduce a state system of insurance against the need for long-term care financed by an increase in the employers' payroll tax (modelled on the German system). This would increase wage costs and one would expect this to raise the prices of U.K. goods and services. U.K. firms would find it harder, or less profitable, to sell their products abroad. This sounds very much like an expansion of the welfare state leading to Britain being less competitive in world markets, intensified by the globalization of world trade if a much larger fraction of the economy is now subject to competition.

One has, however, to consider the reactions which would be brought into play. If exports fall, and imports rise, then the exchange rate may adjust, with, in the example just given, sterling depreciating so that exports become cheaper in foreign currency or exports receipts become more valuable. This is where the distinction becomes important between trade among currency unions and trade within currency areas. If globalization is taken to mean greater competition in trade outside Europe, then the greater costs of a European country's welfare state, or the European welfare state as a whole, can be offset by depreciation of the euro vis-à-vis other currencies, such as the dollar. On the other hand, within the European Monetary Union there will not be this instrument of adjustment.

If the exchange rate does not adjust, the demand for U.K. goods will fall, and hence the derived demand for labour. This is likely to cause downward pressure on wages, and here we come to the second prong of the attack: the intrinsic economic impact. If the welfare states are characterized by inflexibility in the labour market, then wages may not adjust. Suppose that unions negotiate a wage which is a mark-up on the level of unemployment benefit, and that people are not willing to work in the non-union sector for less than the benefit level. Then wages remain rigid, and the effect of the welfare-state expansion is a rise in unemployment. The lack of competitivity of European welfare states shows up in their higher unemployment.

Here we come to the crux of the matter. What people in fact mean by 'being competitive' is being able to maintain their present and future levels of income. Unemployment lowers living standards. When European leaders are concerned about lack of competitiveness, they are in effect concerned about jobs. Of course, if wages do adjust, then standards of living are also affected. But then we are simply saying that welfare-state expansion has a cost – there is no free lunch. As with other spending programs, we have to weigh the cost against the benefits – and I do not discuss in this essay the benefits from the welfare state.

In this sense, it is the second prong of the argument that should really concern us here: the specific features of the welfare state that make its costs greater by causing unemployment or adversely affecting economic performance in other ways, such as slowing the rate of growth. Elsewhere (Atkinson 1995, 1999), I have considered the relation between the size of the welfare state and the rate of economic growth; here I concentrate on unemployment.

Empirical Evidence about Unemployment for OECD Countries

Does social protection cause unemployment? For some people, the empirical evidence is clear. According to Paul Krugman, 'cross-country regressions, like those of Layard, Nickell and Jackman (1991), do find that measures of the level of benefits have strong positive effects on long-term averages of national unemployment rates' (1994, 59).

Cross-Country Evidence

The results of Layard, Nickell, and Jackman (1991) are based on a statistical regression equation seeking to explain the average unemployment rate in 1983–8 in twenty OECD countries in terms of labour-market institutions, such as the benefit variables, spending on active labour-market policies, and wage-bargaining institutions.[2] Their work represented a major step forward in that it based the statistical analysis on an explicit theoretical model of the macro labour market. It was not just a case of rounding up the usual suspects and putting them into a regression equation.

It is therefore not surprising that the conclusions of the Layard, Nickell, and Jackman study have been widely quoted. For example, the review for the OECD by Elmeskov of the causes of high and persistent unemployment cites their findings that raising the replacement ratio by 10 percentage points could raise the average (over time) unemployment rate by 1.7 percentage points. (The replacement ratio is the ratio of unemployment benefit to wages.) Increasing the maximum duration of unemployment benefit by one year could increase the unemployment rate by 0.9 percentage points. These are large effects: they mean that Germany with long benefit duration and a replacement rate of 63 per cent would be predicted to have, on average, an unemployment rate more than 5 percentage points higher than the United States.

It should be noted that the Layard, Nickell, and Jackman findings differed from those of earlier studies, which had found no relation between benefits and aggregate unemployment. These earlier studies included that by the OECD Employment Outlook in 1991, which related unemployment in 1987 (as a percentage of the population of working age) to the average replacement rate for three different family situations. They concluded that 'there is no correlation between this general replacement rate indicator and the overall employment rate' (1991, 204–8). There were some countries, such as the United States and Japan, with low benefits and low unemployment, but others, such as Scandinavia, with high benefits and low unemployment.

In the subsequent Jobs Study, the OECD set out three reasons why its earlier findings may have been misleading (1994, 177):

- causality may be difficult or impossible to establish;
- aggregate measures of benefit generosity may be too crude;
- a more subtle analysis of the time path of responses may be necessary.

These are all serious points. The first, in my view, threatens to undermine any cross-country analysis of this type. It may be that there is a relation between benefit generosity and unemployment, but that this is obscured by both variables being related, in opposite ways, to a third variable. The OECD refers to the example that Southern European countries with high levels of agricultural employment, self-employment, and concealed employment may have also high reported unemployment, but the same factors have retarded the development of benefit programs. On the other hand, there may be reverse causation, with either sign. Countries with low unemployment can 'afford' more generous unemployment benefit programs, or countries prone to unemployment 'need' more extensive programs (we would not be surprised to find more malaria hospitals in tropical countries).

Benefit Generosity

Second, the problems with defining benefit generosity will be evident to anyone with any knowledge of the working of social security. Unemployment insurance and social-welfare systems are highly complex, and their impact on the individual depends on many elements. To attempt to characterize these in terms of a single variable is a heroic endeavour. This has certainly proved to be the case with replacement rates. They depend on family circumstances, on past labour-market history and levels of earnings, and on the duration of unemployment.

The duration of benefit should be singled out, since one of the conclusions of recent research seems to be that duration has greater impact than benefit rates. This has been found in a number of micro studies of individual unemployment spells, and it is given greater weight in the Layard, Nickell, and Jackman study. Their data for the two variables are plotted in figure 2, where duration of benefits is shown on the horizontal axis. This immediately brings out several aspects. The first is the concentration on four years. In fact they treat cases with an indefinite period as four years, so that what we have in effect is a distinction between those with time-limited and those with indefinite benefits. It is more a 0/1 difference. Then there is the curious position of the Scandinavian countries. Curious, in that we would expect them to be among the generous, whereas they are shown as having short benefit durations. In fact this seems to be a misreading. According to a comparative study organized by the Dutch government,'in Sweden it is possible to renew the benefit period by claiming a "job-offer" before the initial period expires … This can be repeated over and over again' (Ministry of Social Affairs and Employment 1995, 44). The OECD Jobs Study similarly states that,

> in Denmark, Norway and Sweden, the guarantee for the long-term unemployed of a place on an active labour market programme, which lasts just

long enough to generate a new period of benefit entitlement, has made it possible to receive insurance benefits almost indefinitely: Sweden becomes a country with high rather than low benefit entitlements when this is taken into account. (1994, 176)

If we were to shift Scandinavia to the indefinite category, we would get a rather different picture. Most of Europe would be on the right, with only Italy, Portugal, and Switzerland on the left. There are really two spikes, and there is evidently a lot of variation at both spikes.

Clearly the statistical analysis is more sophisticated than simply looking by eye at a graph, but equally I believe that one has to ask what lies behind the econometric results. How far are we identifying the contribution of the particular policy variable? Can we separate out the impact of benefit duration? I referred earlier to the importance of seeing economic and social arrangements as parts of an interrelated system, citing the work of Richard Freeman. Drawing on the NBER-SNS study of Sweden (Freeman, Swedenborg, and Topel 1997), he concludes that it is 'a highly interrelated welfare state and economy in which many parts fit together ... in ways that maintained high employment and wage compression, that offset work disincentives from welfare benefits and high taxes' (1995, 18).

The interrelations of the system are one reason that I am not myself convinced that we can learn a lot from this kind of cross-country evidence. Countries differ in a variety of ways, and I am not sure that one can pull out one variable as responsible for the observed differences in performance.

Dynamic Responses

Implicitly, I have been considering a contemporaneous relationship between social transfers and unemployment, but it may be a dynamic one in the sense that behaviour adjusts only with a lag. Assar Lindbeck (1995a and 1995b) has argued that individual responses are influenced by social norms which adapt over time. Initially the welfare state did not affect labour-market behaviour, but over time people became more willing to live off unemployment benefits, and the negative impact began to be important. In order to test this hypothesis, evidence is required about the formation of social norms and their impact on labour-market behaviour.

In aggregate terms, we need to allow for lagged effects (see for

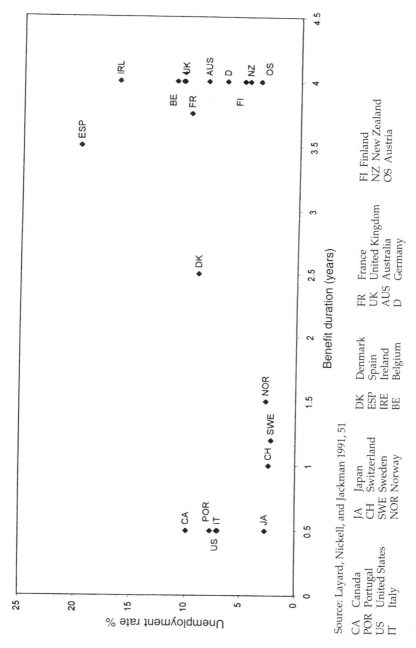

Source: Layard, Nickell, and Jackman 1991, 51

CA	Canada	JA	Japan	DK	Denmark	FR	France	FI	Finland
POR	Portugal	CH	Switzerland	ESP	Spain	UK	United Kingdom	NZ	New Zealand
US	United States	SWE	Sweden	IRE	Ireland	AUS	Australia	OS	Austria
IT	Italy	NOR	Norway	BE	Belgium	D	Germany		

Figure 2. Unemployment and Benefit Duration

example OECD 1994), but the specification is a matter where we need to exercise considerable care. As emphasized by Layard, Nickell, and Jackman (1991), the welfare state may affect the *speed of response* to exogenous shocks. Unemployment may have risen initially for reasons unconnected with the welfare state, and these shocks may have affected all countries in much the same way, but, on this argument, those countries with smaller welfare states responded more quickly. The econometric estimates of Layard, Nickell, and Jackman based on both cross-country and time-series variation bear this out to the extent that the degree of persistence of unemployment depends significantly and positively on the benefit-duration variable (but not on the replacement rate). Adjustment is faster in countries where benefits are paid for shorter periods.

I am cautious about accepting these findings in an unqualified way, in view of the concerns expressed earlier about how far it is possible to separate benefit duration as distinct from other dimensions of the European welfare state, but the dynamics do bring me to the theoretical underpinnings, since I believe that this poses the question in just the right form.

The Welfare State in Theory

As you will have deduced from what I have said so far, I am sceptical as to the possibility that we can draw definitive conclusions from the empirical cross-country evidence. The findings are interesting but not conclusive as to the impact of the welfare state on competitiveness (jobs). To this you may respond by saying that the empirical evidence is necessary only to measure the extent of the effect; its existence, on the other hand, is obvious from theoretical considerations. If there were no unemployment insurance, then unions would adjust more speedily their wage demands in response to changes in labour-market conditions, such as those arising from globalization. If there were lower mobility costs, then labour markets would clear more speedily. Such theoretical predictions are the subject of this section. What can we in fact learn from economic theory?

Much economic theory of the labour market is concerned with equilibrium or steady state situations, but what is more relevant is the differential response, depending on the size of the welfare state, to *changes in the economic environment*. It is the dynamic, rather than static, picture which was highlighted by the White Paper titled *Growth, Com-*

petitiveness, Employment. Concerned with Europe's capacity to compete, the European Commission noted that, 'although we have changed, the rest of the world has changed even faster' (1993, 10).

More appropriate, therefore, is a theory of economic change, rather than of steady state. A macro-economic approach to adjustment costs is adopted by Layard, Nickell, and Jackman (1991); here I consider a more disaggregated model of structural change (drawing on Johnson and Stafford 1993), which posits a stylized world divided into OECD economies, on the one hand, and newly industrializing countries (NICs), on the other. There are three types of goods: (a) high-tech, in which OECD countries have a continuing productivity advantage; (b) medium-tech, produced by both OECD and NICs, where the OECD has an initial productivity advantage; and (c) low-tech, produced exclusively in NICs. Goods are made using solely labour and subject to constant returns to scale. All consumers spend the same fraction of their income on the different goods. (These assumptions potentially affect the conclusions drawn, but are not material to the points I want to make here.)

Suppose that globalization leads to a steady rise in labour productivity in medium-tech goods produced by the NICs. In other words, they catch up with the OECD technology for, say, automobile production. In a fully flexible economy, it is possible that the improvement in technology in NICs leads to a fall in real wages in the OECD.[3] What happens is that the OECD economies reduce their production of medium-tech goods, transferring workers to the high-tech sector, and the demand for the high-tech goods is growing on account of the increasing wealth of the NICs. In time, the adjustment will be complete, so that the OECD is specialized in high-tech production. This will happen before NIC productivity reaches the OECD level, and if the gain continues in the NICs, then the OECD countries now benefit, since the terms of trade turn in their favour.

The question we have now to ask is how the welfare state affects this structural transformation. In seeking to answer this question, we have to be careful not to build in the answer by the assumptions made. It cannot simply be assumed that we are starting from a first-best fully flexible world in which any government intervention is necessarily a step in the wrong direction. Most important, we cannot take it for granted that the labour-market adjusts immediately to the changing conditions of international trade. If employment does not change, we will see a wage differential emerging as those in the import-competing sector of OECD economies face increased competition, whereas those in the export sector benefit from improved terms of trade. The wage differential widens until workers begin to move to the high-tech sector, at which point the differential remains as long as there are still workers in the medium-tech industry. The more that the differential widens, the longer is the total transition period.

The question is – how soon will the adjustment be made? Suppose we look at the individual worker contemplating 'migration' to the high-tech sector. I use the word 'migration' advisedly because there is a definite parallel with the migration of people from the agricultural to the industrial sector. There may be no literal geographic mobility, but some of the same considerations apply. There are costs of making the move. There is uncertainty as to what such a move will bring. As in models of migration in developing countries (the Harris-Todaro model), the incentive to make the transition depends on the wage differential and the probability of employment. Where there is an uncertain matching of potential workers and vacancies, there is a probability of initial unemployment. This now brings in a further consideration: the degree of social protection. The existence of unemployment insurance, or equivalent transfer programs, increases the total expected remuneration in the new sector, and hence reduces the wage differential required. This is one example of how social protection may have a positive rather than a negative impact.

The idea that the welfare state may have positive as well as negative consequences for economic performance will not come as a totally alien idea to most non-economists. Historically, social insurance grew up as a complement to the modern employment relationship, guaranteeing workers against catastrophic loss of income through accident, sickness, or unemployment, and hence providing an incentive for people to enter industrial employment (Atkinson 1996, ch. 11). In current times, as mature economies transform, it is recognized that people may be more willing to take risks, to retrain, and to change jobs, in a society in which there is adequate social protection. In policy terms, unemployment benefits have long been used as a tool to ease structural change: for example, in the United Kingdom in the 1960s earnings-related benefits were introduced precisely in order to encourage the reallocation of labour. As argued by Abramovitz,

> the enlargement of the government's economic role, including its support of income minima, health care, social insurance, and other elements of the welfare state, was ... not just a question of compassionate regard ... It was,

and is – up to a point – a part of the productivity growth process itself. (1981, 2–3)

The welfare state can work with, rather than against, the grain of economic growth.

I am not asserting that all aspects of social protection have positive effects on structural adjustment; there may also be negative effects. As stressed earlier, we need to look at the whole package. The different elements may be mutually offsetting. In related context, Bertola and Rogerson have argued that worker dismissal regulations in Europe have a negative effect on job creation and job destruction, but that this tends to be offset by greater wage compression, relative to the United States: 'wagesetting institutions and job-security provisions differ across countries in ways that are both consistent with rough uniformity of job turnover' (1997, 1147).

Two countries may have different combinations of welfare-state provisions, but the same net effect on employment and growth. Where there may be important divergences is in the distributional outcome. Earlier, I referred to 'competitiveness' as being ultimately concerned with maintaining living standards, but there remains the question – whose living standards? I have just sketched an example where domestic wage differentials emerge as a result of increased international competition. The quotation from the IMF at the start of this essy recognized that scaling back social protection has distributional consequences. These are political issues, involving distributional judgments, and politics is the cue for my conclusions.

Conclusions: Which Direction for the Future?

Faced with an essay whose title contains a question, the reader may reasonably expect an answer – although I do not myself believe that the most useful contribution of economists is to give definite answers. Rather, they should help others make up their minds. Quite a lot of my time has indeed been devoted to clarification of the question – what we mean by terms which appear frequently in public debate, such as the welfare state, globalization, and competitiveness.

My own personal judgment is that I am not convinced that welfare states cannot compete in a global economy. If this were a court of law, and the welfare state were charged with undermining competitiveness, then I would put it to the jury that the case has not been proved beyond reasonable doubt. The empirical evidence is often quoted as though it were definitive, but I do not regard it as conclusive. The cross-country statistical work is based on comparing social systems which contain interacting and interlocking elements. One cannot isolate one element of the 'social settlement' and attribute to this the observed difference in economic performance. Nor is the conclusion self-evident from theoretical considerations. What may seem like an obvious deduction from the simplest economic models appears less so when we allow for a more realistic point of departure.

What I would stress is that I believe that there *are* choices to be made. It is not the case that all countries are driven by economic imperatives to follow a particular line. The attempt by bodies such as the IMF to impose a particular approach based on labour-market flexibility and dismantling of social protection is not justified by appealing to economics. It involves a political judgment as well, and this is a matter where we can legitimately disagree.

Notes

1 Revised text of Vancouver Institute Lecture, University of British Columbia, 4 October 1997, and Public Sector Economics Research Centre Lecture, University of Leicester, 23 October 1997.
2 A more recent study combining the data for 1983–8 with those for 1989–94 has been carried out by Nickell (1997).
3 This is only one of the possible outcomes. If, for example, productivity also improved in the low-tech sector at the same rate, then the terms of trade gain to OECD from its cheaper imports of the low-tech good would leave unaffected its real wages overall.

References

Abramovitz, M. 1981. 'Welfare Quandaries and Productivity Concerns.' *American Economic Review* 71: 1–17.
Atkinson, A.B. 1995. 'The Welfare State and Economic Performance.' *National Tax Journal* 48: 171–98.
– 1996. *Incomes and the Welfare State.* Cambridge: Cambridge University Press.
– 1999. *The Economic Consequences of Rolling Back the Welfare State.* Cambridge, MA: MIT Press.

Bertola, G., and R. Rogerson. 1997. 'Institutions and Labor Reallocation.' *European Economic Review* 41: 1147–71.

Elmeskov, J. 1993. 'High and Persistent Unemployment: Assessment of the Problem and its Causes.' OECD Economics Department Working Paper 132. Paris: OECD.

European Commission. 1993. *Growth, Competitiveness, Employment: The Challenges and Ways Forward into the 21st Century*. White Paper. Luxembourg: European Commission.

Freeman, R. 1995. 'The Large Welfare State as a System.' *American Economic Review: Papers and Proceedings*, vol. 85: 16–21.

Freeman, R., B. Swedenborg, and R. Topel, eds. 1997. *Reforming the Welfare State: The Swedish Model in Transition*. Chicago: National Bureau of Economic Research and University of Chicago Press.

International Monetary Fund. 1994. 'World Economic Survey.' *IMF Survey*, 16 May 1994, pp. 153–6.

Johnson, G.E. and F.P. Stafford. 1993. 'International Competition and Real Wages.' *American Economic Review: Papers and Proceedings*, vol. 83: 127–30.

Krugman, P. 1994a. 'Competitiveness: A Dangerous Obsession.' *Foreign Affairs* 74/2: 28–44.

– 1994b. 'Past and Prospective Causes of High Unemployment.' In *Reducing Unemployment: Current Issues and Policy Options*. Kansas City: Federal Reserve Bank of Kansas City.

– 1996. 'Making Sense of the Competitiveness Debate.' *Oxford Review of Economic Policy*, Autumn: 17–25.

Layard, R., S. Nickell, and R. Jackman. 1991. *Unemployment*. Oxford: Oxford University Press.

Lindbeck, A. 1995a. 'Hazardous Welfare-state Dynamics.' *American Economic Review: Papers and Proceedings*, vol. 85: 9–15.

– 1995b. 'Welfare State Disincentives with Endogenous Habits and Norms.' *Scandinavian Journal of Economics* 97: 477–94.

Ministry of Social Affairs and Employment. 1995. *Unemployment Benefits and Social Assistance in seven European countries*. Werkdocumenten 10. The Hague: Ministry of Social Affairs and Employment.

Nickell, S.J. 1997. 'Unemployment and Labor Market Rigidities: Europe versus North America.' *Journal of Economic Perspectives* 11/3: 55–74.

Organization for Economic Cooperation and Development [OECD]. 1991. *Employment Outlook*. Paris: OECD.

– 1994. *Jobs Study*. Paris: OECD.

– 1995. *Historical Statistics*. Paris: OECD.

– 1996. *Beyond 2000: The New Social Policy Agenda*. Paris: OECD.

11

Social Justice and Citizenship: Dignity, Liberty, and Welfare

EDWARD BROADBENT

When I was a student many years ago, I was inspired by Albert Camus. Unlike many intellectuals such as Jean-Paul Sartre, he was critical of the Soviet Union's denial of political freedom. But unlike so many others in the West during the Cold War, Camus refused to say that we must choose political freedom over economic justice. There was, he rightly contended, a necessary reciprocity between the two. Speaking to a group of workers in the early 1950s, he said: 'If someone takes away your bread, he suppresses your freedom at the same time. But if someone takes away your (political) freedom, you may be sure that your bread is threatened; for it depends no longer on you and your struggle but on the whim of a master.'[1]

For many of my generation, the post–Second World War years can be seen as the struggle to put in place the link Camus made between politics and economics. The agenda can be summed up in two propositions. If humans are to be free, they need all the traditional political rights associated with our liberal heritage. On the other hand, for freedom to be real in the daily life of the majority, the deep inequality and insecurity of capitalism has to be removed.

For many years after the war, it seemed that the battle was being won. During a period of almost four decades, a new notion of social citizenship based on a broad concept of freedom appeared to have acquired a permanent acceptance. Unimpeded capitalism, with a concept of citizenship narrowly restricted to political rights, seemed as dead as the Depression of the 1930s. In its place was a new system that amalgamated a market economy with social rights. This was the Golden Age of the North Atlantic democracies, when individual and collective well-being reached an unprecedented level. Employment remained high, laws based on discrimination were abolished, vacation time expanded, most forms of censorship were eliminated, real incomes grew annually, and, for the first time, for an ordinary person to become elderly or seriously ill did not constitute a sentence to poverty. In short, more people enjoyed more freedom that in any other society in human history.

As the century closes, however, the struggle between those who believe in this vision and those who don't is clearly unresolved. As a reality, social citizenship has become more precarious. As an ideal, its origins need to be understood. It also needs to be defended, not in detail but in principle, by all those who believe in the possibility of combining social justice with a market-based economy.

The Birth of Social Citizenship

The notion of social citizenship was born of a fortunate combination of popular struggle and political leadership in the North Atlantic world. Following the war, citizens in the established democracies (Canada, the United States, the United Kingdom, Holland, France, and Scandinavia) no longer accepted the pre-war view that the state should remain simply the agent of law and order and the guarantor of civil and political rights. They demanded that their governments also respond to their social needs. It was not surprising that the ideological leadership for social rights came from politicians on the left. However, at this crucial time they were joined by a number of other parties and leaders, traditionally on the conservative side of the ledger. They agreed with the left that *laissez-faire* capitalism had contributed significantly to producing the two great horrors of the 1930s: Nazism and the Great Depression. They, too, wanted government to play an ongoing equalizing role in the economy.

The most notable among such figures was Franklin Delano Roosevelt. He has been the only American president to advocate adding social rights to his country's democratic legacy. In his last address to Congress in 1944, he pointed out that civil and political rights alone were 'inadequate to assure us equality in the pursuit of happiness.' He urged, without success, American legislators to adopt an Economic Bill of Rights: 'We have come to the clear realization of the fact that true individual freedom cannot exist without economic security and independence: "necessitous men are not free men".'[2]

These words of Roosevelt illustrate how far certain important leaders in Western democracies had come. In England, both Winston Churchill and Harold Macmillan supported the creation of the welfare state. In his book, *The Middle Way*,[3] written before the war, Macmillan had called for a mixed economy state with expanded social obligations. And it was Churchill's wartime coalition cabinet that made the decision not only to establish social rights in Britain, but also to make a comprehensive rights-based program a crucial part of the postwar global agenda.[4] Hence, when a Canadian, John Humphrey, prepared the first draft of the Universal Declaration of Human Rights, it was seen that the 'inherent dignity' of human beings required the inclusion of social and economic as well as political and civil rights. It was adopted in 1948 by the newly created United Nations.[5]

While the ideological leadership for social rights clearly came from the democratic left, the point I wish to emphasize is that the immediate postwar period produced an important consensus in asserting the need for the democratic state to play a crucial role in the economy. John Maynard Keynes's view, that during the inevitable cyclical downturns, the state should intervene by means of fiscal stimulation rather than by budget cutbacks, became the new orthodoxy of macro-economic policy. The twin goals of government were an expanding fully employed market economy and a new set of social rights. These objectives were shared by politicians across the ideological spectrum.

This view was not only to be found among the Allies, as revealed in their declaration of war aims. It was also an important element in the traditional thinking of many Continental Christian Democrats, particularly in Germany, where the Christian Democratic Union view of a 'social market economy' to this day differs from that of the Social Democrats more in detail than in principle. Both agree on the need for a rights-based welfare state. In Canada, postwar federal governments, responding to new demands from returning veterans, as well as many others who wanted no return to the 1930s, brought in new universal social programs in unemployment insurance, family allowances, health services, and pensions.

Morality and practicality came together in this period. If greater equality and more stability were to be achieved, capitalism could not be left to its own devices. Political action was needed. In deliberately creating the welfare state at home and putting in place the stabilizing Bretton Woods financial institutions abroad (also intellectually inspired by Keynes), leaders rose above the short-run ad hoc nature of most democratic decision making. They had reflected on the pre-war sources of conflict and put in place institutional changes as remedies. They concluded that the democratic state must intervene in the economy, not intermittently, but on a continuing basis. A new social foundation for democratic citizenship had to be established which would ensure greater stability by producing greater equality.

The belief that certain aspects of life must, in principle, be de-linked from the market place was scarcely new. After all, virtually all religions and moral systems hold such a position. What was new was the political view that the democratic state should incorporate this principle in its laws as an aspect of citizenship. Access to health, education, and retirement with dignity were to be established by democracies not as minimal-level safety nets for the poor, but for everyone. These essential requirements for a dignified life had hitherto been the guaranteed privilege of only the wealthy. They were now to become de facto citizens' rights. Added to this was the expectation that the state, through its management of the economy, would ensure virtually full employment.

Subsequently, during the heyday of the welfare state, ordinary working families throughout the North Atlantic region demonstrated a level of openness and tolerance that had not been seen before. Affirmative-action programs for women and visible minorities were launched either with the support or without significant opposition from male industrial workers who themselves had come to believe that the state had finally accepted its social responsibilities towards them. More openness and tolerance at home were accompanied by support for foreign aid programs abroad. Economic debates in the North Atlantic democracies increasingly ignored challenges and responses about the fundamentals of the system. Politicians were more likely to focus on the speed, not the principle, of extending the welfare state.

In retrospect I believe we should see this postwar development as a period of transformation. There was in a sense a historic class compromise in the developed democracies. Instead of the open and often violent conflict that had characterized the first three decades of this century, workers and their families in the North Atlantic world came to accept the in-built market inequality that comes with capitalism in return for equality in social rights. The holders of capital, in turn, obtained the degree of social peace necessary for a market economy to operate. On these fundamentals, there was an unstated but functional social contract. Apart from the United States, citizens in virtually all other North Atlantic democracies gradually came to view citizenship and social rights as being inextricably connected.

What distinguishes contemporary welfare states from our liberal roots is the view that, for democracy in an industrial age, political and civil rights are insufficient either to ensure a minimal level of justice or to produce a stable peace. The classic liberal argument of John Locke, with its provision of such rights, including the guaranteed protection of economic inequality based on the rights of property, had proven to be sufficient inducement for the middle classes to support the state. Why should working people, however, reach a peaceful accord with such entrenched market-based inequality? In an industrial or postindustrial era with universal political rights, one practical solution seemed to have been found in the provision of equality-based social rights. Not only was this seen in a steady decline in popular support for Communist parties in Continental Europe, but also in perceptible changes in the programs and rhetoric of successful social-democratic parties. Whether in government or in opposition, it was during the heyday of the welfare state that most social-democratic parties moved away from seeing their goal as achieving substantial state ownership to seeing it as one of producing greater degrees of equality.

A broad range of social policies, including taxation and minimum-wage legislation, did produce a greater degree of monetary equality in strong welfare states than was to be found in other industrial democracies.[6] What has been key to the transformation of the nature of citizenship, however, is that there has been a net increase in access to what the leading theorist of the welfare state, T.H. Marshall, fifty years ago called 'a civilized life' for the majority.

The objective of social policy as a right of citizenship has been to ensure a high level of community standards equally accessible to all. The consequence of doing so is that money incomes have become less important in their social consequences. Much of the social conflict derived from income inequality can be eliminated.

It is, of course, advantageous to have a larger pay cheque. But the advantages can be made to have a limited impact. Put in terms appropriate to contemporary life, as long as ordinary citizens can send their children to good schools, have comprehensive health facilities, benefit from income compensation programs when they are unemployed, have an annual paid vacation and access to healthy air and clean beaches, and retire in comfort, they will be indifferent to the more exotic advantages that come from being wealthy. It is within this kind of welfare state arrangement – one with equal social incomes running side by side with unequal money incomes – that a kind of social justice can be achieved.

In Canada, for example, federally initiated universal social programs led to the emergence of a qualitatively different sense of citizenship. For the first time in history, everyone was provided education, health care, pensions, and adequate financial support when unemployed. It's these social rights, not their traditional political and civil rights, that account for Canadians describing themselves as belonging to a 'sharing and caring' nation. Canadians would not have described themselves in this way before the Second World War, for the perfectly good reason that, at that time, apart from some provinces providing minimal levels of social assistance for the poor, the state neither shared nor cared. Similarly, it's been the welfare state's use of both market and non-market principles to provide two different sources of income that resulted in a majority of Canadians as well as other citizens in the North Atlantic world describing themselves for the first time as 'middle class.' In this regard the United States is not an exception.[7]

With diminished consequences of class differences and a dignified life a probability for most working families, the North Atlantic democracies became much more tolerant and stable than in the pre-war period. More social equality meant a more civilized society. And if the move towards the political centre tended to blur the distinctions between conservative parties and their democratic competitors on the left, this was in part because the conservatives of the time had made the fundamental compromise in accepting the welfare state and its universal rights-based social agenda.[8] It was this compromise with the forces of the market plus economic growth – not isolated, individual initiative – that made 'middle class' life a subjective reality for the majority of ordinary people.

The Ideological Attack on Social Citizenship

Just as the welfare state came into being in the postwar period in part because of the ideological commitment of many of the leading politicians, so, too, did ideology play an important role in undermining its continuation. And if one breed of conservatives had helped make or sustain the original consensus on the need for a positive state, so, too, conservatives of a different kind were now decisive in its break-up. It was in the so-called Anglo-Saxon countries (Britain, the United States, and Canada), not Continental Europe, that the national political consensus began to unwind. Coming to power at the time of mounting fiscal pressure on the state produced by a combination of major global price increases for petroleum and lower growth rates, newly elected conservative heads of government led the assault.

The contrast between Ronald Reagan and Margaret Thatcher with their conservative predecessors was clear. Richard Nixon's domestic policy had included support for affirmative-action programs for women and extending the state's role in health care. Winston Churchill's wartime government not only supported the introduction of social rights. Much earlier, he had expressed a principled commitment to such an approach. Writing about the positive impact state involvement could have on the individual, he had asserted, 'I do not agree with those who say that every man must look after himself, and that intervention by the state ... will be fatal to his self-reliance, his foresight, and his thrift ... Where there is no hope, be sure there will be no thrift.'[9] In Canada, the government of Brian Mulroney embarked upon cutbacks on social programs and signed the Canada–U.S. Free Trade Agreement, initiatives that were accompanied by neo-conservative justifying arguments.

In their critiques of the established policies in their respective countries, these leaders, notably Thatcher and Reagan, disconnected a key element embodied in the heart of the welfare state from its surrounding framework. They converted self-interest into selfishness. The social rights–based welfare state does contain important elements of altruism, for example, in the affirmative-action programs and special entitlements for the poor. However, it is not dependent on generosity of spirit. Its psychological foundations are more complex. In the intimate or loving relationships of the family – whether of the traditional or post-traditional type – men and women are quite capable of high levels of unreciprocated generosity on a long-term basis. However, the democratic state is not a family. It is not intimate. Democratic citizenship entails a *quid pro quo*. For citizens, a give-and-take among themselves, and between themselves and the state, is expected. In the welfare state neither egotism nor altruism dominates, but both are bordered or touched upon. Taxes in the welfare state needed for universal social services obtain widespread support precisely because I or my children will be a beneficiary tomorrow. I am even willing to pay more than 'my share,' for example, for targeted programs, providing others do their share of work and the overall level of social programs continues to meet my needs.

There is, however, an aspect of all welfare states that is directly related to the potential for selfish or greedy behaviour: the market. The market allows for the normal disposition of most people to work on a regular basis simply in terms of self-interest. This is not to say they are selfish. Nor, *a fortiori*, is it to say they are *driven* by economic greed. Some, however, are so motivated. And the market, by definition, provides legal leeway to this minority. In its embrace of the market mechanism, the welfare state therefore runs the continuing risk of selfishness becoming more widespread. The marriage of the welfare state brings together the two dispositions of altruism and self-interest. Like all marriages, it is precarious. Balance is required. If self-interest is replaced by selfishness or if altruism is expected to prevail over self-interest, the welfare state runs into trouble. The avoidance of either of these possibilities is pre-eminently a matter of political leadership. Ideas and values count.

Margaret Thatcher and Ronald Reagan helped tip the balance. Where the founders of the welfare state openly justified the functional necessity of recognizing individual self-interest as a means of producing enough wealth to ensure an adequate level of social rights, Thatcher and Reagan, taking advantage of fiscal pressures, attacked the same social rights as an unjustified burden on individual self-realization. Rejecting the social legacy of Churchill and Macmillan, Thatcher denied society's significance. It is only individuals who exist, she proclaimed. If only isolated individuals are seen to be real, and society is viewed as a mere artificial construct, then it can be argued that natural justice or the conditions for a virtuous life are achieved by liberating people from all inessential obligations imposed by the state. According to this version of self-fulfilment, the pursuit of personal satisfaction alone can be virtuous. Self-interest thus becomes selfishness. Neo-conservatism is born.

For the neo-conservative, citizenship is far from being a comprehensive concept combining the notion of personal happiness with a commitment to social institutions of the state for achieving the common good. Instead, the good life is seen essentially as a private matter to be exercised in the family and neighbourhood. It is to be lived out in the marketplace, as worker or consumer. 'Welfare' itself is converted from meaning maximizing the common good for all to refer more narrowly to special provisions for the poor. Reagan was quite clear about his agenda. Expenditures by the state on social programs, apart from minimal support for the absolutely destitute, is really a misplaced sense of charity which should remain a private virtue, not a public obligation. It was time, he argued, to stop advocating such spending of other people's money.[10] In this thinking, a citizen's public role and responsibilities have become so slight they almost disappear. If a defining characteristic of totalitarianism is the elimination of the personal in favour of the collective, neo-conservatism eliminates the political pursuit of the common good in its triumphant version of the restricted self.

The attack by the new conservative leadership in the 1980s on the welfare state was not designed simply as a warranted criticism of some insensitive bureaucracies or as a necessary but temporary measure for coping with the oil shock and other fiscal pressures which emerged in the 1970s. It had other immediate objectives as well as broader ideological ambitions. Nor were its these ambitions restricted to national boundaries. In London in 1983, Margaret Thatcher hosted the founding meeting of the International Democratic Union, a new global body of conservative parties which currently has members in more than fifty countries. Unlike the Christian Democratic International, which endorses social rights as well as political and civil rights, the International Democratic Union officially supports only political and civil rights.[11]

In terms of government policies, the intention was for the state to reduce its commitments, and therefore its expenditures on social programs. The goal was to stimulate more market activity by shifting financial resources to richer individuals and to effect a broadly based attitudinal change in the population as a whole, so that citizens who had begun to internalize the cooperative values of the welfare state would cease doing so. Program reductions, privatization, and deregulation in a welfare state with a market economy inevitably result in widening the gap in monetary incomes and reducing the impact of non-monetary incomes. In addition, if democratic electorates could be persuaded of the desirability of a significant shift in emphasis towards seeing lower taxes and private consumption as *the* goal of the good life, then the possibility of a return in the future to a program agenda of an activist equalizing state, even when controlled by parties traditionally seen on the left, would be significantly reduced.

There can be little doubt that the very success of the welfare state in establishing a higher and more secure economic level had the unintended consequence of increasing the number of ordinary families open to neo-conservative arguments. Like others who become accustomed to economic well-being, more workers were now ready to believe it was their effort alone, not the complex social and economic institutions of the welfare state, that accounted for their success. Convinced of their own virtue, more became open to the lures of private solutions to what had once been seen as common problems. Increasingly insecure because of a perceived threat by capital to go abroad, they also became less willing to pay taxes to support programs for the poor. Instead of seeing abuses of welfare as exceptions that needed to be corrected, more were inclined to believe the cruel propaganda that serious abuse and dependency were endemic to all social programs.

During the past fifteen years, most North Atlantic democracies have seen a reduction in the state's role. There has been an increased emphasis on the pursuit of personal gain and the freezing or abolition of social and economic entitlements. While national debts have been reduced, inequality has deepened. It is severe in both the United Kingdom and the United States. In the latter, inequality is reaching record levels. Since 1979, while the family income of 80 per cent of the population has stagnated, the rich have become richer and the number of millionaires (adjusted for inflation) has increased by 500 per cent. The gap within the working class is also widening.[12] In Canada, while the rich make unprecedented demands for a new Mercedes Benz, the income of average workers is lower today than it was in 1989, and the fate of the poor worsens each year.[13] Markedly influenced by the privatized state at home and by the unregulated mobility of capital globally, insecurity is now pervasive in most occupations throughout the North Atlantic.

However, reaction has been unfolding. In Britain's 1997 election, voters massively rejected a Conservative government, according to polls in good measure because of the consequences of its education and health policies. In the same year, both the French and the German government announced their intention to make reductions in their social benefits in order to meet the deficit criteria of the planned European currency. The reaction in France was to defeat the government and elect a Socialist-dominated National Assembly. In Germany, massive public demonstrations caused Chancellor Kohl to modify his proposals. In Britain and on the Continent, major nation-wide debates about the place of the 'social agenda,' particularly in the context of globalization, have been launched. In Canada, near record levels of unemployment and cutbacks in social programs contributed to the loss of Liberal seats in the 1997 national election.[14]

Thoughts on the Current Situation

The democratic state came of age in the North Atlantic region during the four decades following the war. It was based on the view that human beings, while individuals, are also inescapably social. This in itself is a banal fact. What flows from it is not. We have both private and public desires, as well as personal and community responsibilities. Our human dignity requires a political order that makes each a possibility. From its birth as a nation, Canada's political tradition has always recognized that nation-building required the state to intervene in the economy. There has been an understanding that the market alone should not be allowed to shape industrial priorities. In the postwar period, political leaders sought to give this belief a deeper foundation by developing a sense of citizenship based on social equality. As with other North Atlantic democracies, with the notable exception of the United States, the means was to be a marriage of a market economy with a broad system of social rights. While the Americans retained an anti-state notion of citizenship grounded exclusively on political and civil rights, all others in the North Atlantic region went on to endorse and implement the U.N. Covenant on Economic, Social, and Cultural Rights. Such rights cannot persist without the constant determination by governments to ensure that sufficient revenue is taken out of the consumer-driven marketplace. Political decision making, not just supply and demand, must shape the allocation of resources.

However much they otherwise differed ideologically, the innovative politicians in the postwar era shared two important practical attributes: the desire to avoid a repeat of the turmoil and violence that emerged in the 1930s, and the understanding that a large part of the problem of that decade could be assigned to unregulated capitalism. The major contribution of the founders of the welfare state is not to be found in the details of their prescriptions. Rather, it is in their understanding of the related points, that economic and social rights at a level beyond scarcity require a market economy – and that a democracy with a market economy requires an intervening government to ensure such rights if it is to avoid growing inequality and instability.

As we close off the century, it is important to note the emergence of structural changes and new problems of social life during the period of the welfare state's ascendancy. Among these are the consequences of the combination of lower rates of economic growth, greater proportional costs of social programs, technological change that is destroying more jobs than it creates, and the evolution towards a global market economy without borders. There has also been radical change in the nature of families and the role of women in the economy. The negative effects of large public and private bureaucracies must also be addressed.

For those valuing a social sense of citizenship, there cannot be, therefore, a simple-minded return to the 1960s. Clearly initiatives are required at the local level, in communities and in places of work, both to enable people to have a greater sense of participation and to develop feelings of obligation to their society. All such innovations, including some privatization, are important in the building of strong participatory civil societies. Indeed, in a number of welfare states, many have already taken place.

In general, however, responses can take two possible directions. They can be measures aimed at reducing deficits or removing undesirable bureaucracies or reforming unhealthy dependencies. Such changes are desirable and are compatible with postwar social citizenship. However, changes can also be ideologically motivated, with the purpose of driving the state out of social life. The great contribution of the postwar democratic leaders was their insistence on the need for social equality and the related need for the state. The state was essential to ensure universal social and economic rights precisely because of a market economy's inherent thrust towards greater inequality. The material aspect of such rights is important. However, their significance is more than monetary. As with similarly motivated community activities in civil society outside the state, social rights are expressions in the political domain of our human disposition to cooperate. They intensify and reaffirm our solidarity with one another and with our country. And, liberating us from the anxiety needed to purchase their equivalents in the market, they enable us to live, quite literally, more freely. Having provided for our health, education, and pensions socially, we become more free to choose what gives us personal pleasure, whether it's painting, playing soccer, reading, fishing, listening to Bach, or drinking beer on a sunny afternoon with family and friends. Life need not be an incessant quest for security and consumption. Only by making such a civilized life possible for the majority of ordinary people can the democratic capitalist state become morally legitimate.

From the experience of the 1980s we now know the consequences of neo-conservatism. Margaret Thatcher was honest in seeing social rights and neo-conservatism as an oxymoron. As she and others did not grasp, however, neo-conservatism in practice, domestically and internationally, exacerbates class and regional conflict. It undermines the very economic order it seeks to justify.

Dignity, Liberty, and Welfare: What Can Be Done?

I make six suggestions.

1/Politicians must provide ideological leadership. It was politicians, responding to the postwar pressure of working people, who created the welfare state. They led where their electorates in an unfocused way wanted to go. Those believing in social rights must do so once again. They don't have the political advantage that was provided in the early post–Second World War leadership consensus. Neo-conservatism has emerged as a powerful force in new or existing parties. In part, the neo-conservative revolution of the 1980s became a political success because of the obvious conviction of Reagan and Thatcher, its ideological leaders. The democratic right put the emphasis on the first half of the private-egoist and public-fairness disposition of the modern citizen while denying the very legitimacy of the other half. Withstanding the impact of right-wing think-tanks and a consumer-oriented media, recent studies have shown that citizens in modern states have retained a commitment to certain core values and institutions of the welfare state.[15] People are not one-dimensional. However, those who believe in the citizenship equality made possible by social and economic rights must counter the political strength of the new radical conservatives by providing an explicit alternative social philosophy. It must be an elaboration of the two balancing components of the welfare state. First, there should be recognition of the positive social role of competition and private economic gain, which avoids the error of equating self-interest with selfishness or greed. The private sector is essential if we are to produce efficiently beyond the level of scarcity and as a counterbalance to the state. Second, they should speak with equal conviction about our public needs and duties, about the profoundly human disposition to cooperate with others, about the need for state guaranteed social and economic rights. Neo-conservatism should be described and attacked for what it is: a narrow consumption-based materialist view of human nature, unworthy of a free people.

2/Citizens' rights must be related to responsibilities. In 1937, some of my uncles were involved in the strike that brought industrial unions, one of the key institutions of the welfare state, to Canada.[16] They and most others in their generation believed that all citizens in such a state have an obligation to work in order to make their contribution. Today, they would understand initiatives designed to head off a culture of dependency. Who can argue against that in principle? However, such programs require obligations not just of their participants. Obligations are required on both sides of the class divide. That was the original argument of the welfare state and it remains valid today. If contemporary governments expect a young single mother to work or be retrained, they are obliged to provide her with adequate care for her children. Otherwise they will not only deny her right to human dignity as a mother but will cruelly make victims of her children as well.

3/The alarming trend of increasing inequality in tax burdens must be reversed. The share of taxes paid by the rich and by corporations have dropped significantly in most OECD countries. The average rate of corporate income tax fell from 43 per cent in 1986 to 33 per cent in 1995. The highest marginal rates of income tax have also been significantly reduced. The average top rate was 59 per cent in 1975 and only 42 per cent in 1995. At the same time, marginal tax rates for average workers increased from 32.6 per cent in 1978 to 38.4 per cent in 1995. Additionally, governments have steadily increased regressive consumption taxes, while retaining tax expenditure programs disproportionately beneficial to the wealthy.[17] Corporations and the rich must pay more. To make this most effective would require multinational cooperation.

4/However, all citizens must continue to pay what are conventionally regarded as high taxes if we are to retain social rights and social peace. This has been much better understood and accepted in continental Europe, where market-based individualism is not nearly so strong as it is in the United States or even in the United Kingdom. Having built the world's strongest welfare states, Continental Europeans seem more prepared to see taxes as the price of a civilized society. How else can we have clean cities, first-rate education, support for the arts and social justice?

As a former politician I do not underestimate the challenge. However, I observe that during the 1997 election in the United Kingdom, polls indicated citizens of all classes were prepared to pay the higher taxes urgently needed for health and education.[18] Nonetheless, neither major party pointed out that if the British paid taxes simply at the same level as their neighbours in Germany and France they would be able to *double* their spending on these services and social security.[19]

5/There must be more informed public debate on the economic costs and benefits of the welfare state. In most such discussions today there is an unstated and unproven assumption that welfare states are an economic burden which reduces a nation's international competitiveness. This is seen most flagrantly in misleading comparative assertions about percentages of GDP absorbed by the public sector which ignore the fact that the spending of an equivalent or greater percentage on a particular service may go on in the private sector of one of the countries in question. In either case it is an economic 'cost.' Nor is it usually pointed out that in a number of cases the effect of putting such spending in the public sector is simultaneously a net reduction in the economic cost to society, a more comprehensive coverage and the source of a competitive advantage. For example, Canada spends a lower percentage of its GDP in providing public health insurance services for its whole population than does the United States. (In the United States, an estimated 35 million have no health insurance.) Canada's public health service also provides the country with an important competitive *advantage* in some sectors: it can attract major private corporate investment which would be expected to include a health plan in an employee's benefit package in the United States, for example, in the steel and automotive sectors. More analysis about the real economic costs and benefits of the existing welfare state and what they would be if programs were reduced or dismantled is now under way.[20] However, it is nonetheless a sad truth that a large majority of professional economists – unlike in the postwar period – remain wedded in their preoccupations to a *laissez-faire* model for both national and international economic analysis. This is not merely a question of technical analysis. It is also ideological.[21] Regrettably, this currently fashionable ideology has an effect on setting limits on what is seen to be possible in social policy. Value-laden ideas are passed on as scientific fact.

6/The negative effects of globalization on social citizenship need to be addressed, not ignored. While it is clear that the expansion of world trade in goods and services cannot and should not be reversed, it is equally clear that imaginative policies are needed to deal with two related aspects of this trade: the increase in corporate power and the chaotic flow of capital. Unfortunately, up to now, the G7 countries have shown no serious interest in measures intended to deal with these concerns. While economic globalization threatens the tax base of welfare states and undermines the authority of Third World governments alike, proposals – including an Economic Security Council and sophisticated versions of taxation on international flows of capital – are rejected out of hand. Such inaction confirms the continuing ideological ascendancy of neo-conservatism in the minds of political leaders.[22]

In the development of the North Atlantic democracies, regulations by the state were applied to corporations involving tax policy, workers' rights, and environmental standards. While considerable autonomy still remains with the nation-state in these matters, globalization unquestionably is tipping the balance in the direction of corporate power.[23] At the same time, the totally unregulated flow of capital continues to contribute to the radical overnight reduction in living standards of whole nations. In part, what is needed in the new globalized market economy is a degree of international re-regulation and cooperation between states that is equivalent in its effects to what was once done nationally by successful welfare states.

Conclusion

Citizenship based on social as well as political rights has been the outstanding democratic achievement of the North Atlantic countries. For ordinary working people who constitute a majority everywhere, this rich notion of citizenship, based on the understanding that humans are both self-interested and cooperative, was a remarkable improvement over the old liberal idea of competitive individualism, restricted as it was to political and civil rights. Social citizenship presumes that democratic governments will make possible our desire for personal happiness *and* public good. It embodies the truth that human nature is neither intrinsically altruistic nor reducible to market-calculating behaviour. It insists that we citizens see our governments, including the required public spending, as desirable and necessary agents in creating more non-commercial space in our daily lives. As such it can constitute a potential model of citizenship in a world that is becoming a market without borders.

As the century closes, the reality is that we can move in either direction. However, the consequences for human beings of increasing inequality and insecurity should now be transparent. Only the mendacious or those ignorant of history can argue that *laissez-faire* capitalism let loose on a global basis can produce a level of justice and stability that it could never achieve within the nation state. Fifty years ago, with social rights guaranteed by the democratic state, imaginative politicians provided an innovative answer. Rather than abandon a commitment to such rights, today's leaders must innovate again. They must produce the appropriate mix of national and international reforms which will permit the market to do its job, but which will also enable governments to fulfil their much broader obligations to their citizens.

Postscript

A few years ago I travelled to Berlin in hope of seeing Willy Brandt before he died. I was too late. However, he would have been proud of the young woman cab driver who took me to the airport. At one point she looked out the window of her car, at the remarkable commercial vitality of her home town. 'It's nice,' she said with emphasis, 'but we have to make more room for "soul" in our lives.' She was right. That's what social citizenship is all about.

Notes

1 Albert Camus, *Resistance, Rebellion and Death* (New York: A. Knopf, 1960), p. 94.
2 Address by President Roosevelt to the United States Congress, 11 January 1944.
3 Harold Macmillan, *The Middle Way: A Study of the Problem of Economic and Social Progress in a Free and Democratic Society* (London: Macmillan, 1938).
4 I am indebted to Claire Palley for pointing this out: *The United Kingdom and Human Rights* (London: Stevens & Sons/Sweet & Maxwell, 1991), 45.
5 The words 'inherent dignity' not only appear in the preamble to the Universal Declaration of Human Rights, but are found also in the preambles to the Covenant on Economic, Social and Cultural Rights, and the Covenant on Civil and Political Rights, adopted by the United Nations in 1966.
6 This difference persists today. According to 1995 data from seventeen industrial countries published in *The Economist* of 20 September 1997, stronger welfare states have a significantly more equitable distribution of after tax income: the poor have more in absolute and relative terms than the poor in other states, and the rich have less in absolute and relative terms than their equivalents in other states. The fact that incomes now

tend to be polarizing in all North Atlantic democracies is an important but different point.

7   It is often asserted that the United States is an exception to what I have just said. The widespread belief that Americans have always described themselves as middle-class is not true. The reality is that the absence of feudalism, 'manhood' suffrage before industrialization, and liberal political institutions since the birth of the nation did encourage more Americans than others in the North Atlantic states to believe they could one day *achieve* middle-class standing. Before the Second World War the groundbreaking studies by the Lynds documented the seriously felt nature of class divisions in American life. (See in particular S.R. and H.M. Lynd, *Middletown in Transition: A Study in Cultural Conflicts* [New York: Harcourt, Brace, 1937].) When this began to change, much more than economic growth was involved. It was not until 1959, twenty-five years after Roosevelt launched the welfare state with social security, and after the growth of strong industrial unions, that most Americans subjectively identified themselves as being middle class. Growth plus a vast array of welfare-state initiatives had done their work. Housing subsidies, unemployment insurance, union rights, veterans' programs, pensions, loan guarantees, tax-subsidized mortgages, and state-provided university education had transformed the life of the ordinary citizen. The United States is not a social rights–based welfare state. But it is a welfare state. See J. Madrick, 'Social Security and Its Discontents,' *New York Review of Books*, 19 December 1996. Robert N. Bellah, Richard Madsen, William M. Sullivan, Ann Swidler, and Steven M. Tioton, in *The Good Society* (New York: A. Knopf, 1991), point out that it was between 1940 and 1959 that the real income for most of the population in the United States doubled. This was precisely the great period of growth of the welfare state. See also the early chapters of John Updike's *In the Beauty of the Lilies*, and all of E. Annie Proulx's remarkable novel *Accordion Crimes* for vivid recent fictional portrayals of working-class life in early-twentieth-century industrial America, of life before the welfare state.

8   In a different context a recent author illustrates my point with the assertion, 'If [today's conservatives] could design their ideal welfare state, it would consist of nothing but means-tested programs' (Paul Pierson, *Dismantling the Welfare State?* [Cambridge: Cambridge University Press, 1994], 6).

9   Winston Churchill, *Liberalism and Social Problems* (London, 1909), 209; cited in N. Timmins, *The Five Giants* (London: Fontana, 1996).

10 Outlined in a speech given by Ronald Reagan as president in 1984 and cited in R.N. Bellah, R. Madsen, W. Sullivan, A. Swidler, and S. Tipton, *Habits of the Heart* (Los Angeles: University of California Press, 1985), 263.

11 See 'The Battle of Ideas,' a document about goals produced by the International Democratic Union, 32 Smith Square, Westminster, London.

12 See Jeff Madrick, 'In the Shadows of Prosperity,' *New York Review of Books*, 14 August 1997, 40.

13 Between 1993 and 1996 the average total family income of the bottom quintile dropped by 3.1 per cent, while that of the top quintile increased by 1.8 per cent. Source: Statistics Canada.

14 The shift in financial responsibility for social welfare back to the provinces in a federal state has important long-range negative consequences, affecting both the amount of spending and its redistribution effects. See Keith Banting, *The Welfare State and Canadian Federalism* (Montreal and Kingston: McGill-Queen's University Press, 1982). In 1996 the Canadian Imperial Bank of Commerce/Wood Gundy Securities Inc. *Report* (22 August 1996) pointed out that the principal reason for Canada's unemployment being as high as it is was the federal government's 'excessive' fiscal-restraint policy. The 1997 budget confirmed the point when it was revealed that the federal government was $5 billion ahead of its deficit-reduction target.

15 The results of a comprehensive survey published in the *Globe and Mail* of 10 November 1997 revealed that 70 per cent of Canadians favour new government spending aimed at strengthening social programs. For data on the United States and Britain see chapter 6 of Pierson, *Dismantling the Welfare State?* See also Bellah et al., *Habits of the Heart*, and Bell et al., *The Good Society*. The latter two books provide richly documented evidence supporting the view that even Americans, the most anti-state of all citizens in the North Atlantic world, have maintained in their personalities dispositions favourable to both private consumption and social programs.

16 The strike against General Motors took place in 1937 in Oshawa, Ontario, and resulted in the establishment of a local of the United Automobile Workers of America.

17 See *The Economist*, 20 September 1997. *The Economist* quite specifically relates this serious increase in inequality to the effects of globalization. The rich and capital of all kinds are more mobile than labour; therefore, governments have backed away from the former and imposed ever more burdens on working people. For an analysis of the regressive nature of Canada's tax system, see Richard Shillington, 'The Tax System and Sound Social Policy,' chapter 7 of *Remaking Canadian Social Policy*, ed. J. Pulkingham and G. Ternowetsky (Halifax: Fernwood, 1996).

18 This was confirmed in countless polls, such as that published in *The Independent* on 21 November 1996. In the United States, social security, which provides substantial pension benefits for over 90 per cent of those of retire-

ment age, has remained untouchable by the neo-conservatives, in large measure because of the political strength of organized seniors who come from every income category.

19 See Andrew Dilnot, 'Crisis in Welfare?' in P. Askonas and S. Frowen, eds., *Welfare and Values* (London: Macmillan, 1997).

20 See A.B. Atkinson's *The Economic Consequences of Rolling Back the Welfare State* (Cambridge, MA: MIT Press, 1999).

21 See Robert Heilbroner and William Milberg, *The Crisis of Vision in Modern Economic Thought* (Cambridge: Cambridge University Press, 1995).

22 The Commission on Global Governance, *Our Global Neighbourhood* (Oxford: Oxford University Press, 1995). This report of the Commission on Global Governance made many practical proposals. Although written by twenty-nine former heads of government, senior ministers, and international officials, this thoughtful document seems to have been completely ignored by those currently with power.

23 Until quite recently most discussions about the impact of globalization on the welfare state, whether from the left or from the right, have left little hope for an activist government. More recently, there has been a questioning of this pessimism. See Paul Hirst and Grahame Thompson, *Globalization in Question* (Cambridge: Polity Press, 1996), and Linda Weiss, 'The Myth of the Powerless State, ' *New Left Review* 225 (Sept.-Oct. 1997): 3–27.

Notes on Contributors

Anthony Atkinson is Warden of Nuffield College, Oxford University. He is the founding editor of the *Journal of Public Economics* and his most recent book is *The Economic Consequences of Rolling Back the Welfare State* (1999).

Ronald Beiner is Professor of Political Science, University of Toronto. His recent books include *What's the Matter with Liberalism?* (1992) and *Philosophy in a Time of Lost Spirit: Essays on Contemporary Theory* (1997).

Edward Broadbent is Visiting Fellow, Department of Political Studies, Queen's University. For fifteen years he was leader of the New Democratic Party of Canada, during which time he also worked globally as vice-president of the Socialist International.

David J. Elkins is Professor of Political Science, University of British Columbia. His most recent book is *Beyond Sovereignty: Territory and Political Economy in the Twenty-First Century* (1995).

Richard Ericson is Principal of Green College and Professor of Law and Sociology, University of British Columbia. During 1998–9 he was a Canada Council Killam Research Fellow and Visiting Fellow of All Souls College, Oxford. His most recent book is *Policing the Risk Society* (1997).

David Held is Professor of Politics and Sociology, Open University, and a member of the editorial board of Polity Press, Cambridge. His most recent books are *Democracy and the Global Order* (1995) and *Global Transformations: Politics, Economics and Culture* (1999).

Barry Hindess is Professor of Political Science in the Research School of Social Science, Australian National University. His most recent books are *Discourses of Power: From Hobbes to Foucault* (1996) and *Democracy* (2000).

Warren Magnusson is Professor of Political Science, University of Victoria. His most recent book is *The Search for Political Space: Globalization, Social Movements, and the Urban Political Experience* (1996).

Claus Offe is Professor of Political Science, Humboldt University. His most recent book is *Modernity and the State* (1996).

Nikolas Rose is Professor of Sociology, Goldsmith College, University of London. His most recent books are *Inventing Ourselves* (1996), *Governing the Soul* (2d ed., 1999), and *Powers of Freedom: Reframing Political Thought* (1999).

Dietrich Rueschemeyer is Charles C. Tillinghurst Jr. Professor of International Studies and Professor of Sociology, Brown University. His most recent book is *Capitalist Development and Democracy* (1992).

Nico Stehr is Professor Emeritus of Sociology, University of Alberta, and DAAD Professor of Sociology, University of Duisburg. His most recent book is *Klima-Wetter-Mensch* (1999).